AF096404

COINAGE AND HISTORY IN THE SEVENTH CENTURY NEAR EAST

7

Edited by

TONY GOODWIN

Proceedings of the 17th Seventh Century Syrian Numismatic Round Table

Held at Corpus Christi College Oxford on the 26th and 27th of September 2022

The Legends of the Most Common Variety of the Two Imperial Bust Type of Arab-Latin Gold Coinage from North Africa 185
David Woods

Umayyad Caliphal Seals 191
Nitzan Amitai-Preiss

The Significance of the Monetary Reforms of ʿAbd Al-Malik 205
Marcus Phillips

PREFACE

This volume contains 16 papers presented at a two-day conference organised by the Seventh Century Syrian Numismatic Round Table and held in Oxford in September 2022. The Round Table aims to bring together numismatists, historians and archaeologists with an interest in the Near East around the time of the Arab conquests and in the early years of new Umayyad empire. The period covered runs from the early seventh century to the first decades of the eighth, and the geographical focus is mainly on Syria and the Eastern Mediterranean, although three articles deal with North Africa and Sicily.

The central focus of the Round Table has always been the Arab-Byzantine coinage of Greater Syria, but this volume contains rather more than previously on the Byzantine coinage of the seventh century; in fact there are almost equal numbers of papers covering Byzantine and Early Islamic numismatics. As editor I am once again hugely impressed by the number of original ideas, details of new types of coins and new historical insights from the various contributors. In many cases their papers are the result of a formidable amount of detailed numismatic work and it is interesting to note how the nature of this work has changed over the past couple of decades. Twenty years ago a die study or the construction of a detailed typology would have inevitably involved many visits to view private and museum collections. For rarer or more valuable coins this would have been supplemented by a long trawl through old auction catalogues in a specialist library, but most of the coin series covered here (e.g. folles of Constans II, Pseudo-Byzantine coins or Standing Caliph fulus) were rarely illustrated. However, increasingly over the past few years, very many images of low value copper coins have become available on-line, and the quality of images presented in web auctions or on websites such as zeno is now generally more than sufficient for most numismatic research. So it is now possible to access a much greater sample of these coin series and several contributors have made full use of these new resources. There has also been some useful progress by museums in making their collections available on-line, although the emphasis is often initially on imaging objects of more general interest to the public. Finally it is sad to note that the tragic situation in Syria continues, exacerbated by the recent earthquake, and precludes any significant archaeological work in that country. Some useful results have emerged from neighbouring countries, but, with a few notable exceptions, there is still much room for improving the quality of numismatic reports from excavations.

Tony Goodwin   March 2023

The Heraclian Mint of Isaura

Tony Goodwin[1]

During the Persian wars two temporary mints, Seleucia Isauriae and Isaura, operated briefly in south east Asia Minor. The two mints were active from 615 to 618 and produced copper folles of three different types (see Fig. 1 below): at the important coastal town of Seleucia a two-bust type struck in years 6 and 7 followed by a larger emission of a two standing figure type in years 7 and 8. Minting then apparently moved inland to the more easily defensible town of Isaura which struck two-bust coins in year 8. There are also very much smaller emissions of half folles from both mints. Frank Trombley's article of 2015 gives a comprehensive overview of the historical background and a corpus of examples from his own collection. In this article I will concentrate more narrowly on the smaller mint of Isaura to see what we can learn from a detailed look at the numismatics, including a die study, and then how this might help our understanding of the broader picture.

a Seleucia years 6 and 7 **b Seleucia year 7** **c Isaura year 8**

Figure 1. The three types of follis issued by the Isaurian mints in years 6, 7 and 8 (615/6 to 617/8). All show Heraclius and Heraclius Constantine on the obverse (approximately 1.5x actual size).[2]

[1] Tony Goodwin is an independent scholar a.goodwin2@btopenworld.com

Historical Background

The historical background is well covered in Trombley's paper, so I will confine myself to summarising a few main points. The sketch map below (Fig. 2) shows the geographical location of the two mints and by 615 Seleucia was effectively a Byzantine frontier town facing Tarsus, which was under Persian occupation. So the existence of the two mints is clearly connected in some way to the military situation, which by 615 was extremely serious for the Byzantines.

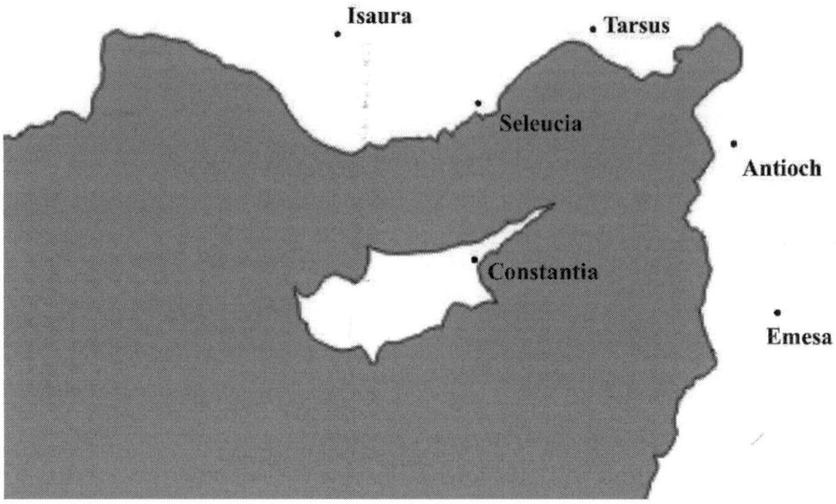

Figure 2. Sketch map showing the location of the Isaurian mints.

The surviving written sources tell us very little about how the war progressed during this period and there is no mention of the role, military or otherwise, of the two Isaurian cities. However, we know that in 615 the Persian general Shahrbaraz led an army through Asia Minor as far as Chalcedon on the Bosphorus coast opposite Constantinople. This was probably not a serious attempt to take Constantinople, but was more probably designed to weaken and thoroughly alarm the Byzantines, and it certainly succeeded in doing so. The Senate dispatched a grovelling letter to Khusru (which is reproduced in the Chronicon Pascale) offering terms which would have effectively reduced the Byzantine state to the role of a vassal. But Khusru refused to negotiate and sent two separate raiding parties deep into Asia Minor under his generals Shahen and Shahrbaraz. After sifting the very meagre historical evidence James Howard Johnston has concluded that these raids probably took place in 617.[3] We do not know whether Seleucia was directly threatened by the raids, but it seems very likely that they prompted the move of the mint to the more secure location of Isaura. The next key event that the sources are reasonably clear about is the fall of Alexandria in 619. Trombley suggested that this shut off grain supplies to Seleucia, and so made the military presence unsustainable.[4] Howard-Johnston suggested that the removal of the army resulted from the Byzantine's realisation that the Persians were now concentrating on Egypt rather than Asia Minor.[5] Both suggestions explain the closure of the mints by 619, although Howard-Johnston's suggestion would probably make it a few months earlier.

---

[2] Coin a CNG auction 93, 22.5.13 lot 1352, coin b CNG auction 102, 18.5.16 lot 1149 and coin c Cat. 10 below.

[3] Howard-Johnston 2021 pp. 120-127.

[4] Trombley 2015 p. 259.

[5] Howard-Johnston 2021 p. 127.

Studies of the Isaurian mints

Folles from both mints were known in the 19th century and the mint name of Isaura was correctly identified, for example by Sabatier in 1862,[6] but the Seleucia mint name caused numismatists some puzzlement and was variously read as a blundered rendering of Ephesus or Antioch. All the confusion was cleared up in a seminal article by Philip Grierson in 1951 which established our modern understanding of the two mints and their relationship with each other. He included one type of Seleucia half follis and identified the second type two years later.[7] It is interesting to note that in the 1950s the folles of Isaura were extremely rare and Grierson was able to illustrate only one example compared with 14 of Seleucia.[8] The Isaura half follis was still unknown and, so far as I can ascertain, was first published by Wolfgang Hahn in 1981.[9] In the 70 years after Grierson's article a number of short surveys were published (notably Grierson in 1968, Phillip Whitting in 1973, Grierson again in 1971 and Hahn in 1981), but these mainly repeated Grierson's original interpretations with some elaborations. Finally Trombley's 2015 article is the most comprehensive survey of the two mints to date. A number of observations and generalisations run through this literature and can be summarised as follows:[10]

1. One Seleucia obverse die became the principal (probably only) die used at Isaura

2. Only two obverse dies were used at Isaura

3. Folles were minted at Isaura in years 8 and 9 of Heraclius

4. All Isaura obverse legends are heavily blundered

5. Both Seleucia and Isaura were 'military mints' striking coins for military pay and purchases

6. Mint personnel from Alexandria were diverted to Seleucia to open a mint there

7. Heavy folles were shipped from Constantinople for overstriking

8. Perhaps re-striking was an attempt to impress the inhabitants with the presence and power of the emperor

My interest in Isaura was initially aroused by the first two assertions that there were only one or two obverse dies, as I could see from my own collection that there were at least three. This prompted me to attempt a die study and, as this progressed, I began to doubt some of the other assertions. As I hope to show in this article all of them require at least some reappraisal, in the light of the much larger number of Isaura coins that are now available for study.

The Isaura Obverse

Before dealing with the detailed results of the die study it is worth noting some aspects of the obverse and reverse images and legends (see Fig. 1c above). Like the first emission from Seleucia

---

[6] Sabatier 1862 p. 278 and pl. XXX no. 3.
[7] Grierson 1953.
[8] In his 1951 article Grierson listed 5 other specimens, 4 of which were only known to him from engravings in older catalogues. The fifth in the British Museum was described as 'very badly preserved'.
[9] MIB Heraclius 197.
[10] Most of these are based on Grierson's original observations, but all those listed appear in at least two of the articles or books mentioned and none of them are contradicted. Those in inverted commas are actual quotes.

(Fig. 1a) the obverse depicts busts of Heraclius and Heraclius Constantine. This image first appeared on the solidus and was subsequently used on copper coins at Alexandria and at most western mints, although not at the major eastern mints of Constantinople, Nicomedia or Cyzicus. However, a quick glance at a few Isaura folles (see catalogue at the end of this article) is enough to show that there is not a close resemblance between the Isaura image and any possible prototypes, including Seleucia. Apart from the crude style, the image has two very distinctive features: firstly the heads are unusually small with rather untidy, wispy beards and secondly both emperors have a very prominent rhomboidal object on their chests. These are schematic representations of the *tablion*, a richly embroidered rectangle of cloth fastened to both the inside and outside of the emperor's chlamys, so that it overlaps the edge. This item of imperial regalia is not shown on the solidi or on the Alexandrian coppers, but it is usually depicted at Seleucia, albeit much less prominently than at Isaura. Why it should have been given so much prominence at Isaura is a mystery, but it may well be just a stylistic trait of the principal die engraver which was copied by other engravers. It should also be noted that the Isaura obverses are very different from anything found on the Alexandrian coppers, where the heads of the busts are proportionally larger and the *tablion* is never depicted. The Seleucia obverses are somewhat closer in style to Alexandria, but still distinctly different,[11] so I feel that there is no real evidence at either mint for the presence of Alexandrian die engravers.

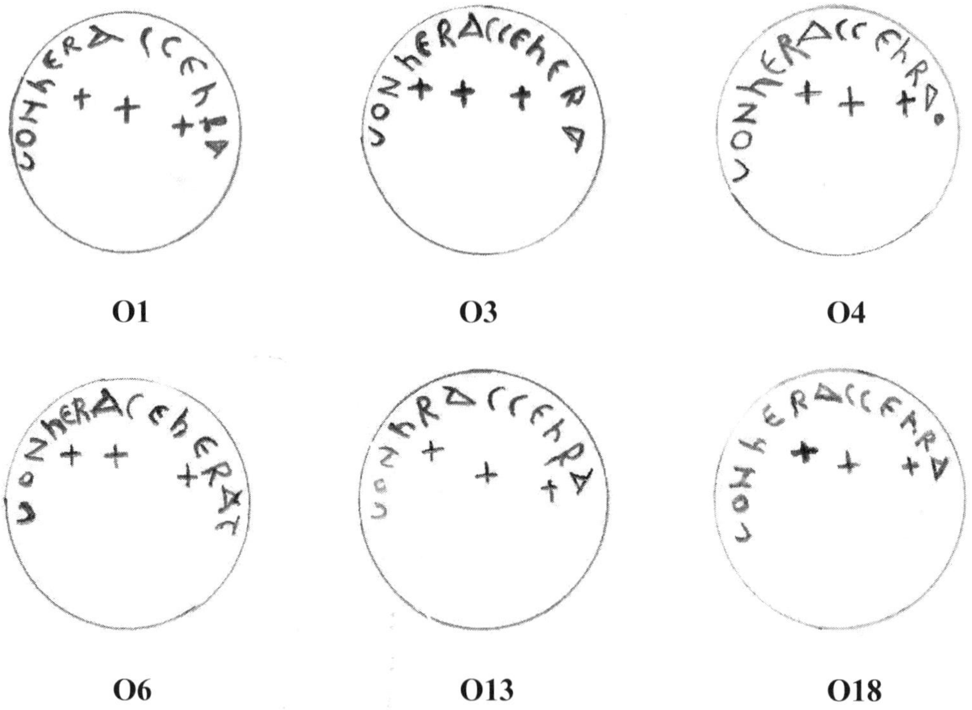

Figure 3. Composite drawings of the obverse legends for six different Isauria obverse dies.

At first sight the obverse legend appears to be completely garbled, but as the die study proceeded, I was able to piece together most of the legend for 12 different obverse dies and was surprised to find that it was actually legible and quite consistently written, although with crudely engraved letters. Six examples are shown in Fig. 3. The first two letters are puzzling and look like UO, but if we assume that they are intended to read əə, all the legends can be read as əəN hЄRACL E hЄRA, i.e. a

[11] For example, at Seleucia the bust of Heraclius Constantine is proportionately smaller than at Alexandria, the crowns are significantly different and the tablion is usually depicted.

reasonably normal truncation of the Latin legend 'DOMINI NOSTRI HERACLIUS ET HERACLIUS CONSTANTINUS'[12]

These odd initial two letters could possibly reflect a local cursive style of writing, perhaps normally used for another language, as Latin would not have been a spoken or commonly written language. It is interesting to compare the Isaura legend with the legend on a contemporary follis of the Syrian mint, struck in the area occupied by the Persians, perhaps at Emesa (Fig. 4). This has a legend which is more blundered than the Isaura coin, although the letters are generally better formed, and which also starts with two letters apparently reading OU.

Isaura **Syrian Mint**

Figure 4. Legends on the obverse of an Isaura follis compared with those on a contemprary follis from the Syrian mint. The Syrian mint legend is more blundered, but both use the same initial two letters OU *for* ƏƏ.

The Isaura Reverse

The reverse dies (Fig. 1c) are more neatly engraved than the obverses and there is very little variety; all have ANNO - ƓII either side of the M and ISAYR in exergue, with no significant blundering. There is always a plain cross above the M rather than the Christogram used by Seleucia and the officina letter is always A. This level of accuracy and consistency is perhaps surprising and contrasts with the Seleucia mint where blunderings are fairly common and at least five different officina letters are used.

The Die Study

By searching published reference books, private collections, museum holdings, auction catalogues and internet sales I was able to find images or actual examples of 97 Isaura folles for which at least one die was eventually identifiable and for 86 of these the weight was also available.[13] For comparison I collected data on 68 Seleucia folles of the two-bust type (59 with weights), but I did not attempt to carry out a detailed study and so the data from the Seleucia sample should be regarded as approximate. The main findings from the study were as follows (data for the Seleucia sample in brackets):

[12] Assuming that the legend is in the nominative case, but there is nothing in the abbreviation to suggest which case is intended. A few dies have traces of one or two uncertain letters after the final A.

[13] I would like to thank all those who assisted me in locating images, particularly Mikhail Myskin, Steve Mansfield, Maria Vrij and Piotr Tomczyk.

1.19 obverse and 17 reverse dies were identified[14] – many more than originally expected (Seleucia 16 obverse and 18 reverse). The similar number of dies for the two mints suggests that the Isaura emission of folles was of a similar order of magnitude to the earlier emission of two-bust folles by Seleucia.

2. The majority of coins were overstruck on earlier folles (in one case on a half follis), none of which appear to have been clipped.

3. No year 9 examples were found.

4. The mean weight was 11.27g and the median 11.24g (Seleucia 11.48g and 11.09g). The maximum and minimum weights were 15.18g and 8.3g excluding the single example overstruck on a half follis, which was 7.54g (Seleucia 17.08g[15] and 8.79g).

Initially the die study proved to be quite difficult as almost all coins were poorly struck with only parts of the image or legend visible and often with much of the undertype showing. There was also a certain amount of double striking, sometimes due to die clashing and sometimes apparently due to the mint operative striking the upper die twice. All these factors could make it difficult to distingusih two very similar dies produced by the same die engraver, but the problems eased as more examples of each die were found. Another problem arose because the mint tended to work their dies hard, so the development of a die flaw or even a die beginning to break up could give the appearance of two distinct dies. An example of this is shown in Fig. 5 where a die (R3) starts to break up in the vicinity of the date numeral. Then a piece of the edge of the die probably broke away and the resulting cavity was smoothed or filed to reduce the risk of further cracking. Alternatively the mint operative may have decided to take action as soon as he observed the die starting to crack. Whatever the exact sequence of events the die must have lasted well following the repair as I recorded seven examples of coins struck from the die in its final state. This is a particularly obvious example of a die flaw, but close examination of the catalogue will reveal a number of others and, as the die study progressed, these occasionally proved useful in identifying dies on coins for which only a part of the image or legend was visible.

Figure 5. Die deterioration. Three coins struck from the same reverse die (R3). In the second example the die is beginning to break up in the vicinity of the date numeral and in the third example a piece has broken off the edge of the die.

[14] Shortly before going to press an Isaura follis appeared at auction (Bucephalus auction 14,10.1.23, lot 1171, weight 12.11g, catalogued as 'Pseudo-Byzantine imitating Constans II'). The reverse die was clearly R11. Less than half of the obverse was visible, but it appeared to be a new die, of typical style, provisionally designated O20.

[15] Two outlying examples in the Seleucia sample weighed close to 17g, but the next highest weight was 15.26g.

Perhaps the most surprising result of the study is the unexpectedly large number of dies. As mentioned above the reverse dies are all quite similar, but the obverse dies fall into two groups. The first, comprising 11 dies (Cats. 1-20 below) are in a similar 'Typical Isaura Style' and are probably the work of a single die engraver. The second, smaller, group comprises eight dies and could be the work of two or more die engravers. The style is varied and in general slightly cruder than for the first group, but the distinguishing feature of the group is the varied depiction of the emperors' crowns (Cats. 21-31 below). In some cases the crowns appear somewhat fantastical (e.g. O18, Cat. 29) and on one die (O16, Cat. 26) the crosses on top of the crowns are replaced by trefoils. An example of the 'typical' group is compared with two examples of the second group in Fig. 6.

At first sight this second group might be regarded as contemporary imitations, but there is no difference in the reverse style of the two groups and there are a number of die links between them (see Fig. 7), so they must all be products of the same mint.

Figure 6. Coin a (die O4)is an example of the 'Typical Isaura Style', whilst coins b and c (dies O17 and O8) are from the smaller group of obverse dies which have varied and unusual shapes of crown.

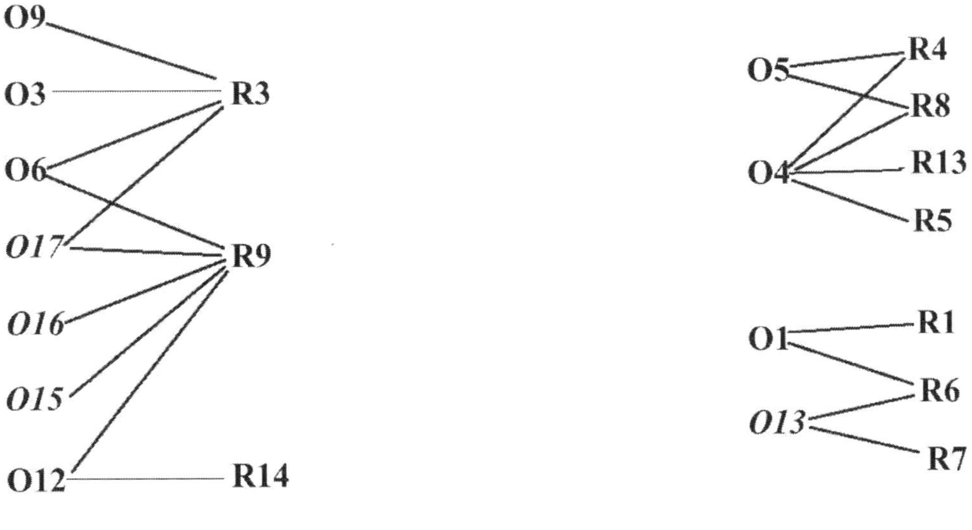

Figure 7. Die links. The die numbers in italics are for the smaller group of dies with varied crowns

Die links between Seleucia and Isaura

Two questions which the die study attempted to answer were whether the Isaura mint started operations with an old Seleucia obverse die and whether die engravers were transferred from Seleucia to Isaura. In general terms the second question can be answered with some confidence; the style of almost all Isaura dies, both obverse and reverse, is very different from the style of almost all Seleucia dies. It is therefore clear that most of the Seleucia die engravers did not go on to work at Isaura. However, I did find two die links between the mints, so the answer to the first question is possibly affirmative, but the evidence is somewhat equivocal. The first die link (Cats. 11 and 12) involves an obverse die of typical Isaura style (O5, see Fig. 8 below) which is known from six examples paired with two different Isaura reverse dies. It is only known paired with a Seleucia reverse from one example (Cat.12), but this Seleucia reverse die, of normal style, is known paired with two Seleucia obverse dies of normal Seleucia appearance. There are no other known Seleucia dies which bear the slightest resemblance to O5. Two interpretations of this evidence are possible:

1 A new die engraver was employed just before the Seleucia mint closed and he cut a single die (O5) which was briefly used. Both he and his die were then transferred to Isaura and the die engraver went on to cut all the other dies of 'typical style'.

2 O5 was one of the dies cut at Isaura by the die engraver who was responsible for all dies of the 'typical style' At some point Isaura broke its only reverse die and, whilst waiting for a new one to be cut, made short term use of an old Seleucia die.

My feeling is that the second interpretation is more plausible and would explain why we only have one surviving example of O5 paired with a Seleucia reverse. Unfortunately this one example is quite corroded, but if a better example is found, it may be possible to check whether the die was less worn when paired with the Seleucia reverse. This would provide strong support for interpretation 1, although not actual proof.

O5 **O14**

Figure 8. Two dies which are paired with both Isaura and Seleucia reverses (see Cats. 11, 12, 23 and 24).

The second die link (Cats. 23 and 24) is also rather enigmatic and involves obverse die O14 (see Fig. 8). This is known from a single example paired with a normal Seleucia reverse and a single example paired with a slightly atypical Isaura reverse (R10, Cat. 23) on which the reverse **M** has different proportions to that on all other Isaura reverse dies. O14 is very different in style to almost all Seleucia dies and, whilst O14 would fit comfortably into the group of Isaura obverses with unusual crowns, there are no other Isaura dies that look like the work of the same die engraver. However, there is one Seleucia obverse die, again only known from a single example, which is clearly the work of the same die engraver and also is paired with the same Seleucia reverse die as Cat. 24 (see Fig. 9 below). It therefore seems most likely that die O14 started life at Seleucia and was subsequently re-used at Isaura, but whether it was the first Isaura die is less certain. There are no other Isaura dies that can be attributed to this die engraver and no indication of his style influencing the style of any other Isaura dies.

O14 **Seleucia**

Figure 9. Isaura O14 compared with a Seleucia follis with an unusual obverse which is clearly the work of the same die engraver.[16] *Note the unusual crowns and the sharply angled folds of Heraclius' robe.*

Overstriking

Out of 97 coins recorded 66 had a visible undertype.This is certainly an underestimate as in some cases the coin had thick patination and in others the image from an old auction catalogue was of poor quality. In fact I strongly suspect that all Isaura folles were overstruck on earlier coins. In many cases there was insufficient of the undertype visible to allow precise identification but I was able to identify 7 undertypes of Justin II, 24 of Maurice and 2 of Phocas. This was a little surprising as I had expected to find more examples of Phocas, the previous emperor and Heraclius' enemy, so clearly the overstriking was not carried out with the objective of eliminating his memory. The identifiable mints were 16 of Antioch, 4 of Constantinople, 4 of Cyzicus and 3 of Nicomedia. Given that Antioch was the nearest main imperial mint to Isaura, it looks as if old folles had been collected for overstriking either locally or perhaps by the retreating frontier armies when they abandoned Syria. If they had been sent out from Constantinople we would expect to see a much higher proportion from the mint of Constantinople.

I did not carry out a similar detailed search for undertypes on the comparative sample of Seleucia two-bust folles, but my impression is that a similar proportion of these show traces of an undertype and that, like Isaura, probably all coins were overstruck on earlier folles. The very similar average weights, and range of weights, for the two mints suggests that Seleucia had also collected folles for overstriking either locally or in Syria.

---

[16] Nomos auction e17 lot 810, 12.43g.

The half folles

The Isaura half folles are extremely rare with only two examples known (see Cat. 33 below), both of which were probably struck from the same dies.[17] The obverse is in the 'typical Isaura' style with a full legend and the die appears to be smaller than the follis dies. The reverse has a date numeral 8 and the mint name ISЄ. Recently two rather crude half folles with a two-bust obverse and dated to year 8, but with no mint name, have appeared at auction (see Cat. 34 below).[18] Both are struck from the same die pair. The style of the obverse is very different from that of the Isaura folles and there is no legend, but it is possible that they represent a small emission from Isaura.

A 'Military Mint'?

There can be little doubt that the two Isaurian mints were set up because of the military presence in the area, so in this sense it is reasonable to describe them as 'military mints'. But were the coins they produced intended for soldiers' pay as assumed by most commentators? In the late Roman Empire soldiers were normally paid in gold, although clearly there would have been a need for some small change to make local purchases. It seems likely that late sixth century practice in peacetime was to pay soldiers allowances in cash so that they could purchase provisions and maintain their equipment,[19] but during periods of active service direct provisioning of the troops was probably the norm. We also know that the emperor Maurice (582-682) had made strenuous efforts to control military expenditure and had moved towards more direct provision of food and other necessities to the troops. Much of this would have been obtained by taxation in kind of the local population. Unfortunately we have no relevant contemporary sources for normal practice during the early years of Heraclius. The situation in Anatolia during the Persian war has been discussed by John Haldon who concluded that at least some military pay in Anatolia was in copper coin and he cites a report that Heraclius had to melt down a statue in Constantinople to produce copper coin for military pay in Pontus.[20] So military purchases may have been partly by the army (or the local civil administration on the army's behalf) and partly by the soldiers themselves.

Given the likely need by the military for at least some small change, it seems at first sight obvious to regard the Isaurian coinage as fulfilling this need. However, one then has to ask why the hard-pressed (and presumably practically minded) Byzantine military would not just use their supply of perfectly good Imperial folles to make small purchases or pay troops? We know from the evidence of the die study that this supply comprised coins in current circulation. Instead why did they go to the expense and effort of setting up mints and carelessly overstriking these locally familiar coins with a crude and unfamiliar design? The result must have been much less acceptable to both soldiers and to the local population. Furthermore the crude new coins would certainly not have projected a positive image of the emperor and his son. In considering this question it is instructive to compare the Isaurian coins with other near-contemporary emissions from what are now generally

[17] MIB 197 (now in the Manchester Museum) and EBCC Supplement 209 (Cat. 33). The two reverses are definitely struck from the same die, but it is not possible to be absolutely certain about the two obverses as the image in MIB is quite poor.

[18] NBS web auction 10, 9.1.22 lot 241, now EBCC Supplement 210 (Cat. 34) and Dara Antiques Museum auction E 4, 19.2.22 lot 544.

[19] The Strategikon, a military manual written at the end of the sixth century, mentions soldiers receiving an allowance for maintaining their weapons. See Dennis 1984 pp. 18-19.

[20] See Haldon 1990 p. 220 ff for a discussion of the provisioning of the armies in Anatolia and p. 224 for the melting down of the statue. Of course this could not refer to the Isaurian folles as these were all restrikes and not freshly minted coins.

accepted as military mints. The most important of these is the large group of late 6th century folles and half folles struck in the name of Justin II (565-578) and first properly described by Wolfgang Hahn as 'Moneta Militaris Imititiva'.[21] These coins are generally carefully struck from well engraved dies on freshly prepared flans. A second probable military mint operated in Cyprus under Heraclius from years 17-19 (MIB 198), i.e. around 10 years after the Isaurian issues, and this also produced quite high quality coins struck on fresh flans. Both emissions seem to be the logical result of action by the state to produce a large volume of currency to support a miliary campaign and which would project a favourable impression to the local population.

A fiscal explanation?

In contrast the standards of the Isaurian mints do not fit in with those adopted by other known military mints. In fact the careless overstriking is much more in line with many of the slightly earlier Class 2 Constantinople folles of Heraclius and much of the Constantinople copper of Constans II (641-668). This practice of frequently overstriking earlier coins, often those of the same emperor, is almost certainly associated in some way with the fiscal system and allowed the Byzantine state to cream off a little extra revenue from the process of tax collection. The mechanism was discussed by Michael Hendy who cites a description in a twelfth century treatise dealing with a series of tax reforms undertaken by Alexius 1 between 1106 and 1109.[22] When the tax collector was receiving tax payments which included a fraction of a solidus he took payment of a whole solidus and gave change in copper coin. The 'new' (overstruck) copper had to be bought by the tax collector from the civil authorities at a premium. In a possible variation of this for small tax liabilities the payer could pay in copper coin, but again this had to be 'new' (overstruck) copper and had to be bought from the civil authorities at a premium. The precise mechanism used in the seventh century will probably always be unknown, but the evidence of repeated careless overstriking particularly at the Constantinople makes it certain that something similar was common practice. It therefore seems plausible that this was the prime purpose of the Isaurian coinage from both mints and it would mean that the coins were issued by a nominally civil authority rather than the military themselves. This seems to me a more logical interpretation of the Isaurian coinage, although we cannot entirely rule out the 'soldier's pay' interpretation, however illogical it would have been under the prevailing circumstances.

Whichever interpretation of the Isaurian coinage one favours, a further question that needs to be answered is 'what was the origin of the supply of folles which were overstruck by the two mints?' As we have seen from an analysis of the Isaura undertypes, it is highly unlikely that a supply of old folles was sent out from Constntinople. Perhaps the most likely answer is that a large quantity of copper coins, sufficient to last the mints for 2 or 3 years, was brought to Seleucia by the retreating armies following the abandonment of Antioch and other cities in Syria and southeastern Asia Minor.

Conclusions

The conclusions of the study are listed below and the numbers in brackets refer to the eight observations or assertions by earlier authors which I listed on page 3:

[21] Hahn and Metlich 2009 p. 33 and pl. 9.
[22] Hendy 1984 pp. 285-289.

The mint of Isaura was considerably larger than previously realised and used at least 19 obverse and 17 reverse dies. This is comparable with the number of dies used for the emission of two-bust folles from Seleucia (1 and 2).

There is no evidence of the extensive use at Isaura of either dies or die engravers from Seleucia and the styles adopted by the two mints were very different. But there are two examples of die links between the two mints which indicate the brief re-use of Seleucia dies (2).

The legends on the Isaura folles are less blundered than has been generally thought; the obverse legends, where visible, are readable and the reverse legends are always correctly written (4).

No examples dated year 9 were found (3).

All, or very nearly all, Isaura folles were overstruck on earlier folles, particularly those of Antioch. It therefore seems very likely that these were collected locally and not sent from Constantinople (7).

The Isaurian coins may not have been produced to to pay soldiers, but it is more likely that old folles were overstruck as part of the normal practice of maximising state revenues from the process of taxation (5).

Addendum – the 'Barbarous Mint'

In 2015 Henri Pottier described a group of crudely engraved folles of Heraclius which were quite distinct fom the folles of the Syrian Mint which he had published some years earlier.[23] He appropriately named these coins 'barbarous folles' and suggested that they were struck from 612 onwards by a small mint located in the area of Persian occupation. He catalogued 39 examples, all of which had a two standing figure obverse and completely blundered obverse legends (Fig. 10 a and b). The reverses were also heavily blundered, but in some cases a date numeral could be read which he suggested might be meaningful and including in a few cases year ϚII (8). Pottier's article was very much a report on 'work in progress' and his conclusions were provisional, but there is no doubt that the majority of these coins form a coherent group. Since then a number of other coins from the group have appeared including one with a new type of obverse showing busts of Heraclius and Heraclius Constantine (Fig. 10c) which presumably copies (approximately) either Seleucia or Isaura.

The reason for mentioning the 'barbarous folles' in this article is that many of them are overstruck on regular, unclipped Byzantine folles of Justin II, Maurice and Phocas (for example Fig. 10a). This is exactly the same as the practice at Isaura and would seem to rule out a completely illegal mint, as a forger would have no incentive to overstrike good folles that were currently in circulation. It also raises the possibility that the mint was operating for the same reason as Isaura i.e. to produce 'new' folles which could be used for payment of tax or given as change for tax payments in gold. So some remnant of Byzantine civil authority may have attempted to levy taxes in the usual way for a short period despite lacking a die engraver with even the most basic skills. The 'barbarous mint' could even have been an immediate successor of the Isaura mint, but this suggestion should be regarded as speculative.

[23] Pottier 2015, for a full description of the Syrian Mint coins see Pottier 2004.

Figure 10. Three examples of folles of the 'Barbarous Mint'. All three coins show Heraclius and Heraclius Constantine and have completely blundered legend. Coin a, 12.81g 4h, is overstruck on a regular follis of Justin II; Coin b, 10.29g 12h, is overstruck on an uncertain undertype; Coin c, 10.94g 1h, has a two-bust obverse, probably copying either Seleucia or Isaura (approximately 1.5x actual size).[24]

Catalogue (all coins shown approximately actual size). Unless otherwise noted the type and legends are as follows:

Obv: Facing busts of Heraclius and Heraclius Constantine, both wearing crown with cross and chlamys, cross between heads. Around (sometimes slightly blundered: ƏƏN hЄRACL E hЄRA.

Rev: Large M with cross above, officina A, ANNO - ϚII either side, ISAYR in exergue. MIB 196 (dies O15/R9).

1. O1/R1. 10.09g, overstruck on an Antioch? follis of Maurice. CNG auction 76, 12.9.07 lot 3421.

[24] Coin a private collection, coins b and c courtesy of Leu Numismatik.

2. O1/R6. 10.10g. Elsen auction 121, 14.6.14, lot 511.

3. O1/R12. 12.17g, overstruck on a follis of Maurice. Trombley 2015 Cat. 25.

4. O2/R11. 9.90g, Sternberg auction VIII, 16,17.11.78 lot 831(=Stack's 12.1.09 lot 3135).

5. O3/R3. 11.13g 1h, overstruck on an uncertain follis of Antioch. Roma e-auction 2, 30.8.18 lot 942.

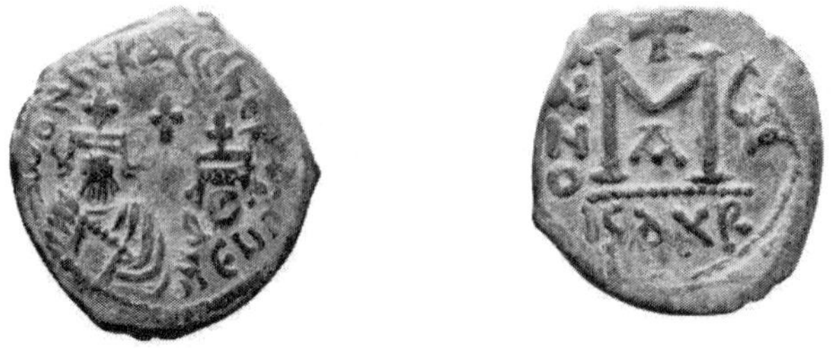

6. O4/R4. 10.83g, overstruck on a follis of Maurice. Triton VIII auction, 12.1.05 lot 1365 (= Sear 1987, 848).

7. O4/R5. 11.65g 12h, overstruck on a Constantinople follis of Maurice. Barber Institute of Fine Arts B3495.

8. O4/R8. 11.72g, overstruck on a follis of Phocas, Constantinople or Nicomedia. ebay March 2022.

9. O4/R13. 7.54g, overstruck on a half follis of Justin II. Roma auction 24, 30.1.16 lot 763.

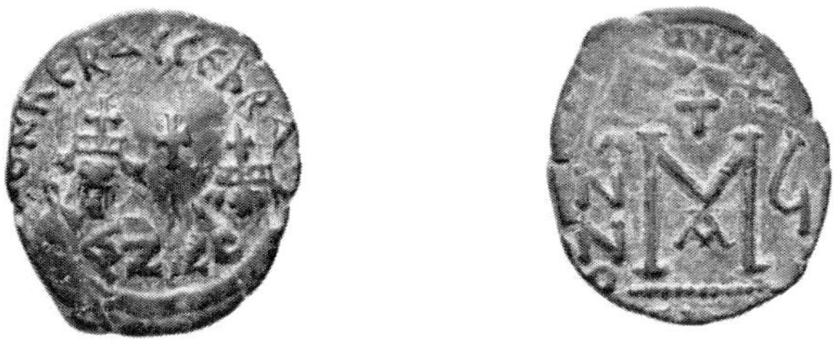

10. O5/R4. 9.40g. CNG auction 326, 7.5.14 lot 622.

11. O5/R8. 11.72g 6h, overstruck on an Antioch follis of Maurice. Dumbarton Oaks collection BZC.1980.5.

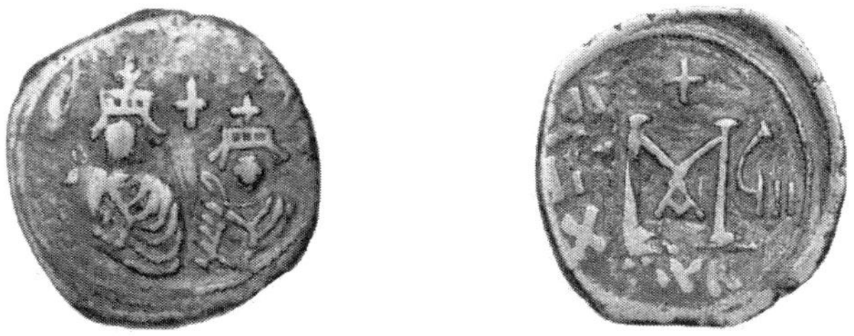

12. O5/Seleucia. 10.17g. Roma auction 78, 17.12.20 lot 1927.

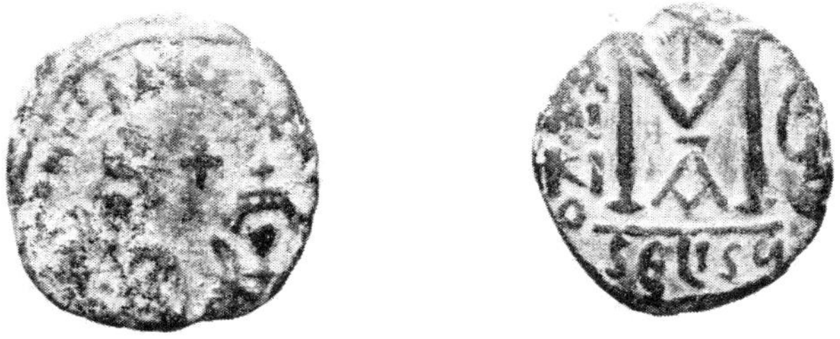

13. O6/R3. 11.99g, CNG auction 355, 15.7.15 lot 673.

14. O6/R9. 10.44g 8h, overstruck on a Cyzicus(?) follis of Maurice. Private collection

15. O9/R3. 10.46g 12h. CNG mail bid sale 66, 19.5.04 lot 173.1 (= Sommer 2010 11.84).

16. O10/R2. 11.18g, overstruck on a follis of Maurice. Sternberg auction VIII, 16,17.11.78 lot 832 (=Sotheby 5.12.90 lot 299 part).

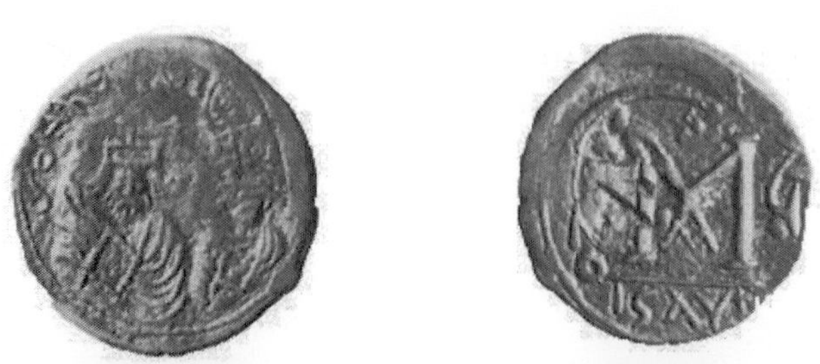

17. O19/R16. 12.50g, overstruck on a follis of Justin II. Numismad auction 24.7.22 lot 1108.

18. O19/R12. 10.37g. Savoca Blue auction 147, 13.11.22 lot 1386.

19. O11/R2. 10.51g, Künker auction 216, 8.10.12 lot 1476

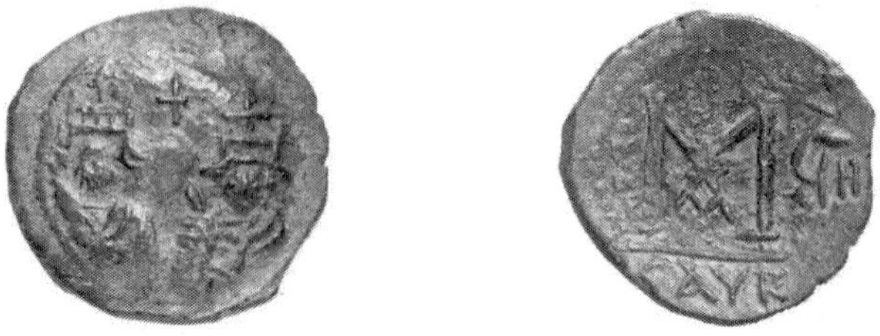

20. O12/R9. 11.65g 6h, overstruck on a Nicomedia follis of Justin II. Private collection.

21. O13/R6. 12.46g, overstruck on a follis of Maurice. CNG auction 37, 20.3.96 lot 2078.

22. O13/R7. 11.53g, overstruck on a Nicomedia follis of Maurice. Numismatik Naumann auction 52, 2.4.17 lot 734 (= Hirsch 25.9.14 lot 3281).

23. 014/R10. 12.04g 3h. Barber Institute of Fine Arts B3494

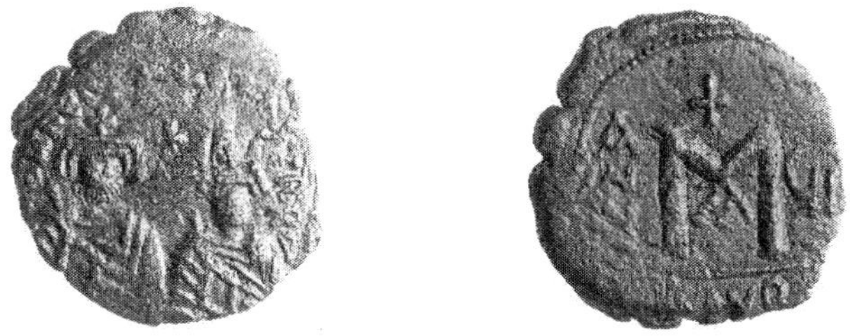

24. O14/Seleucia. Private collection.

25. O15/R9. 12.72g. CNG auction XIX, 19.2.92 lot 331.

26. O16/R9. 10.55g. *Obv.* Trefoils instead of crosses on top of crowns. Numismatik Lanz on ebay 11.20.

27. O17/R9. 11.15g. CNG auction 61, 25.9.02 lot 2237.

28. O17/R3. 10.20g 1h. CNG auction 88, 14.9.11 lot 1636.

29. O18/R15. 11.19g 10h. CNG mail bid sale 84, 5.5.10 lot 1617.

30. O7/R2. 11.2g. Private collection (zeno.ru website #178100).

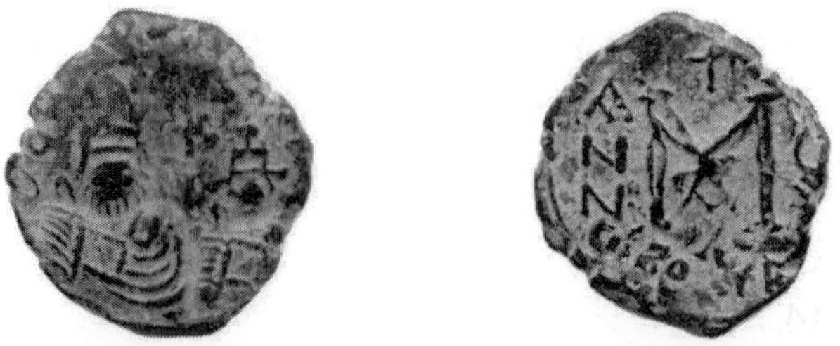

31. O8/R2. 11.08g 12h, overstruck on an Antioch follis of Maurice. Private collection.

32. O?/R14. 12.03g. Biga auction 7, 4.12.21 lot 940.

33. Half follis. 5.39g. *Rev*: large **K** with cross above, **ANNO - ϚII** either side, **ISE** below (MIB 197). EBCC Supplement 209.

34. Irregular half follis imitating Isaura? 6.03g. *Obv*: as above, but no legend. *Rev*: large **K** with cross above, **ANNO - ϚII** either side, Λ below EBCC Supplement 210.

Die duplicates of the catalogued coins[25]

O1/R1: Berk-England 7.12.89 lot 139 12.19g, Numismatik Naumann 80, 4.8.19 lot 675 10.19g, Private collection 9.92g 12h. O1/R6: Savoca 28.12.18 lot 1600 11.03g. O1/R12: Leu 6, 9.12.18 lot 1311 13.53g.

O2/R11: EBCC 18.115 11.83g, Berk list 4 1976 no. 209, Bucephalus 28.7.22 lot 793 12.46g.

O3/R3: Private collection 11.13g 8h, Sotheby 5.12.90 lots 296 and 297 11.86g and 12.77g, Heritage Europe 58, 15.5.18 lot 3239, Private collection 12.4g.

O4/R4: BM Heraclius 267 = Grierson 1951 Pl. X no. 7 and Grierson 1982 Pl. 25 no. 431, 11.87g, Numismatica Ars Classica 95, 26,27.10.95 lot 825 11.78g, trade 2019 11.13g, EBCC 18.116 10.42g, CNG XVIII, 3.12.91 lot 937, Elsen 16.3.19 lot 299 9.90g, CNG 325, 23.4.14 lot 724 3.61g,

[25] Examples without known weights or where one or both dies are uncertain are not included in this list.

Kasdagli 2018 Cat. 660 (weight given as 6.2g, but this appears to be an error as it repeats the weight of the smaller half follis Cat. 658), Zeus 19, 8.8.21 lot 741 11.6g. O4/R5: CNG 404, 23.8.17 lot 605 8.67g, Leu web 19, 28.2.22 lot 3295 9.35g 1h. O4/R8: Trombley 2015 Cat. 28 15.12g.

O5/R4: CNG mail bid 64, 24.9.03 lot 1292 11.14g, Freeman and Sear list 10, 2000 lot 79 11.44g, Savoca 14.7.18 lot 1636 10.49g. O5/R8: Roma 17.12.20 lot 1927 14.06g 6h.

O6/R3: Barber B3493 9.80g 12h, Sotheby 5.12.90 Lot 298 11.76g, Savoca 14.7.18 lot 1638 11.37g, Elsen 152, 9.9.22 lot 1121 11.76g. O6/R9: CNG XIX, 19.2.92 lot 332 11.34g, Barber B3496 = Whitting 1973 no. 208 (rev only shown),13.63g 6h, trade 2019 8.3g, Hirsch 16.2.17 lot 2205.

O8/R2: Ares web 11, 30.8.20 lot 819 11.8g 12h, Leu web 23-24.2.19 lot 1517 1.42g 2h, Hess Divo 317, 27.10.10 11.51g, CNG XXV 24.3.93 lot 953 10.00g, CNG 334, 3.9.14 lot 410 12h (weight given as 20.56g, which seems very unlikely as it is overstruck on a regular Antioch follis of Maurice).

O10/R2: Private collection 10.83g, 12h, BN Is/AE/o1 10.46g 12h.

O11/R2: Private collection 9.52g.

O12/R9: Private collection 11.36g, CNG XXIX, 30.3.94 lot 1154 13.76g.

O13/R6: cgb.fr 2020 11.27g 3h, CNG XIII, 4.12.90 lot 570 11.53g. O13/R7: Gorny and Mosch 122, 10.3.03 lot 2337 11.16g, Trombley 2015 27 12.89g 8h.

O15/R9: Zeus 17, 5.6.21 lot 1048 12.3g., MIB 196 = Morton and Eden 1,2.12.16 lot 511 (part).

O19/R12: Private collection 11.45g 10h.

Bibliography

BM = Wroth, W., 1908, ***Catalogue of the Imperial Byzantine Coins in the British Museum, Vol. 1***, London.

BN = Morrisson, C., 1970, ***Catalogue des monnaies byzantines de la Bibliothèque Nationale***, Paris.

Dennis, G. T. (translator and editor), 1984, ***Maurice's Strategikon***, Philadelphia.

DOC = Grierson P., 1968, ***Catalogue of the Byzantine Coins in the Dumbarton Oaks Collection and in the Whittemore Collection II. Phocas to Theodosius III, Part I. Phocas and Heraclius (602-641)***, Washington, D.C.

EBCC = (Mansfield, S.), 2016, ***Early Byzantine Copper Coins,*** Manchester.[26]

EBCC Supplement = (Mansfield, S)., 2022, ***Supplement to Early Byzantine Copper Coins***, London.

[26] Also available on the website byzantine-ae.info.

Grierson, P., 1951, 'The Isaurian coins of Heraclius' in ***The Numismatic Chronicle***, pp. 56-67.

Grierson, P., 1953, 'A new Isaurian coin of Heraclius' in ***The Numismatic Chronicle***, pp. 145-146.

Grierson, P. 1982, ***Byzantine Coins***, London.

Haldon, J., 1990, ***Byzantium in the seventh century***, Cambridge.

Hahn, W. and Metlich, M., 2009, ***Money of the Incipient Byzantine Empire Continued (Justin II – Revolt of the Heraclii 565-610)***, Vienna

Hendy, M., 1985, ***Studies in the Byzantine Money Economy c. 300-1450***, Cambridge.

Howard-Johnston, J., 2021, ***The Last Great War of Antiquity***, Oxford.

Kasdagli, A-M., 2018, ***Coins in Rhodes***, Oxford.

MIB = Hahn, W., 1981, ***Moneta Imperii Byzantini III. Von Heraclius bis Leo III. / Alleinregierung (610-720)***, Vienna.

Pottier, H., 2004, **Le monnayage de la Syrie sous l'occupation perse (610-630)**, Paris.

Pottier, H., 2015, '7th Century 'barbarous' Folles; a Secondary Mint in the Eastern Part of the Byzantine Empire under Persian Rule' in ***Coinage and History in the Seventh Century Near East*** 4 (A. Oddy, ed.) pp. 17-25, London.

Sabatier, J., 1862, ***Description Génerale des Monnaies Byzantines***, Paris

Sear, D., 1987, ***Byzantine coins and their values***, London.

Sommer, A. U., 2010, ***Die Münzen des Byzantinischen Reiches 491-1453***, Regenstauf.

Trombley, F., 2015, 'The coinage of the Seleucia Isauriae and Isaura mints under Herakleios (ca. 615-619) and related issues' in ***Coinage and History in the Seventh Century Near East*** 4 (A. Oddy, ed.) pp. 251-272, London.

Whitting, P., 1973, ***Byzantine Coins***, London.

Some Observations on the Copper Coinage of Thessalonica under Heraclius

S J Mansfield[1]

Introduction

This paper considers how studying the pattern of copper coinage from the Thessalonica mint can throw light on the history of the Byzantine Empire in the seventh century. It follows the approach taken by Dr Phillips, in relation to the Nicomedia mint[2] and, as respects the Heraclean dynasty more widely[3], by Fr. Maxfield.

In addition to providing an update to the standard works of reference, the paper seeks to encourage archaeologists to describe their coin finds in greater detail and to urge museums to incorporate numismatics as part of mainstream study.

It is worth making four points at the outset. First, the Dumbarton Oaks system, which classifies Byzantine copper coins on the basis of obverse iconography, can no longer be regarded as satisfactory and should be reconsidered – there is a considerable corpus of previously unrecorded types and dates. Second, academics, particularly those interested in the recording of hoards, should pay greater attention to typology. Coins with an *X* or an *I* on the reverse are almost always dekanummia but are differentiated by other factors such as iconography, the forms (or absence) of mint marks and the dates shown. It is frustrating to read of the finding of Heraclian "rare ¼ folles" without reference to typology or dates.[4] Third, it would be appropriate if professionals, particularly in museums, were to assist amateurs more enthusiastically. Fourth, we have to recognise the severe limitations on the credibility of what dealers tell us.

All these issues come into particular focus when addressing some coins of Thessalonica that represent here *a study within a study* – they are the reasonably common but enigmatic "anonymous" dekanummia of Heraclius in profile, anonymous in that they have no mint mark. Can these have been produced for export to Cyprus? The evidence available at present is slight and the conclusions tenuous. Enquiries made to academics and curators on the island have not resulted in useful information. Dealers can sometimes be a little more helpful but what reliance can be placed on what they say?

---

[1] Steve Mansfield is an unaffiliated scholar; sandkmansfield@aol.com

[2] M. S. Phillips, ***The Mint of Nicomedia and Cyzicus during the Persian War 610-620***, in ***Coinage and History in the Seventh Century Near East 5***, London, 2017, pp. 11-32.

[3] S. J. Maxfield, ***Using the iconography and inscriptions on Heraclean Dynasty coins to construct an historical narrative of the 7th century Byzantine Empire***, in ***Coinage and History in the Seventh Century Near East 6***, London, 2020, pp. 19-34.

[4] A. Gandila, ***Early Byzantine Coin Circulation in the Eastern Provinces – A Comparative Statistical Approach***, American Numismatic Society, 2009, p. 190.

Figure 1. Thessalonica and Cyprus.

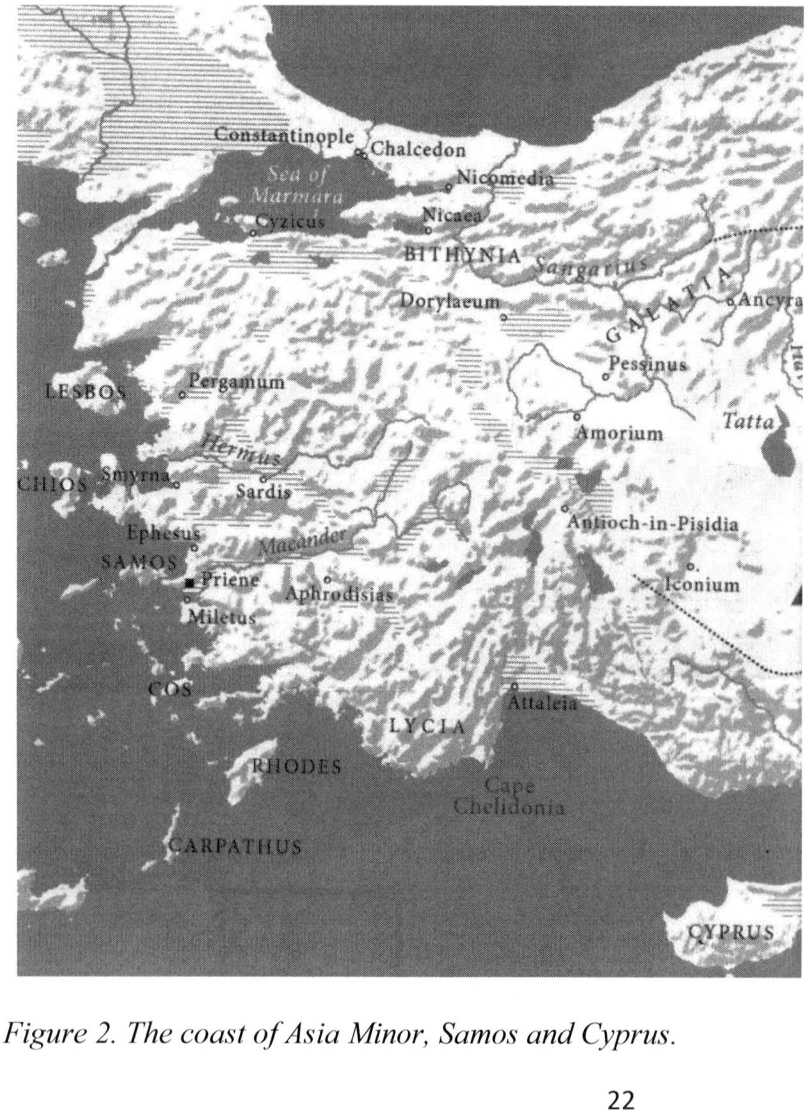

Figure 2. The coast of Asia Minor, Samos and Cyprus.

Thessalonica, a port city, is located in north central Greece at the head of the Gulf of Thermia, part of the Aegean Sea. In late Antiquity it belonged to the Diocese of Moesia, part of the Prefecture of Illyricum, and its large and secure harbour provided for good sea communications with Constantinople, the coast of Asia Minor and the Middle East littoral as well as the western part of the empire. Road systems connected Thessalonica to the capital, the rest of Greece and the range of Byzantine provinces to the north separated from Barbaricum by the River Danube. In the last case, the road network may have been for a largely military purpose as the area was a war zone – the city itself coming under frequent pressure from the Avaro-Slav khaganate.[5] The frequent close sequestering of the city and the suggestion that several sieges took place indicate the importance of sea routes. Figure 2 shows the location of the island of Samos which plays a part here.

The copper coinage of Thessalonica

In the Dumbarton Oaks catalogue[6] volume 2 part 1 Grierson applies a descriptive framework to the coins similar to that used at the other major mints of Constantinople, Nicomedia and Cyzicus. This is, generically, the familiar "family coinage" of the Heraclian dynasty: class 1 shows Heraclius alone; class 2 with his then only son Heraclius Constantine, on classes 3 and 4 they are joined by a female figure, either Eudocia the emperor's first wife or his second wife (also his niece) Martina; class 5 reverts to two figures with Heraclius in military costume; the rare and enigmatic class 6 at Thessalonica has three figures all apparently male. Classes 3 and 4 are combined at Thessalonica and all the fractional denominations are gradually phased out.

The other major work of reference – Moneta Imperii Byzantini[7] employs quite a simple numeric system. Counting the numbers (while discounting minor variations) 15 categories of coins are listed therein. By contrast, this paper shows that 11 different iconographical combinations of obverse and reverse exist among the five denominations[8] making 19 sub-categories in all. Each is represented by a figure in the catalogue at the end of this paper. A further 16 regnal years, not previously published, are also noted.

Thus the coinage is more complex than set out in DOC and MIB. Three of the 19 "Types" (which is the terminology adopted for this paper) have innovative designs and two may now be attributed more firmly to Thessalonica. Each new Type is examined in light of events in the western part of the empire. Another Type, a dekanummium with a profile bust but without a mint mark, may be associated with Byzantium's response to events in the war against its eastern rival, Sasanian Persia.

The basis for a new typology

The typology is constructed as follows. The Type of the coin for each of the five denominations is specified in terms of three attributes (a fourth – whether the issue is dated or undated – can be discarded as only the pentanummium is undated):

1. the form of portrait ("iconography");

[5] A term used for convenience. For the subordination of the Slav tribes to the Avars, J. V. A. Fine, ***The Early Medieval Balkans***, Ann Arbor Mich., 1983, pp. 29-33. Much of the historical background to Avaro-Slav activity as described here is derived from this work.

[6] P. Grierson, ***Catalogue of the Byzantine Coins in the Dumbarton Oaks Collection and in the Whittemore Collection, Volume Two Phocas to Theodosius III (602-717) Part 1 Phocas and Heraclius (602-641),*** Washington DC, 1968.

[7] W. Hahn, ***Moneta Imperii Byzantini, Volume 3 From Heraclius to Leo III (610-720),*** Vienna 1981.

[8] Being the follis of 40 nummi (f); three-quarter follis of 30 (tqf); half follis of 20 (hf); dekanummium of 10 (d) and pentanummium of 5 (p).

2. the denomination and the form of the denomination mark (in Greek or Latin);

3. the mint mark (if any).

Where a combination of the three attributes forms a "whole" that is unique (thus differentiating one Type from another) this is given a Type number. To assist clarity an abbreviation representing the denomination – *f* for the follis; *tqf* for the (very rare) three quarter follis; *hf* for the half follis; *d* for the dekanummium and *p* for the pentanummium – is attached to the Type number. The 19 Types are illustrated as plates in the catalogue at Annex 2. In five instances (totalling 13 Types) the sole distinction is the denomination although only in a single case are all the four most common denominations (f; hf; d and p) present. The three-quarter follis (tqf) was first struck, and then only very briefly, in regnal year 20 (629/30). The other six Types (4d; 5d; 7hf; 8hf; 9f and 12f) may (to varying degrees of probability) represent trial strikes or experimental issues – all are rare.

To make this paper easier to read the table of Types is relegated to an Annex (1) and this is followed by the associated catalogue of Types at Annex (2).

Several high level points may be noted (these are repeated at Annex 1). Coins seem to have been issued by the Thessalonica mint in every regnal year except year 11 (620/1) down to year 20 (629/30) - the accepted date of its closure - despite the recurrent threat to the city by the Avars and Slavs. For denominations and mint marks both Latin and Greek forms are used although Greek is used almost exclusively after about year 5. The mint "tinkers" with the coinage, for example substituting the Greek M for the Latin XXXX on the follis between regnal years 3 and 4 and inserting the Latin form again amidst a sea of Greek, but seemingly very briefly, in regnal years 17-19. But it is the dekanummium that is particularly interesting. Four Types exist (1d; 2d; 4d and 5d) overlapping with each other up to and including regnal year 7 at which point the anonymous profile bust Type 5d[9] takes over and was apparently struck until year 15 and possibly to year 20. Why should the mint have produced such different forms of small change – something that could only have confused the local city population?

The possible circumstances surrounding the striking of the Type 5d dekanummium are explored in detail subsequently.

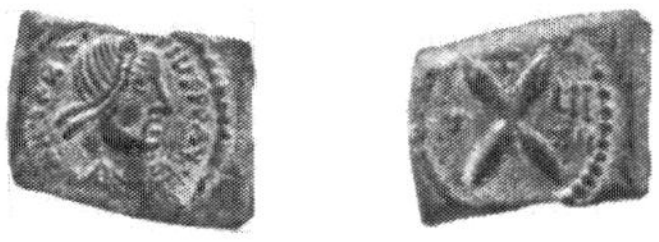

Figure 3. Type 5d dekanummium of regnal year 8. 2.11g. MIB 232. Mansfield collection – Dumbarton Oaks Gift.[10]

There are health warnings with a certain amount of the Thessalonican coinage. Issues of Phocas and Heraclius are difficult to tell apart unless there is a fairly complete obverse legend, which is rarely the case. Also, many of the regnal years are hard to read on account of wear, sloppy striking and, in particular for this issue of dekanummia, the restriking of quartered flans of earlier coins with the result that some part of the date arrangement may be off-flan.

There are five proposed revisions or additions to the DOC arrangement of the coinage and it is convenient to address these in chronological order:

---

[9] Some dekanummia with a facing bust are similarly "anonymous".

[10] At Oxford there was a short discussion concerning a possible marking to the left of the reverse X – perhaps a II. It is not possible to resolve this at present as the coin is now in Washington DC – where it may be examined.

- The “anonymous” facing bust dekanummia (Type 1d): years 1-7;
- The “military” half folles (Type 7hf): years 3-4;
- The “enthroned emperors” (Type 8hf): years 9 and 20;
- The XXXX denominational mark (Type 9f): years 17/18 or 18/19;
- The late anomalous follis (Type 12f): year 31.

Figure 4. Attribution of the Type 1d anonymous facing bust dekanummium to Thessalonica (obverses @ twice actual size).

Thessalonica 40 nummi regnal year 3 with mint mark TES. Type 2f. Byzantine Coinage in the East vol. II, Edizioni D’Andrea 2020, no. 875. MIB 217. Wt. unknown.

“Anonymous” dekanummium regnal year 1. Type 1d. 2.76g. MIB 231. Mansfield collection – Dumbarton Oaks Gift.

In DOC, Grierson attributes this dekanummium issue (Type 1d) to Constantinople although he says “while probable, it is not certain.. . .”.[11] Comparison of the two obverse portraits shown above leaves practically no doubt that the dekanummium belongs to Thessalonica. Thus, there are two types of anonymous dekanummium with different iconographies that belong to the mint.

Figure 5. Type 7hf half folles – emperors wear military dress.

Thessalonica half folles of regnal years 3 and 4 (612-614). 5.24g & 5.63g. Mansfield collection – Dumbarton Oaks Gift.

On the second coin in particular the belted tunic and pteruges (reinforced strips of leather designed to protect the groin) worn by both figures are clearly shown. Both emperors hold long crosses. These coins are rare, and hitherto probably unpublished, but folles and half folles were struck (the latter more intermittently than the former) at Thessalonica with the emperors wearing the civilian dress from regnal year 3 (catalogue figs. 10-11). The origin of the military style may of course lie with the idiosyncratic practices of an individual die-cutter although the retention of the design into regnal year 4 perhaps tells against this.

[11] ***DOC Volume 2, Part 1*** nos. 85 to (88) and also p. 230.

Folles with the emperors holding long crosses were produced at Constantinople and Nicomedia during 612-4 – in these cases it is the chlamys that is worn, however.[12] Combined with military dress, why the long crosses? The state religion of the Sasanian Empire was Zoroastrianism and although Christian minorities existed within its frontiers persecution was not unknown. The Avars were pagan Animists. The cross, given a prominent position on the coins, sent a message of militant Christianity. It seems that the Thessalonica mint may have authorised an issue projecting a more aggressive image at this time.

Figure 6. Type 8hf half folles – emperors enthroned.

Thessalonica half folles of regnal years 9 and 20. 6.17g and 3.66g. DOC 144.1 and Mansfield collection – Dumbarton Oaks Gift.

The iconography of these rare half folles is also unexpected and the apparent gap of 10 years between the issue of the only two examples known cannot be explained. The differences in style and production standards are obvious. Neither Grierson nor Hahn note any particular significance, the former limiting his comments to the quality of the manufacture of the coin at Dumbarton Oaks.[13] On the face of it the second coin was struck in the last year (629/30) of the accepted period of operation of the mint. These comments aside, it is clear what is being portrayed and it may be that the coins represent test strikings for issues intended at various times to promote imperial prestige in a city continually hard-pressed by the enemy.[14]

Figure 7. The brief life of the XXXX denominational mark at Thessalonica; years 17-18 (626-8).

Follis (XXXX) (Type 9f). In trade 2022 (Sol Numismatik). Probably regnal year 17. 5.75g.

Similar. In trade 2022 (Sol Numismatik). Probably regnal year 18. 4.96g.

These interesting, again rather rare, coins can be dealt with briefly. Where one would expect to see M, the reverse says XXXX. The coins may simply represent the playful work of a die-cutter about to knock off from his shift. The interchangeability of Greek and Latin for the denomination marks has already been remarked upon. Because of some uncertainty in interpreting the second digit – the stigma - it is possible that this issue was also struck into year 19.

---

[12] ***MIB Volume 3, pl. 10***, 159 for Constantinople. The Nicomedia folles (not recorded in MIB), while much rarer, are iconographically similar.

[13] ***DOC Volume 1, Part 2*** no. 144.1.

[14] Interestingly, the Dumbarton Oaks collection includes a follis of broadly similar design (DOC 134) produced even earlier – in regnal year 4 (613/4).

Figure 8. The anomalous late follis issue (Type 12f); year 31.

Follis "year 31" (Type 12f). Early Byzantine Copper Coins[15] 19.50 & 19.51. 10.18g & 7.90g. Mansfield collection – Dumbarton Oaks Gift.

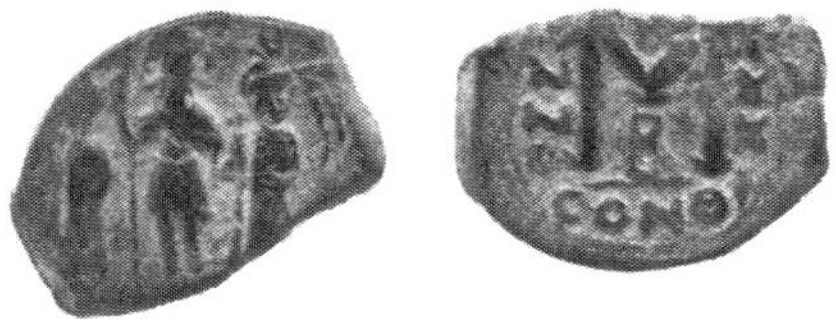

Figure 9. Constantinople follis of regnal year 31 (MIB 167).

Only about half a dozen specimens of the Type 12f follis, a very perplexing coin, are known, struck, if the regnal year is to be taken at face value, 11 years after the accepted date for the closure of the Thessalonica mint in 630. It is difficult to believe that the die-cutter mistakenly added the digits X & I to existing dies as no coin is known for certain of year 21 – a possible specimen recorded by Ratto cannot be verified. A possible explanation is based on the existence of some, reasonably common, coins bearing the mint mark CON followed by a theta (Θ) and the date arrangements for years 30 and 31 (fig. 9) which may have been produced for some purpose at Thessalonica. If so, Type 12f may have been part of this project, the different iconographies of the obverses indicating, perhaps, that there were two separate stages to it.

The West – war against Avars and Slavs (Types 7hf; 8hf & 12f)

The western theatre of war saw the empire confronted by a generally firm alliance of Avars and Slavs with the former as the dominant partner. For events affecting Thessalonica and its environs in this period there is The Miracles of Saint Demetrius[16], a rich store of contemporary local information telling, if sometimes rather floridly, how the long-dead saint intervened to save his city during its years of crisis.

From an examination of the dates of the coins discussed in the last sub-section we see key regnal years as 3-4 (612-614) for the military half folles; 9 and 20 (618/9 and 629/30 respectively) for the enthroned half follis; and 31 (640/1) for the three figure follis of that year. But the idea of a synthesis of the typology of the coins and the events affecting the Prefecture of Illyricum during the first three decades of the seventh century – in principle an attractive idea advanced below - is at present hard to maintain convincingly.

---

[15] S. J. Mansfield, ***Early Byzantine Copper Coins (EBCC) – Catalogue of an English Collection***, Ex Officio Books, Manchester, 2016.

[16] P. Lemerle (ed.) ***Miracula S. Demetrii***, Paris 1979 and 1981.

The following coin, apparently unique and unpublished, cannot be a product of the imperial mint of Thessalonica – the unusual iconography and the date are all wrong. What is particularly noticeable is the Germanic-style helmet albeit with a trifoliate ornament attached. There is no suggestion that it is an Avar coin but it might well be the result, to adopt Gandila's phrase[17], of some kind of cross-Danubian cultural encounter between the Byzantine Empire and Barbaricum.

Figure 10. "Avar imitation" a cultural encounter?
11.85g; @ twice actual size. Pavlou collection. Courtesy of P S Pavlou.

Byzantium at war on two fronts 611-41

In the early seventh century Byzantium was engaged in the strategist's nightmare of a war on two fronts – against the Sasanian Persian Empire in the East and its ally the Avar Khaganate (together with its Slav clients) in the West. The geographical position of Thessalonica, critically the potential to dominate the Aegean, undoubtedly gave it a strategic role in the wider war but the immediate military threat was confined to that coming from the Avaro-Slavs.

Byzantium enjoyed certain strategic advantages including the natural defence of the Balkans region offered by the Danube and (against the Persians) its client polity of the Christian Arab Ghassanids. There were also the very strong fortifications of the capital and internal communications allowing ease of movement of troops between the two fronts.

This wide-ranging conflict, sometimes described as "The Last Great War of Antiquity"[18;19] commenced in 603 when the Sasanian Great King Khusrau II used the pretext of a regime change, the toppling of the Emperor Maurice (582-602), to declare war on Byzantium. By 615 (probably early in that year, i.e., in regnal year 5) a Persian army was encamped looking over the mouth of the Propontis towards Constantinople. The situation remained critical throughout the 620s but by 625 Heraclius had seized the initiative. The great outflanking march launched in 627 ultimately took his armies to the gates of Ctesiphon leading to a palace coup and the dethroning of Khusrau.

[17] A. Gandila, ***Cultural Encounters on Byzantium's Northern Frontier, c. 500-700, Coins, Artifacts and History***, Cambridge University Press, 2018. This important work, inter alia, examines the export of coins into Barbaricum.
[18] J. Howard-Johnston, ***The Last Great War of Antiquity***, Oxford University Press, 2021.
[19] For a numismatic take on the campaign of 628-9, to a degree speculative, see also S. J. Mansfield, ***An Imitative Mint of the Persian War 602-28*** in ***Supplement to Early Byzantine Copper Coins***, Archetype Publications Ltd and Ex Officio Books, 2022, pp. 59-73.

West	East	Coin Types and dating
	Fall of Caesarea in Cappodacia (611)[20]	
	Byzantine defeat near Antioch (613)[21]	
	Persians under Shahen march to Chalcedon (615)[22]	7hf: military dress 612-4
Slav migration into the Balkans after 610[23]		
	Byzantium hard-pressed; refugees and a currency famine on Cyprus?	5d: profile bust/anonymous 615-25
Slavs encircle Thessalonica 614-6[24]		
Avars ravage Thrace (617 or 619)[25]		8hf enthroned emperors 618-9
Slav attack on Thessalonica (620)[26]		
Lengthy (33 day) Avar siege of Thessalonica in 622[27]		
	First Byzantine counter-offensive (625)[28]	
Avar siege of Constantinople – summer 626[29]	Persians at Chalcedon (June 626)[30]	
	Decisive Byzantine counter-strike (627)	
		9f XXXX 626-9
	Persia accepts unfavourable peace with Byzantium (628-9)	
Decline in power of the Avar Khaganate (630-35 and later)		
	Arabs take Maritime Caesarea (641) – end of Byzantine rule in "Greater Syria"	
Relative peace/economic recovery?		12f three figures 640-1

Figure 11. Key events of the "Last Great War" & issues of the copper coinage at Thessalonica.

[20] Howard-Johnston, ***Last Great War*** p. 81.
[21] ***Last Great War*** pp. 85-6.
[22] ***Last Great War*** p. 105 *et seq*.
[23] Fine, ***Early Medieval Balkan***s, p. 34.
[24] ***Early Medieval Balkan***s, p. 41.
[25] ***Early Medieval Balkan***s, p. 42.
[26] Howard-Johnston, ***Last Great War***, p. 206.
[27] ***Last Great War***, pp. 202 *et seq*. The date is described as powerfully circumstantial and without strong contrary evidence.
[28] ***Last Great War***, p. 217, *et seq*.
[29] ***Last Great War***, p. 268 *et seq*.
[30] ***Last Great War***, p. 274.

It is obvious that there is not a high degree of cohesion here. It is, in fact, somewhat disjointed. Nor has the text yet covered Type 5d – the anonymous profile bust dekanummium. This is proposed to form a part of the "Eastern question". But drawing on the, admittedly crude, chronology set out above it is hard to suggest any very concrete significance for the three particularly innovative Types – 7hf; 8hf and 12f – set against events in the West between 610 and 622, a story of almost continuous pressure on Thessalonica. The military half folles, while probably associated with the similar Constantinople and Nicomedia folles, may have represented a propagandist response to increasing Slav activity. The enthroned type, similarly, could have been an attempt to boost imperial prestige in the light of the Avaro-Slav threat to Thrace. Last, some degree of greater political stability in Illyricum, given the decline of the Avar Khaganate and the lesser threat posed by the more fragmented Slav tribes, might have been reflected in the production of a new coinage in 640 and 641 designed to stimulate economic activity even if this was limited to Thessalonica itself. It is possible the coins signed CONΘ which were struck for regnal years 30 and 31 were the first stage of this project with an issue marked TES in year 31 when the former proved not to be popular. All these suggestions are tenuous.

The East – war against the Persians (Type 5d)

If the Byzantines managed the decline of the Avar Khaganate through its customary underhand diplomacy the Persian war was, until its final stages, more a story of march and counter-march. The focus here is on the anonymous profile bust dekanummium of Type 5d.

In the first four years of the reign of Heraclius, four different dekanummia seem to have been issued by the Thessalonica mint. Two of these (Types 2d and 4d) are very rare coins today and the first is not central to the argument. This leaves Types 1d and 5d – dated coins without any mint signature bearing a facing bust (1d) and a bust in profile (5d) on the obverse.

Figure 12. Differentiating Type 5d - the commoner dekanummia: "Constantinople" (a) and "anonymous" (b & c).

Fig. a. Constantinople (undated) MIB 172.	Fig. b. Thessalonica anonymous Type 1d (year 7). MIB 231.	Fig. c. Thessalonica anonymous Type 5d (year 7). MIB 232.

All ex Mansfield collection now at Dumbarton Oaks – Mansfield Gift.

For the anonymous coins, the above are representative examples only but both may be accepted (subject to caveats) as regnal year 7. In EBCC[31] there are 13 specimens of the two Types – a sizeable holding for what are reasonably scarce coins (for example the DO collection originally had eight – all catalogued as Constantinople). By contrast, MIB gives both to Thessalonica.

The lack of any particularly compelling argument for Thessalonica as the origin of the anonymous issues is frustrating.[32] Type 5d represents the only profile bust dekanummium known apart from those made at Ravenna and appears to be quite easily the largest of all the issues for the denomination. If it

---

[31] Mansfield, ***Early Byzantine Copper Coins***, digital edition 2019.

[32] DOC gives them to Constantinople. MIB prefers Thessalonica (as above). Grierson (in DOC p. 230) suggests Constantinople "partly on the evidence of letter forms" and that "future research may show them to be Thessalonica".

is from Constantinople why were there two contemporaneous issues, one with the mint signature CON and one without it? Of course, the same could be said for Thessalonica. It helps to note a distinction in the quality of production of the two Thessalonican issues. The facing bust type is for the most part struck on well prepared flans and the profile type mostly on quartered remnants – possibly suggesting a degree of urgency in their production.

For Type 5d, it may be that the following coin (only known from a handful of examples) was a short-lived prototype.

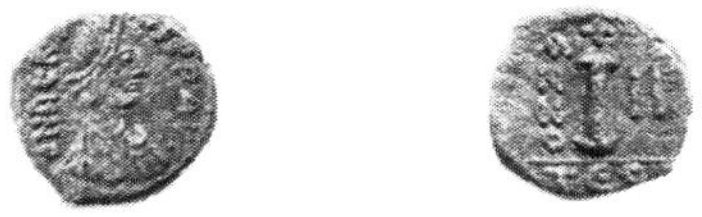

Figure 13. "Prototype" Thessalonican dekanummium of regnal year 2.

Type 4d (regnal year 2). MIB 230.
2.08g. Mansfield collection – Dumbarton Oaks Gift.

During the last decade whenever the Type 5d dekanummia have been offered for sale it has normally been by dealers based on Cyprus;[33] certainly five out of eight examples in EBCC came from Cyprus. There is provenance for the other three but they do not ever appear to be listed by dealers known to be associated with Turkey, Jordan or Israel. Of course, this risks bad numismatics. Ignoring this risk might lead us to think, as has been pointed out, that the only sure provenance for many ancient coins is the international transit lounge at Zurich airport.[34] Dealers buy coins in one place and sell them from another.

Nonetheless, why should Thessalonica need two separate but overlapping issues of the dekanummium? Is it possible that Type 5d was connected in some way with Cyprus? And, if so, might this reflect some aspect of the Persian war?

Whither the coins?

In 2018, Gandila wrote: "*It has been repeatedly suggested that the main purpose of the moneta publica of Thessalonica was to meet the needs of the Macedonian metropolis and to supply the Danube frontier in northern Illyricum.*"[35] Of the later period, however, he writes:

.. .. the reorientation of Thessalonica southward towards the Aegean and the Mediterranean after 75 years when its efforts had concentrated primarily on the Balkans .. .. was signalled by the growing influx of Thessalonican half-folles to provinces in Palestine and became clearer in the early decades of the 7th century. With its back against the wall – literally because of Avaro-Slavic attacks that targeted the city itself - Thessalonica had no choice but to redirect its dwindling mint output towards the sea ***using the islands as stepping stones****. There are very few 7th-century coins in the eastern Balkans and no hoards with Thessalonican coins are so far known after 600.*[36] [My bold]

[33] Clearly this is a matter of the author's perception.
[34] M. S. Phillips, ***Currency in seventh-century Syria as a historical source***, Byzantine and Modern Greek Studies 28 (2004) pp. 13-31.
[35] A. Gandila, ***The Mint of Thessalonica and the Mediterranean Economy in the 6th–7th C.***, Revue Belge de Numismatique, Brussels, CLXIV-2018, Abstract.
[36] ***Mint of Thessalonica***, p. 464.

Numismatists might challenge the idea of a dwindling mint output during the reign of Heraclius – in public and private collections and in trade Thessalonican folles struck down to 630 are today quite plentiful. Although blockaded on its landward side, the mint could, one imagines, supply coin to other provinces by sea relatively easily. The city's large artificial harbour, according to Zosimus, dates from the civil wars in the time of Constantine the Great.

Our particular interest is in the dekanummia. Where do these occur (or not)?

Thessalonican dekanummia of Heraclius do not appear to be specifically recorded in the database of the Israel Antiquities Authority (IAA) for the provinces of Palaestina Prima and Secunda (some 45,000 coins).[37] Bijovski (IAA) adds: "The mint of Thessalonica, which was a main supplier of copper coinage during the second half of the sixth century, played no significant role in monetary circulation in Palestine during the reigns of Phocas and Heraclius."

Gandila lists three hoards and 30-odd Thessalonican "*half folles and fractions*" found in Asia Minor.[38] Byzantine hoards in Asia Minor (the Diocese of Asia) have also been addressed by Morrisson, Popovic and Ivanisevic but the work was subject to a critical review, mainly on grounds of its lack of completeness, by Curta.[39;40]

Today, Thessalonican coins of Heraclius are found plentifully in the Lebanon. A hoard (or part hoard) of 231 folles and five half folles probably found at Sarhine (in Lebanon's Bekaa Valley) with a tpq of 630 contained 16 Thessalonican folles of Heraclius.[41] But as (in all probability) this was a savings hoard the absence of dekanummia might not perhaps be surprising.

While the foregoing paragraphs cannot be regarded as a comprehensive survey or to be conclusive, it appears that there is no concrete evidence for circulation of the dekanummia in the Balkans, Asia Minor or "Greater Syria".[42] One would wish nevertheless for greater granularity. Even where dozens of relevant hoards are listed (for example in the work of Curta and Gandila on the Balkans[43]) without more detail the value of the information has its limits. For example, Gandila[44] refers generally to Thessalonican *half folles and fractions* without distinction – even if dekanummia were distinguished in coin lists as specific follis fractions it could only be via a comprehensive illustrated database that the *type* of dekanummium noted might be known for certain. His remark about the islands as "stepping stones" is intriguing. In a work of 2009[45] (at page 190), Gandila notes the finding of a number of Heraclian "rare ¼-folles" in the Eupalinian tunnel on Samos. Are they the anonymous dekanummia of Type 5d perhaps deposited while en-route by sea from Thessalonica to Cyprus? We do not know.

---

[37] G. I. Bijovski, ***Gold Coin and Small Change: Monetary Circulation in Fifth-Seventh Century Byzantine Palestine***, Edizioni Università di Trieste, 2012, p. 386.

[38] Gandila, ***Mint of Thessalonica***, p. 475.

[39] C. Morrisson, V. Popovic and V Ivanisevic, ***Les trésors monétaires des Balkans et D'Asie Mineure (491-793)***, Réalites byzantines, 13, Paris, 2006.

[40] F. Curta in ***Byzantine and Modern Greek Studies 31***, no. 2 (2007).

[41] S. J. Mansfield, ***Three Byzantine Hoards***, Numismatic Chronicle, 2013, pp. 391-413.

[42] The author owes this point to Tony Goodwin.

[43] F. Curta and A. Gandila, ***Hoards and Hoarding Patterns in the Early Byzantine Balkans***, Dumbarton Oaks Papers Volumes 65-66, Washington DC, 2011-2012.

[44] ***Mint of Thessalonica***, 2018.

[45] A. Gandila, ***Early Byzantine Coin Circulation in the Eastern Provinces, A Comparative Statistical Approach***, American Numismatic Society, AJN Second Series 21, 2009, pp. 151-226.

"*Semper Chypre*"

The dekanummia were certainly present on Cyprus in the seventh century. Relevant coins were found during the French excavations at Salamis (ancient Constantia) in 1964-74.[46] Large numbers of Byzantine, and both earlier and later coins, have been recorded. Some 750 identifiable Byzantine coins were found on the site of the Basilica at Salamis alone, of which 207 are from the reign of Heraclius. No Thessalonican folles or half folles of Heraclius have been found but the dekanummia recorded are as follows:

Classification	Type	Regnal years	Total number
DOC Class 1 (Constantinople)			6
Thessalonica	1d	4	1
Thessalonica	5d	8 (two); 9 (one); uncertain (three)	6

This is helpful – a ratio of 1:6 for Type 1d to Type 5d aligns roughly to an (admittedly rough and ready) estimate about the respective size of the two issues. But other records lack the desired detail. Byzantine hoards are known for Cyprus but (for example) *Byzantine Cyprus* (Nicosia 2009)[47], while listing the hoards by name, provides little useful detail on their composition. Regrettably, the Department of Antiquities on Cyprus has not answered a query as to whether the Type 5d coins are present in old museum collections on the island.[48]

A coinage for Cyprus?

Georganteli and Shea[49] write

The strong presence of Herakleios's copper coins in Cyprus reflects the position of Cyprus as a way-station between Syria and Constantinople .. .

Oddy and Mansfield[50]

.. .. . the importance of Cyprus to the Byzantine Middle East is unquestionable. The Persian and Arab wars gave rise to twists and turns in Byzantine political and economic decision making. Cyprus seems frequently to have played a significant part.

Woods[51]

the island .. .. . may simply have been experiencing a growing shortage of copper coinage . .. . This difficulty would have been exacerbated by the massive influx of refugees into Cyprus.

---

[46] O. Callot, ***Salamine de Chypre XVI Les Monnaies***, Fouilles de la Ville 1964-1874, Paris 2004.

[47] M. D. Metcalf, ***Byzantine Cyprus 491-1191***, Cyprus Research Centre Nicosia, 2009.

[48] Equally, the author has never been offered these coins by dealers known to be based in Lebanon, Jordan or Israel.

[49] E. Georganteli and J. Shea, ***Numismatic considerations of Byzantium's border with the caliphate***, Journal of the Oriental Numismatic Society (JONS) 193 (Autumn 2007) Supplement, pp. 1-3.

[50] W. A. Oddy and S. J. Mansfield, ***The "Neapolis" Mint and the Cypriot Coinage of Heraclius***, Israel Numismatic Research 16/2021, pp. 213-42.

[51] D. Woods, ***The Nea(polis) Folles of Heraclius***, Israel Numismatic Research 12/2017, pp. 159-72.

But the suggestion that Type 5d was produced for Cyprus still presents difficulties. The Persians were, intermittently, able to raid Cyprus and the Aegean islands, but whether at this time, they possessed a sufficient advantage in sea power to seal off Constantinople and Thessalonica from Cyprus is debatable. The archaeological evidence from the island is not extensive. The issue of Type 5d seems to have been both long lasting (it will be recalled that a specimen dated as late as 630 has been noted), but also – like a lot of the coinage – still somewhat intermittent – a strange profile for a necessity coinage. The export of dekanummia would also leave Thessalonica without the denomination post-617 - although equally the cities of Nicomedia and Cyzicus seem to have managed without these low value coins and they are scarce even for Constantinople.[52]

It could be that the DOC Class 1 issue marked CON is a coin that could be more directly associated with the Cypriot city of Constantia/Salamis than the anonymous coins discussed here. But Type 5d might have been struck without a mint mark for that very reason - to avoid confusion with the products of the Constantinople mint that we know also circulated on Cyprus.

Did Cyprus have its own coinage as early as 615 – some small change needed to oil the local economy in response to an influx of refugees and a currency famine?[53] And, if so, did it come from Thessalonica? At present there are only tantalising pointers.

Summary

- The coinage is complicated – certainly more so than the that of the Eastern mints.
- Chronologically, the "Types" overlap – there is also considerable interchange of iconography, denomination marks and mint signatures.
- The city was blockaded by land for much of the reign – economically did Thessalonica reorientate itself southward as Gandila suggests?
- Is both a "city coinage" and an "export coinage" for the dekanummia a viable idea?
- Specifically, was Type 5d intended for Cyprus where there may have been some kind of currency famine? But the evidence is circumstantial.

---

[52] Grierson (in DOC p. 230) suggests that lower price levels "in the provinces" (assumed to mean remote from Constantinople and the Propontine mints) may have resulted in more abundant striking of the lower denominations at Thessalonica. He makes no suggestion of an export coinage.

[53] The supply of small change under such circumstances might exacerbate an already inflationary situation and this represents a potential source of enquiry. It is a topic outside the scope of the present paper.

ANNEX 1: TABLE OF TYPES

Iconography (1)	Denomination mark (2)	Mint mark (3)	Type	Regnal year(s)	DOC	MIB	Notes (1)	Fig.
Facing bust	XXXX	TЄS	1f	1; 2; 3	Cl 1a; (130)	216		1
Facing bust	M	TЄS	2f	4	-	217		2
Facing bust	XX	TЄS	1hf	1; 2; 3	Cl 1a; 131	225		3
Facing bust	K	TЄS	2hf	3; 4	Cl 1b; (132)	226		4
Facing bust	X	-	1d	1; 3; 4; 5; 6; 7		231a-b	Plume on helmet & cross on crown	5
Facing bust	I	TЄS	2d	4	-	-	(2)	6
Facing bust	Є	-	3p		-	233	MIB: DOC (n. a.) (3)	7
Profile bust	I	TЄS	4d	2	Cl 1; (133)	230		8
Profile bust	X	-	5d	5; 8; 9; 13; 15; 20 (4)	Cl 3; 97	232	DOC: CON	9
2 figures	M	TЄS/ΘЄC	6f	3; 4; 5; 6; 7; 8; 13; 14	Cl 2; 134-138	218-220	Civil dress	10
2 figures	K	TЄS/ΘЄC	6hf	4; 5; 6; 7; 8; 9; 10; 14	Cl 2; 139-143	227-228	Civil dress	11
2 figures	K	TЄS	7hf	3; 4	-	-	Military dress	12a-b
2 figures	K	ΘЄC	8hf	9; 20	Cl 3; 149.1	228, 2	Enthroned (5)	13a-b
3 figures	XXXX	ΘЄC	9f	17 or 18 18 or 19	-	-	Value mark – Latin (6)	14
3 figures	M	ΘЄC	10f	12; 13; 14; 15; 16; 17; 18; 19; 20	Cl 3; (146)-120	221		15
3 figures	K	ΘЄC	10hf	13; 17; 18; 19	Cl 3; 151	229	DOC 151: year 17 (7)	16
2 figures	M	ΘЄC	11f	20	-	222	Military dress	17
2 figures	Λ	ΘЄC	11tqf	20	Cl 5; 152	224	Military dress	18
3 figures	M	ΘЄC	12f	31	-	223		19a-b

Underlining is used in the table to indicate aspects of the coins that have not been noted hitherto: forms of iconography; new iconographical/denominational mark combinations for the mint; unlisted regnal years.

(1) Reference to "dress" is based on the portrayal of Heraclius. Heraclius Constantine usually wears the civilian chlamys.

(2) The attribution is not certain. The coin may belong to Phocas. But its relationship to Type 1d (as here) supports Heraclius. Mansfield, S. J., The attribution of Thessalonica fractional issues of regnal year 4; in the "Supplement".

(3) Seemingly mistaken – the coin is not listed on the DO website.

(4) M. Myskin believes that the date shown is year 21.

(5) Grierson describes the figures as enthroned but comments only on the quality of its manufacture. Neither Grierson nor Hahn give any emphasis to the design. The arm rests of the throne are clearly shown on the DO specimen. There is a similar follis of regnal year 4 (613/45) in the DO collection (134).

(6) Two specimens are recorded. Uncertainty with regard to the digit Ϛ gives two different date sequences. I think that regnal years 17 and 18 are most likely intended.

(7) As above, I believe that the middle digit represents the number five. Thus the date shown is year 17.

Several high level points may be noted. Coins seem to have been issued by the mint in every regnal year except year 11 (620/1) down to year 20 (629/30) - the accepted date of its closure - despite the recurrent threat to the city by the Avars and Slavs. For denominations and mint marks both Latin and Greek forms are used although Greek is used almost exclusively after about year 5. The mint "tinkers" with the coinage, for example substituting the Greek M for the Latin XXXX on the follis between regnal years 3 and 4 and inserting the Latin form again amidst a sea of Greek, but seemingly very briefly, in regnal years 17-19. But it is the dekanummium that is particularly interesting. Four types exist (1d; 2d; 4d and 5d) overlapping with each other up to and including regnal year 7 at which point the anonymous profile bust type 5d takes over and was apparently struck until year 15 and possibly to year 20. Why should the mint have produced different forms of small change – something that could only have confused the local city population?

ANNEX 2: CATALOGUE OF TYPES

Fig. 1: Type 1f regnal years 1-3 (610-3)

Fig. 2: Type 2f regnal year 4 (613/4)

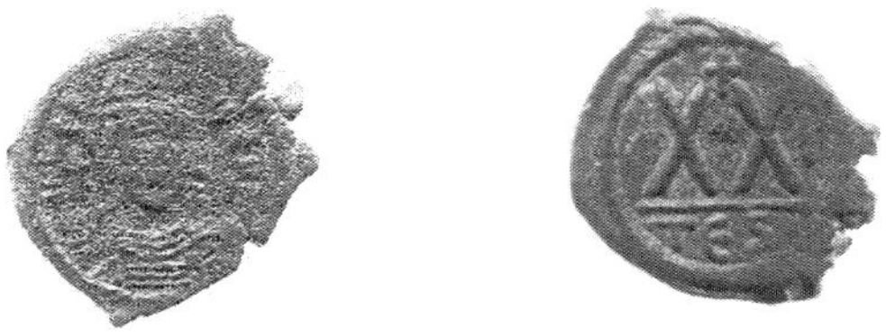

Fig. 3: Type 1hf regnal years 1-2 (610-2)

Fig. 4: Type 2hf regnal years 3-4 (612-4)

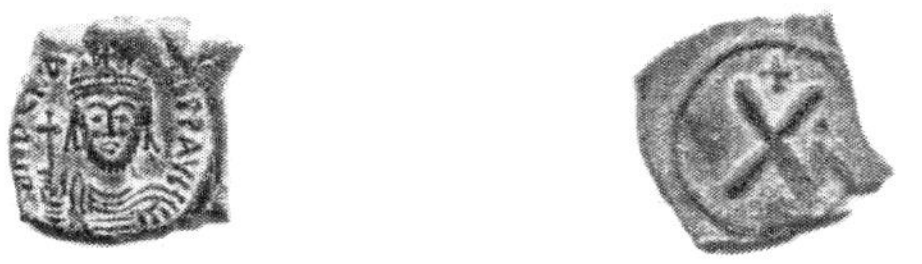

Fig. 5: Type 1d regnal years 1-7 (610-7)

Fig. 6: Type 2d regnal year 4 (613/4)

Fig. 7: Type 3p (undated)

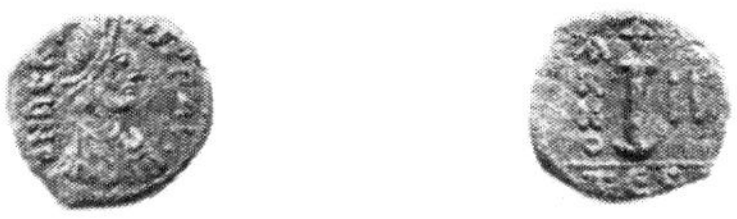

Fig. 8: Type 4d regnal year 2 (611/2)

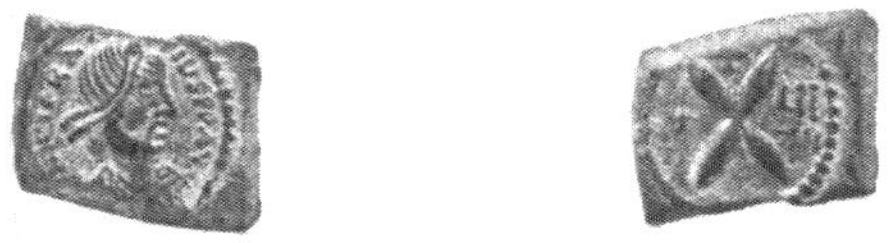

Fig. 9: Type 5d regnal year 5 onwards (615 -)

Fig. 10: Type 6f regnal year 3 onwards intermittently to circa 624

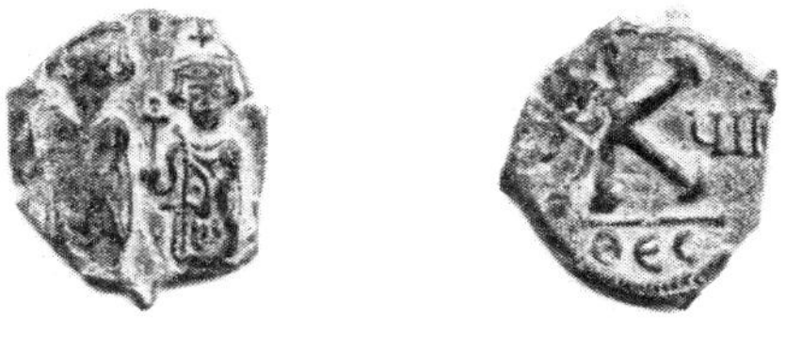

Fig. 11: Type 6hf regnal year 4 onwards intermittently to circa 624

Fig. 12 a-b: Type 7hf regnal years 3 and 4 (612-4)

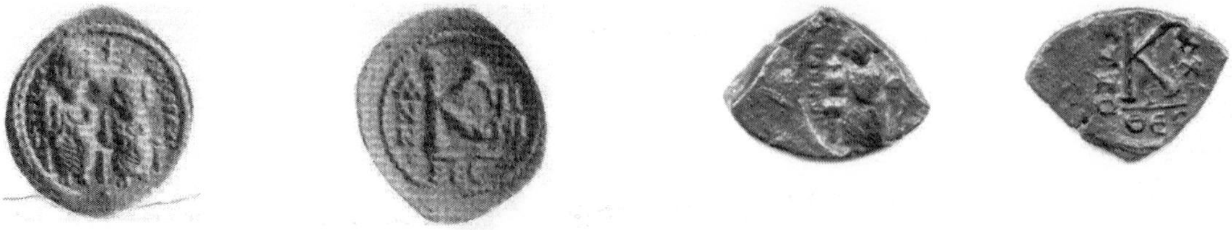

Fig. 13 a-b: Type 8hf regnal year 9 (618/9) and very infrequently thereafter

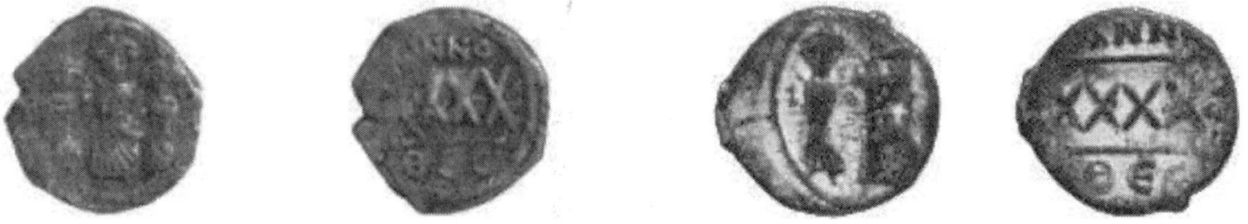

Fig. 14 a-b: Type 9f regnal year 17 & 18 or 18 & 19 (626-9)

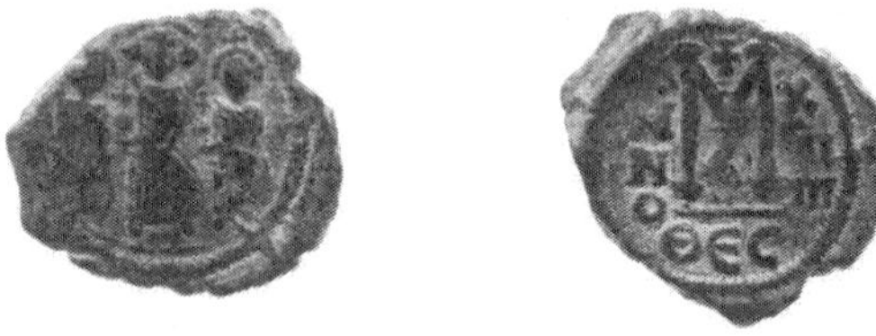

Fig. 15: Type 10f: regnal years 12-20 (619-630)

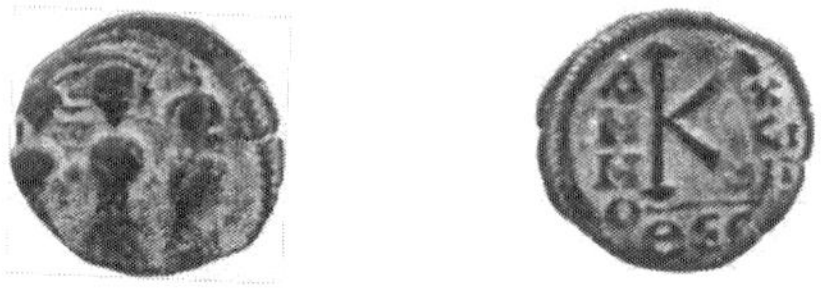

Fig. 16: Type 10hf: regnal years 13 and very intermittently thereafter to 628

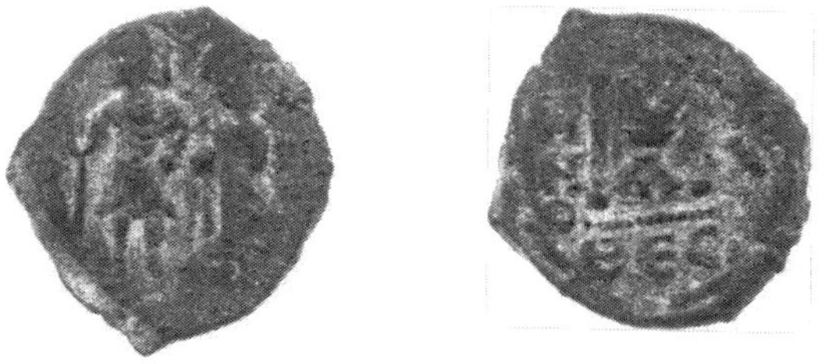

Fig. 17: Type 11f: regnal year 20 (629/30)

Fig. 18: Type 11tqf: regnal year 20 (629/30)

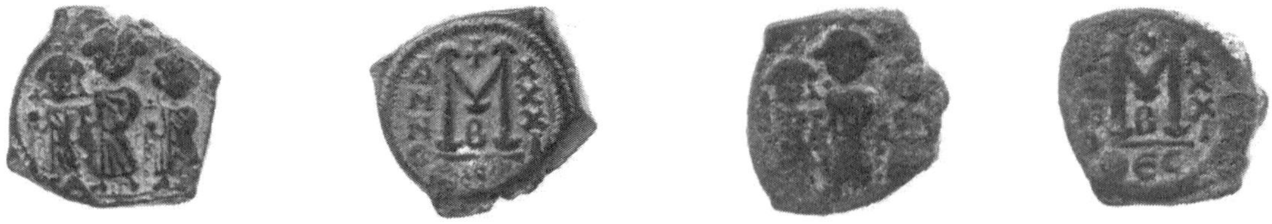

Fig. 19 a-b: Type 12f: regnal year 31 (640/1)

Folles of Heraclius struck in Sicily

Stephen Maxfield[1]

The Folles of Heraclius struck in Sicily are unique in the Byzantine series, interesting and quite attractive from a numismatic point of view. It is my view that they should be considered as overstrikes rather than countermarks[2] as is implied by some authors.[3]

Until year 19 of Heraclius' reign no folles were struck in Sicily. However, because of what subsequently happened to them it can be concluded that folles of all the previous emperors from Anastasios I circulated in Sicily.[4] Generally these were struck in Constantinople though the literature[5] notes that there are a few coins from Antioch, Nicomedia and Kyzikos.[6] None of these were struck in Sicily itself.

However. some "small change" was struck in the city of Catania: pentanummia in the reigns of Justinian I, Justin II, Maurice and Phocas.[7] Many of these coins are dated. (There may be coins from the reign of Tiberius, but these may well be forgeries.[8]) Decanummia and pentanummia were also struck by Heraclius and the decanummia, of which there are two types, are of particular interest. These are struck on quite thick flans and are carefully engraved. They have an image of the Emperor on the obverse with a distinct flat topped crown and an inscription D N ERACLI PP AVG. They are 12mm – 15mm diameter and slightly oval in shape. The reverse has a central I with ANNO to the left, the reign year to the right in Roman numerals and the letters CAT in the exergue. *See figure 1* (It is the first type that is of particular note, the second type have less uniform flans). The first type is dated from year 3 to year 14, the second from 13 to 19. These coins are relatively common.

Around reign year 19, Heraclius must have withdrawn all the folles that were in circulation and required them to be over struck with D.O. Class 1. Dies.[9] These are carefully over struck so that the new striking more or less covers the head of the emperor on the undertype. As the undertype coins have a reverse 180 degrees to the reverse, this means that the original mint of the undertype is often obliterated as well. To have taken such care with the over striking must have considerably delayed the production of these coins.

---

1 Protopresbyter Stephen Maxfield is parish priest of the Greek Orthodox parish, Shrewsbury. He also teaches Liturgy, Church History and Canon Law at the Thyateira Midlands Ecclesiastical Seminary. holy.fathers@gmail.com.

2 An overstrike is where a coin from a previous regime is over struck on both obverse and reverse with a new pattern of coin. A counter strike is where one side is struck, presumably to give some new authentication to the coin. Both types are to be found on Byzantine coins of the 7th Century.

3 See Grierson 1968, p.236

4 Ibid D'A and A p.76

5 D'A page 76

6 D'A and A page 76

7 Grierson 1968 and Wroth 1966 have no knowledge of undertypes from the reigns of Tiberius, Maurice or Phocas, and suggest that only coins with profile busts were overstruck. D'A and A writing significantly later do know of such coins. The author has not been privileged to inspect any of these.

8 Sear 1987 after Grierson 1968, p. 114

9 See Grierson 1968 p.352-4, numbered 241a1- 241e. It is highly unlikely that literally all the folles were collected, but we can say nothing further about those that were not. From the specimens available to us there are some where the undertype is very worn indeed.

Around reign year 22, Class 2[10] appeared, this time over struck on coins of Heraclius Class 5. The over striking is again done with care, but this time the two emperors heads (Heraclius and Heraclius Constantine) are not defaced. The "obverse" of the overstrike may be over struck on the obverse or reverse of the undertype.

A further coin Class 3[11] was struck after year 21, but as the undertype coins are quite small the overstrike can cover most of the undertype. They could have been over struck as late as year 30. In all cases the overstrikes are not dated, the dating derives from the date of the undertype, where this can be read.

There is some controversy as to whether these coins were struck in Sicily or in whether they were struck in Constantinople and then exported to Sicily.[12]

A description of the coins....

Class 1. Over struck on coins of previous Emperors.[13]
Obverse: Bust of Heraclius, bearded, facing, wearing cuirass, ~~and~~ paludamentum and crown with a cross monogram of Heraclius to the right; the whole forming an oval or circular overstrike, which is usually stamped behind or on the head of the previous Emperor.
Reverse: SCLs with bar above (for Sicily) usually stamped so as to obscure the exergue of the over struck coin. *See figure 2*

Class 2. Over struck on early coin of Heraclius Year 20 or 21. (Type 2)
Obverse: Bust of Heraclius, bearded and bust of Heraclius Constantine, beardless, facing; each is draped and wears crown with cross; above cross.
Reverse: SCLs with bar above C and L. Generally, but not always impressed on the lower part of the obverse side of the coin. S*ee figure 3.*

Class 3. Over struck on earlier coin of Heraclius (Type 2 or later)
Obverse: Bust of Heraclius, with moustache and long bearded, and bust of Heraclius Constantine, with close beard, facing. Each draped and wearing crown with cross; above cross.
Reverse: Monogram SCs with bar above S. *See figure 4*

I would like to draw attention to the following:-
1) The dimension of the counter strike impression. This varies slightly between 12mm and 15mm, but within these parameters is remarkably consistent. This size exactly coincides with the sizes of the Sicilian decanummia of the Emperors Maurice through to Heraclius. This could, of course, be pure coincidence. An alternative would be that there was a good supply of unengraved dies in Catania and these were then put to use by engravers to overstrike folles at exactly the point when production of decanummia ceased.
2) If this hypothesis is correct it would suggest that all the folles of Heraclius were over struck **in Sicily** with the undertype coins being sent from Constantinople. It is worth noting further that the engraving of the overstrike is of a high quality, similar to that found on gold coins. The 7th century copper coins of Sicily are generally significantly better engraved than those found elsewhere in the Byzantine Empire.

---

[10] Ibid p.355-6 numbered 242a1- 242b.4
[11] Ibid. p.356-7, numbered 243.1 – 243.10
[12] Ibid p.237
[13] Descriptions follow those in Wroth - British Museum catalogue.

Conclusion

All the folles from Sicily from the reign of Heraclius were over struck with dies that are of similar dimensions to the decanummia of previous emperors. Blank unused dies were engraved in Sicily, probably Syracuse, to create the overstrikes. These took place in Sicily either on coins circulating already in Sicily or on coins imported from Constantinople.

Figure 1. Above left: decanummium of Heraclius struck in Catania year 10. Above right: decanummium of Maurice struck in Catania year six. (die axis 180 degrees). (Author's collection)

Figure 2 Above: examples obverse of Heraclius folles Class I struck in Sicily probably in Syracuse. Below: reverse of the above (die axis of overstrike180 degrees). Author's collection.

Figure 3 Above: examples obverse of Heraclius folles Class II struck in Sicily probably in Syracuse. Below: reverse of the above. (die axis of overstrike180 degrees). Author's collection. Note that the obverse of the overstrike is on the reverse of the undertype.

Figure 4 *Above examples obverse of Heraclius folles Class III struck in Sicily probably in Syracuse. Below reverse of the above. (die axis of overstrike180 degrees). Author's collection. Note that the obverse of the overstrike is on the obverse of the* undertype.

Bibliography

D'Andrea Alberto & **Ginnasi** Andrea Torno ***Byzantine Coinage in Italy Volume II*** 2017 edizioni d'andrea.

Grierson Philip ***Catalogue of the Byzantine Coins in the Dumbarton Oaks Collection and in the Whittemore Collection Volume II Part I,*** 1968 Dumbarton Oaks, Washington D.C.

Kasdagli Anna-Maria ***Coins in Rhodes from the Monetary Reforms of Anastasius I until the Ottoman Conquest (498 – 1522)*** 2018 Archaeopress, Oxford.

Mansfield Steve ***Early Byzantine Copper Coins, Catalogue of an English Collection*** 2016 Ex Officio Books.

Sear David R. ***Byzantine Coins and their Values*** (Second Edition) 1987 Spink & Son Ltd., London.

Wroth Warwick ***Imperial Byzantine Coins in the British Museum*** (two volumes in One) MCMLXVI (1966) Argonaut, Inc., Publishers, Chicago.

Three Unpublished Copper Varieties of Constans II

David Woods[1]

The purpose of this paper is to draw attention to some unpublished varieties of the copper coinage of Constans II (641-68) that have appeared upon the market in recent years, that is, varieties that do not appear in the standard catalogues of the coinage of this emperor by Grierson, Hahn, or even in Mansfield's catalogue of his extensive personal collection.[2]

I. An Unpublished *Dodecanummium* from Egypt

a

b

Fig. 1: a. Dodecanummium of Constans II (20 mm, 7.48g); MIB 188. Ex Classical Numismatic Group, E-Auction 288 (10 October 2012), lot 573;
b. Dodecanummium of Constans II (21 mm, 8.30g); MIB 189. Ex Aquila Numismatics, Auction 5 (25 September 2022), lot 546.

Extensive research has been conducted upon the Egyptian *dodecanummia* of the seventh century in recent years, and it is agreed that the mint at Alexandria struck two main types of *dodecanummium* for Constans II during the brief period between his accession as emperor at Constantinople in September 641 and the final Byzantine surrender of Alexandria to the Arabs in September 642.[3] The

---

[1] David Woods is the Head of the Department of Classics at University College, Cork, Ireland: d.woods@ucc.ie.

[2] P. Grierson, ***Catalogue of the Byzantine Coins in the Dumbarton Oaks Collection and the Whittemore Collection, 2.2: Phocas to Theodosius III 602-717*** (Washington, D.C., 1968); W. Hahn, ***Moneta Imperii Byzantini, 3: Von Heraclius bis Leo III. Alleinregierung (610-720)*** (Vienna, 1981); S. Mansfield, ***Early Byzantine Copper Coins: Catalogue of an English Collection*** (Manchester, 2016) and ***Supplement to Early Byzantine Copper Coins: Four Hundred Coins from an English Private Collection*** (London, 2022).

[3] See e.g. L. Domaszewicz and M.L. Bates, 'Copper coinage of Egypt in the seventh century', in J.L. Bacharach (ed.), ***Fustat Finds: Beads, Coins, Medical Instruments, Textiles and Other Artefacts from the Awad Collection*** (Cairo,

obverse of the earlier type (*MIB* 188) depicts a beardless facing bust with *chlamys* and crown holding a *globus cruciger* at shoulder level in its right hand (Fig. 1a). The associated reverse depicts the numerals I and B on either side of a small cross above a letter M, all above an exergue containing a legend abbreviating the name of Alexandria. The obverse of the later type (*MIB* 189) depicts a beardless facing figure standing and holding a staff topped by a staurogram in his right hand and a *globus cruciger* in his left hand. The associated reverse depicts the numerals I and B on either side of a *globus cruciger*, all above an exergue containing a legend abbreviating the name of Alexandria. In fact, there are two slight variants of this reverse, one that depicts a single large pellet to the left and right respectively of the numerals I and B, and one that does not.

Fig. 2: New dodecanummium of Constans II (19mm, 10.64g). Ex Demos Auctions, Auction 10 (14 May 2022), lot 792.

A new type of *dodecanummium* that appears to combine features of both of the known types recently appeared on the market (Fig. 2). While this specimen is quite worn, and has been struck slightly off-centre, it is clear that the obverse depicts a standing emperor with a staff in his right hand and a *globus cruciger* in his left hand as on the obverse of *MIB 189*. In contrast, the reverse seems to combine features of the reverses of both *MIB* 188 and *MIB* 189. On the one hand, it depicts the numerals I and B on either side of a small cross above a letter, much as on the reverse of *MIB* 188, the main difference lying in the identity of the letter. While *MIB* 188 depicts the letter M beneath the cross, the new type depicts what appears to be an Є there instead. On the other hand, it also depicts a single large pellet to the left and right of the numerals as on the reverse of one of the variants of *MIB* 189. The obvious suggestion, therefore, is that this new type represents a brief intermediate type struck between the end of the striking of *MIB* 188 and the beginning of the striking of *MIB* 189.

The most interesting feature of this new type is the presence of the Є beneath the cross on the reverse. If this is the Greek numeral for five, then it is difficult to understand what it could mean. It cannot denote a regnal year, because 641/42 was the first regnal year of Constans. It cannot denote an indictional year either, because 641/42 was actually the 15th year of the indictional cycle.[4] If one looks to the letter M on the reverse of *MIB* 188 in the hope that it may cast some light upon this problem, one is quickly disappointed, because the meaning of that letter is not much clearer. Comparison of the occurrence of the M on the reverse of the *decanummium* to its occurrence on the reverse of other denomination coins struck at widely differing dates and locations throughout the Byzantine empire suggests that the common factor is association with a cross, so that it probably abbreviates some term

2002), pp. 88–107; M. Metlich and N. Schindel, 'Egyptian copper coinage in the 7th century AD. Some critical remarks', ***Oriental Numismatic Society Newsletter*** 179 (2004), pp. 1–15; T. Goodwin, 'Some aspects of 7th C Egyptian Byzantine coinage', in A. Oddy, I. Schulze, and W. Schulze (eds.), ***Coinage and History in the Seventh Century Near East*** **4** (London, 2015), pp. 27–35; D. Woods, 'Deciphering the *dodecanummia* of Heraclius and Constans II', ***Israel Numismatic Research*** 13 (2018) pp. 195-227.

[4] *Dodecanummia* had not traditionally displayed any form of date. However, the *dodecanummia* struck in the name of 'Abd al-'Azīz ibn Marwān, the Umayyad governor of Egypt in 669-82, seem to have used Greek numerals to denote indictional years. See D. Woods, 'A note on the Arab-Byzantine *dodecanummium* struck in the name of 'Abd al-'Azīz ibn Marwān', ***Israel Numismatic Research*** 16 (2021), pp. 243-53.

used in reference to the veneration of the cross or what it was that the cross symbolized for early medieval Christians. Perhaps the most obvious suggestion is that it abbreviates the Greek term μυστήριον 'mystery', or its Latin transliteration *mysterium*, in reference to what Christians described as the mystery of the cross and resurrection.[5]

The best approach to the problem posed by the presence of the Є beneath the cross on the reverse of the *decanummium* seems to be to approach it in the same way as was done in the case of the problem posed by the presence of the M on the reverse of *MIB* 188, by investigating whether other mints also included it on the reverse of the coins that they struck, and what the common factors were if they did. The simple answer to this question is that the mint at Constantinople used the same mark in the reverse field of several different types of *solidi* struck during the mid-seventh century. However, the same mark does not necessarily mean the same thing in every case, and one needs to pay due attention to context. For example, during the early reign of Constans II, the mint at Constantinople struck *solidi* depicting an Є in the field to the right of the cross on its reverse (*MIB* 9-10). However, it also struck similar *solidi* depicting an S (*MIB* 11-15), Z (*MIB* 16-17), or H (*MIB* 18-19) in the field to the right instead, so confirming that these were all Greek numerals used in reference to the 5th, 6th, 7th, and 8th indictional years respectively (646/47- 649/50). Of much more relevance here is that the mint at Constantinople also struck a *solidus* depicting an Є in the field to the right of the cross on its reverse in about 641 (Fig. 3) when this was not part of some numerical sequence (*MIB* 53). At about the same time, it also struck a *solidus* depicting a K in the field to the right of the cross (*MIB* 52). It is clear from the fact that these coins were struck at about the same time that the marks K and Є must have been co-ordinated in some way, that they share a common theme or purpose, even if this theme or purpose is not obvious now.

Fig. 3: Solidus of Heraclius from Constantinople (19mm, 4.35g); MIB 53.
Ex Classical Numismatic Group, E-Auction 527 (16 November 2022), lot 477.

Hahn attributes *MIB* 52 to the reign of Constantine III as senior emperor and *MIB* 53 to that of Heraclonas (also known as Heraclius II) as senior emperor. He does this on the assumption that the K abbreviates the name Κωνσταντῖνος 'Constantine' in the former case and that the Є abbreviates the adjective ἕτερος 'other, second' in the latter case.[6] As far as the *dodecanummium* under discussion is concerned, one has to admit that the interpretation of the Є as an abbreviation of ἕτερος in reference to Heraclonas is superficially attractive. It would help explain why three different types of *dodecanummia* were struck in such a short period if *MIB* 188 were attributable to Constantine III, the new type to his successor Heraclonas, and *MIB* 189 to Constans II. However, Heraclonas was senior emperor for almost twice as long as his predecessor Constantine III, nearly 6 months against little over 3 months, so that it seems odd that only one specimen of the *dodecanummium* attributable to him should have survived, while that apparently attributable to his predecessor should have survived in such relatively large numbers.[7]

---

[5] Woods, 'Deciphering the *dodecanummia*' (see n. 3), pp. 202-04.
[6] Hahn, *MIB* 3 (1981), pp. 87-8.
[7] On the duration of the reigns of these emperors, see W. Treadgold, 'A note on Byzantium's year of the four emperors (641)', ***Byzantinische Zeitschrift*** 83 (1990), pp. 431-33.

On the whole, it seems more likely that the K and Є of the Constantinopolitan *solidi* abbreviate terms used in reference to the veneration of the cross, or the worship of the crucified Christ, than that they abbreviate imperial names or titles in the manner suggested by Hahn. As I have argued elsewhere, the K probably abbreviates some form of the term κύριος 'lord' used in reference to the crucified Christ, while the Є probably abbreviates the verb ἐλέησον 'Have mercy!', a plea to the crucified Christ.[8] As far as Constantinople is concerned, the plea may have been for Christ to save the emperor Heraclius as he drew ever nearer death, or to relieve the empire from the relentless assaults of the Arab invaders. As far as Alexandria is concerned, however, one may suspect that the prayer was more personal, a desperate plea to prevent the final surrender of the city to the Arabs as agreed in September 641. This is not to claim that whoever was responsible for the design of the reverse of the *dodecanummium* under discussion must have been familiar with the *solidus* displaying the Є in its reverse field. It is a case rather of similar responses to the same desperate political situation utilizing a common liturgical term familiar to every Christian throughout the empire.[9]

II. Star rather than K: A Variant of a *Follis (MIB* 177*)* from Constantinople

The mint at Constantinople struck a surprisingly large number of different types of *follis* under Constans II, and most types can be subdivided into two or more sub-types according to the different marks appearing above the large denomination mark M (or m) on the reverse. Since the time of Anastasius' reform of the coinage in 498, the *follis* had normally displayed a small cross above the denomination M, although this had occasionally been replaced by a chi-rho symbol or a staurogram. During the last years of Heraclius, however, this cross was no longer a permanent feature of the reverse, but was reduced rather to the status of a variable mark that was changed on as regular basis to distinguish one series of production from the next. The mint employed five different devices over the denomination M during the period 629-637, beginning with the traditional small cross (*MIB* 164a) and ending with a form of the monogram of Heraclius' name that included the cross (*MIB* 164d), but there were normally two marks in use at any one time. All of these marks seem to have been Christian in nature, since even Heraclius' monogram now contained a cross.[10] This treatment of the small cross above the denomination M as but one of a series of variable marks continued into the reign of Constans. However, during his reign, the mint only ever used three different marks above the denomination M (or m), the traditional small cross, a star (Fig. 4), and a K.

[8] See D. Woods, 'Respecting the cross: Praying with coins in mid-seventh century Constantinople', ***Studia Patristica*** 104 (2021), pp. 105-14.

[9] On the origin of the prayer *Kyrie eleison* in the Christian mass, see E. Bishop, '*Kyrie eleison*: a liturgical consultation', ***The Downside Review*** *18* (1899), pp. 294–303 and his '*Kyrie eleison*: a liturgical consultation II', ***The Downside Review*** *19* (1900), pp. 44-55.

[10] For a discussion of these marks, and Heraclius' new monogram, see D. Woods, 'Greek monograms and countermarks in seventh-century Syria', in T. Goodwin (ed.), ***Coinage and History in the Seventh Century Near East*** **6** (London, 2015), pp. 101-20, at 101-04.

a

b

Fig. 4: a. follis of Constans II from Constantinople (20mm, 3.92g), dated RY 1 (641/42); MIB 162. Ex Savoca Coins, 106th Blue Auction (27 June 2021), lot 1674;
b. half-follis of Heraclius from Constantinople (22mm, 5.65g); MIB 171a. Ex Savoca Coins, 5th Blue Auction (24 Feb. 2018), lot 1616.

The fact that the mint only used three different marks above the denomination M during the whole of the reign of Constans is noteworthy, as is the fact that the mint had not used either the star or the K in this position before. The decision to set a K there is not surprising, given the frequency with which it had appeared as a mark in the reverse field of the *solidi* and hexagrams struck under Heraclius, when it had almost certainly abbreviated the term κύριος 'lord', as noted above. The star is a rather different case, being a much rarer symbol heretofore. Under Heraclius, it had been used on the reverse of light-weight *solidi* of 23 or 22 carats to identify them as such. One may perhaps doubt its religious symbolism in this case, particularly when one type of light-weight *solidus* had depicted two stars, one to either side of the cross (*MIB* 55). It had also been used once in the field besides the cross on the reverse of a rare issue of hexagram (*MIB* 142). Of most relevance here, however, is the fact that a star sometimes replaced the small cross between the heads of the figures on the obverse of the three-quarter- (*MIB* 168) and half-folles (*MIB* 171) struck during the period 629/36 (Fig. 4b). This strongly suggests that it was thought to possess the same or similar religious significance. As to how or why anyone should equate these two symbols in this way, the answer probably lies in Christ's words to the apostle John at the end of the *Book of Revelation* (22.16):

ἐγώ εἰμι ἡ ῥίζα καὶ τὸ γένος Δαυίδ, ὁ ἀστὴρ ὁ λαμπρὸς ὁ πρωϊνός.
'I am the root and the descendant of David, the bright morning star.'[11]

Hence the three variable marks depicted above the denomination M during the reign of Constans all seem to allude to Christ in some way: the small cross to his crucifixion, the star to his self-identification as the morning star, and the K to his status as the Lord.[12]

[11] For further discussion of Christ as a star, see M.S. Moore, 'Jesus Christ: "Superstar" (*Revelation* xxii 16b)', ***Novum Testamentum*** 24 (1982), pp. 82-91.
[12] There is also a variant with no mark at all.

Fig. 5: follis of Constans II from Constantinople (22mm, 4.42g); MIB 177. Ex Nomos, Obolos 12

The denomination mark M was far less prominent on the three varieties of *follis* struck at Constantinople following Constans' promotion of his two younger sons Heraclius and Tiberius to rank as Augusti in 659. The reason for this was that the coins had now to accommodate the depiction of four different emperors rather than the mere two whose depiction they had had to accommodate during the period 654-59 or the single emperor before that. The result was that denomination M was severely reduced in size and transferred from the reverse to the obverse in the case of *MIB* 175 struck during the period from 659 to 664 (regnal years 19 to 23). A small cross was retained above the denomination M, but no other mark seems to have replaced it during the five-year period 659-64. In the case of *MIB* 176 struck during the year 665/666 (regnal year 25), the denomination M was restored to the reverse and increased in size. The cross was retained above it, but two different forms of the cross were used, one without steps (*MIB* 176a) and one with steps (*MIB* 176b). Hence the traditional differentiation between two series of production, distinguishable by means of the use of different marks above the denomination M, was restored. Finally in the case of *MIB* 177 (Fig. 5), which bears no date but has traditionally been attributed to the period 666-68, the denomination mark is reduced in size again as the busts of all three sons are squeezed tightly around it. This means that there is no space to include a mark above the M, whether the traditional cross or one of the other favoured varieties of mark under Constans, a star or a K. However, a K was inserted in the field to the right of the bust of Constans on the obverse, and a question arises concerning its significance. On the one hand, it may simply abbreviate the official name of Constans in Greek (Κωνσταντῖνος).[13] On the other hand, it may represent the variable mark that has been displaced from above the denomination mark on the reverse.

Fig. 6: Half-follis of Constans II from Constantinople (20mm, 2.62g); MIB 185. Ex Sol Numismatik, Auction 9 (10 December 2022), lot 387.

In favour of the identification of this K as an abbreviation of the imperial name, one notes that it seems to have been used in this way on the obverse of half-*folles* struck in 643/44 (*MIB* 181), 659/60 (*MIB*

[13] So Grierson, *DOC* 2.2, p. 549.

184), and (possibly) 664/68 (*MIB* 185) (Fig. 6). Furthermore, it had often appeared to the side of the figure of Constantine III on the obverse of *folles* struck during the period 629/37 (*MIB* 164). Against this, one notes, it had not been used to identify Constans by name on any of the different types of *folles* struck since his succession as sole Augustus in 641. More importantly, most of these *folles* had not provided any indication of his name. There the matter would have to be left to rest were it not for the fact that two specimens have appeared on the market in recent years revealing that a star was sometimes used on the obverse of *MIB* 177 instead of a K (Fig. 7a-b). While both specimens are rather worn, there can be no doubt that a star appears in the field to the right of the bust of Constans II exactly where one would normally have expected to find a K. The fact that this variant has not been noted previously suggests that it is much rarer than that depicting the K to the side of Constans' bust. However, if previous patterns of production are anything to go by, this is not particularly surprising. For example, in the case of *MIB* 167, the variant with the small cross above the denomination M was struck at between two and four workshops each year for three years (*MIB* 167b), the variant with the K above it was struck at between three and four workshops each year for two years (*MIB* 167d), while the variant with the star above it was only struck at one workshop for one year (*MIB* 167c). Similarly in the case of *MIB* 173, the variant with the K above the denomination was struck at between one and four workshops each year for three years (*MIB* 173d), but the variant with the star above it was only struck at one workshop in one year (*MIB* 173c). In this case, one specimen (Fig. 7a) displays the top of the letter gamma Γ immediately blow the denomination mark, confirming that it was struck in the 3rd *officina*, but the second specimen (Fig. 7b) does not preserve its *officina* number.

a

b

Fig. 7: a. follis of Constans II from Constantinople (25mm, 5.03g). Ex Savoca Coins, 111th Blue Auction (29 August 2021), lot 2158;
b. follis of Constans II from Constantinople (23mm, 5.07g). Ex ebay April 2018.

The fact that the new variant of *MIB* 177 depicts a star where the majority of specimens depict a K suggests that the latter is best regarded as the variable sign that had traditionally appeared over the denomination M, but has been displaced to the obverse in this case.

III. Omega rather than Omicron: Another Variant of a *Follis* (*MIB* 169) from Constantinople

When the mint at Constantinople began striking *folles* in the name of Constans II in 641, it surrounded his figure on the obverse with the legend ЄNTȣTONIKA 'Conquer in this!' rather than his name.[14] This phrase traces its origin back to a phrase that the emperor Constantine I is supposed to have seen written in the sky next to a cross of light sometime shortly before the battle of the Milvian Bridge in 312. According to the famous account by Bishop Eusebius of Caesarea, this phrase ran τούτῳ νίκα 'Conquer by this!' in reference to the cross of light besides it.[15] On the reverse of the new *folles* struck in the name of Constans II, the legend proclaimed ANA and NЄO to either side of the denomination mark in abbreviation of the term ἀνανέωσις 'renewal'.[16] Hence the new coins were consistent in their rendering of what should have been an omega ω, if the legend was written in Greek, as a letter omicron O instead, on both reverse and obverse.[17] This practice continued as long as these legends remained on the *folles*, with one noteworthy exception. Hahn published a variant of *MIB* 169 struck in regnal year 11 (651/52) upon which the omicron of the NЄO on the reverse has been replaced by an omega instead (*MIB* 169.2). Since the obverse of *MIB* 169 depicts a bust of Constans surrounded by an abbreviation of his name rather than the legend ЄNTȣTONIKA, there was nothing to correct in that case. However, I know of two examples of a variant that pairs an obverse depicting a standing Constans surrounded by the legend ЄNTȣTONIKA with the reverse of *MIB* 169.2 (Fig. 8a-b). In both cases, the omicron on the obverse has been corrected to read an omega instead, exactly as on the reverse. It is interesting to note that these two coins were struck from two different obverse dies and two different reverse dies. The differences in the reverse dies include the *officina* number, Γ in the case of Fig. 8a and B in the case of Fig. 8b.

Fig. 8a: follis of Constans II from Constantinople (22mm, 4.05g). Ex Savoca Coins ebay (October 2019)

---

[14] On the earliest *folles*, see T. Goodwin, 'The early *folles* of Constans II', ***Numismatic Circular*** 120.1 (April 2012), pp. 18-20.

[15] Eusebius, *Vita Constantini* 1.28.

[16] On the tendency of seventh-century emperors to represent themselves as a new Constantine (306-37) or a new Justinian I (527-65) set upon renewing the empire once more, see J. Haldon, 'Constantine or Justinian? Crisis and identity in imperial propaganda in the seventh century', in P. Magdalino (ed.), ***New Constantines: The Rhythm of Imperial Renewal in Byzantium, 4th-13th Centuries*** (Aldershot, 1994), pp. 95-108.

[17] It is not clear why the engravers preferred to use omicron rather than omega. One possibility is that the Greek terms were actually written in Latin script, that is, transliterations from Greek into Latin, so that the apparent omicron is really a Latin O. In support of this, one notes that none of the other letters are definitely Greek in form rather than Latin. In that case, the official responsible for the variants discussed here has failed to realize that the legends on Constans' *folles* were in Latin, not Greek, and so corrected something that did not really need correcting at all.

Fig. 8b: follis of Constans II from Constantinople (23mm, 4.32g).

The suspicion that these two variants, *MIB* 169.2 itself and that combining a standing-figure obverse with the reverse of *MIB* 169.2, may have been substantial issues originally is encouraged by the fact that one can discover an Arab-Byzantine imitation of both. In the first example below (Fig.9a), an imitation of the standing-figure variant, one can clearly see the letters TѠ on the right side of the head of the standing figure on the obverse. The most interesting feature of the obverse legend, however, is that the letters O and Y have been separately engraved rather than combined in ligature as Ȣ. On the reverse, one can see the left-hand side of the letter Ѡ where one expects to find it. However, the abbreviation mark below that seems to have been bungled. Another indication that this is an Arab-Byzantine copy, although a very good one by the normal standards of such copies, is that it weighs much less than its Byzantine model would have. Finally, the fact that it depicts the *officina* number A suggests that its model was struck in this *officina*, so that this Byzantine variant was probably produced in at least three *officinae* (A, B, Γ). The second example (Fig. 9b), an imitation of *MIB* 169.2, is a far less accurate copy of its Byzantine model. Nevertheless, one can detect the remnant of the date IA in the presence of a curved I at the bottom left immediately before a large A in the exergue on the reverse. The bust on the obverse does not match that of *MIB* 169.2 in that it clearly does not bear a long beard, but the choice to depict a bust rather than a standing figure here is itself significant, regardless of the fact that the details of the busts do not entirely match. Finally, one should note that, in stark contrast to the previous example, this specimen is far heavier than its Byzantine model would have been.

Fig. 9a: an Arab-Byzantine follis (22mm, 2.91g). Ex Ancientground ebay (May 2020);

Fig. 9b:an Arab-Byzantine follis (28mm, 5.94g). Ex Numismatik Lanz ebay (January 2020).

Reflections on the two different iconographies of Christ on the gold coins of Justinian II.

Stephen Maxfield[1]

The different iconographies of the gold coins of Justinian II are probably well known to most readers. However for those who may not be familiar or need some reminding I will attempt a short summary.

The Emperor Justinian II was a member, the last member to reign, of the Heraclian dynasty. His father was Constantine IV, his grandfather Constans II. He inherited the throne from his father in 685 when he was about seventeen. His first gold coins were traditional, showing in the case of solidi the bust of the emperor on the obverse and a cross on steps on the reverse, with traditional inscriptions. Probably in 687 an entirely new pattern of solidus was introduced, depicting an image of Christ on the obverse and the emperor standing holding a cross on steps, thus demonstrating that this was the reverse. The inscriptions are entirely novel. The obverse states *IhS CHRISTOS REX REJNANTIUM* (Jesus Christ the King of Kings), while the reverse states *IUSTINIANUS SERV CHRISTI* (Justinian the servant of Christ). For reasons that are not entirely clear, these coins were not struck throughout the empire.[2]
After some military disasters, there was a revolt, Justinian was deposed, mutilated (thus making him unacceptable as emperor) and exiled to Cherson in the Crimea. He was replaced as emperor by Leontios (695 – 698) and then Tiberios III (698 – 705). Both these emperors issued traditionally styled gold coins.

However, in 705 Justinian, now equipped with a gold nose, and with the help of the Khazar Khan and the Bulgarians managed to stage a comeback, insinuated his way into Constantinople through a water gate and resumed the throne. The two usurpers were executed and Justinian recommenced striking gold coins as before, but the actual image of Christ on the coins was now entirely different.[3] Given that depicting Jesus Christ on a coin to Orthodox Christians is to depict God Himself, it is extremely odd that the portrayals should be so fundamentally different (*Figure 1*).

---

[1] Protopresbyter Stephen Maxfield is parish priest of the Greek Orthodox parish, Shrewsbury. He also teaches Liturgy, Church History and Canon Law at the Thyateira Midlands Ecclesiastical Seminary. holy.fathers@gmail.com.
[2] Mints that were striking gold coins at this period were Constantinople; Carthage; Sardinia; Syracuse and probably Naples; Ravenna and Rome.
[3] The inscriptions are slightly, but not significantly, different of these second issue coins. The obverse reads D.N. IhS ChS . REX REGNANTIUM (Our Lord Jesus Christ King of Kings), the reverse Ɑ. N. IUSTINIANUS MULTUS AN (Our Lord Justinian Many Years). When Justinain's baby son was crowned emperor he was included on the reverse and the inscription names him.

Figure 1. Left obverse of Justinian II first "Christ" solidus (CNG Triton auction XXIV lot 218). Right obverse of Justinian II second "Christ" solidus (CNG auction 114 lot 1044).

This paper is an attempt to review the evidence and suggest an explanation for this difference. It will demonstrate that the new pattern of coins was a direct result of a church council, that the rejection of the council was perhaps a reason why the first pattern was not struck in Italy and then after Justinian regained his throne why the new pattern was acceptable throughout the empire.

In 686/7, Justinian II now aged eighteen or nineteen, called a council that has a confusing number of names. It may be called "In Trullo" after the hall where it was held, "Quinisext", meaning fifth-sixth in Latin or "Penthekte" in Greek, again meaning fifth-sixth. As there was more than one Council held "In Trullo", the Council will be referred to as the Quinisext in this paper. It was solely concerned with Ecclesiastical Canons, i.e. Ecclesiastical Law. The reason for the name was that neither the Fifth Œcumenical Council 553 nor the Sixth Œcumenical Council 680/1 had passed any Canons, unlike all the previous four councils.

Western historians have frequently derided this council saying that it was called as an example of hubris on the part of the emperor. However, for the Orthodox Church it is the largest body of Ecclesiastical Law passed by any Council. Many of the canons are still relevant and in use. To my mind it seems much more probable that senior churchmen in Constantinople had been advocating the calling of this council and persuaded Justinian to call it. Apart from the canon concerning the status of Justinianopolis (Canon 39: see note 6 below) very few of the others can have been influenced by the young emperor.

However, one of these Canons (82) referred to the way Jesus Christ was to be depicted as follows:-
In some pictures of the venerable icons, a lamb is painted to which the Forerunner (i.e. John the Baptist) points his finger, which is received as a type of grace, indicating beforehand through the Law, our true Lamb, Christ our God. Embracing therefore the ancient types and shadows as symbols of the truth, and patterns given to the Church, we prefer "grace and truth," receiving it as the fulfilment of the Law. In order therefore that "that which is perfect" may be delineated to the eyes of all, at least in coloured expression, we decree that the figure in human form of the Lamb who takes away the sin of the World, Christ our God, be henceforth exhibited in images, instead of the Ancient lamb, so that all may understand by means of it the depths of the humiliation of the Word of God, and that we may recall to our memory his conversation in the flesh, his passion and salutary death, and his redemption which was wrought for the whole world.

There are certain things to note.
1) The Canon refers to a passage from the Gospel of St John:
*The next day he (*i.e. John the Baptist*) saw Jesus coming to him and said "Behold, the Lamb of God who takes away the sin of the world!"* John 1:29 and "*Again the next day, John was standing with*

two disciples. He looked at Jesus as he was walking by and said, "Behold, the Lamb of God!" John 1:36.[4]

2) Ecclesiastical Canons were, and are, promulgated in response to a problem. They do not promote, they correct. So this Canon is intended to deal with a problem, but it is not now clear what this problem was. Perhaps it could be phrased as "**Some people think that Christians worship a sheep**".

3) The Canon is both in favour of icons, but also iconoclast, in that only certain portrayals are acceptable. This may have had an influence on the change in design.

After the Council six copies of the Acts were drawn up with space for all six of the leaders of the autocephalous churches i.e. the Patriarchs of Rome, Constantinople, Alexandria, Antioch, Jerusalem and the Archbishop of Cyprus.[5] Evidently the intention was that each Patriarch would hold a copy with the signatures of all the other patriarchs and Council Fathers.

However, the Patriarch in Rome, Sergios I, flatly refused to sign, or even open any of the copies.[6] This infuriated Justinian who attempted to have the Pope arrested. This failed. So, what reasons might there be for the Pope refusing to sign the acts of the Council?

The matter is expressed in the *Liber Pontificalis*, (which is more or less contemporary with events) thus:

In his (i.e. Pope Sergios') time the emperor Justinian ordered a council to be held in the imperial city (i.e. Constantinople), at which legates of the apostolic see (i.e. Rome) had foregathered, and to whose acts they were deceived into subscribing. He (i.e. Sergios) too was under pressure to subscribe, but he absolutely refused since certain chapters which went outside the usage of the church had been annexed to the acts. .... Instead he rejected them and set them aside as invalid, choosing to die sooner than consent to ***erroneous novelties***.[7]

So, why did the Pope reject the council and what were these "erroneous novelties"? Historians have tended to answer by suggesting two possibilities. The first is that the Council was not properly called as the Pope's delegation did not include bishops. This is predicated on the idea a Council, strictly speaking, is a council of bishops. In fact there were always priest or deacon theologians at Church Councils – there could even be nuns! The LP clearly says that there were legates. No pope had previously attended an Œcumenical Council in person, they had always been represented by legates, and certainly one of the bishops, who we know was at the Council, Basil of Gortyna in Crete, which was at that time under papal jurisdiction.[8]

The second suggestion is that some of the Canons were overtly anti-Western. Canon 13 allows for the marriage of clergy, criticising the Roman tradition of celibate clergy. Canon 55 prohibits fasting on Saturdays again contrary to Roman tradition. However, both these Canons merely restated 4th century Apostolic Canons (so called). Some even suggest that Sergios objected to Canon 36 placing the see of Constantinople as second in honour to Rome, but this was also only the restating of a previous Canon[9].

---

[4] There are at least fifteen other references to Jesus as a sacrificial Lamb in the New Testament. de Young 2021 p.209

[5] The Archbishop of Cyprus was, at this period resident in the city of Kyzikos. This city had been devastated by the Arabs in their siege of Constantinople (674) as they used it as a forward base. One must assume they enslaved or murdered the entire population. Justinian II revived the city by importing new citizens from Cyprus including the Archbishop. He re-named the city "Justinianopolis". However, the Cypriots were not happy in their new home and many including the Archbishop returned to Cyprus. Curiously the Archbishop of Cyprus still today has the title "Archbishop of Justinianopolis"!

[6] Davis 1989 p.86

[7] ibid

[8] Crawford 2021 p185

[9] Canon 3 of the second Œcumenical Council A.D. 381

However, we know from the *Liber Pontificalis*[10] that Sergios was a Syrian by origin, born in Sicily around 650 in the reign of Constans II. It is not unreasonable to suggest that his parents left Syria as a result of the Arab invasions and settled in Sicily. As a Syrian he would have been fully aware of married clergy, the second place of Constantinople, and different traditions as to fasting, which anyway were subject to local rather than universal tradition. There is however a novelty in the Canons which some suggest may indeed have brought about his rejection and that is due to Canon 82 banning the depiction of Christ symbolically as a Lamb. (see above) I find this more convincing.

Using the Lamb as a Symbol of Christ was very popular in Rome. One early example comes from a tomb in the Catacombs[11] dated to the late 4th century (Figure 2) Here we see Jesus Christ portrayed as the good shepherd with the apostles each with a sheep below them.

Figure 2. A 4th Century depiction of Christ as the Good Shepherd with each of the apostles depicted with a sheep, from a tomb in Roman Catacomb. It would seem that a shorthand of this theme developed into the depiction of the sheep alone without the Apostles.

There are a number of churches in Rome that existed at the time of Pope Sergios that still exist today. Many are decorated with mosaics, especially in the eastern apse and many of these feature lambs and sheep. Here are some examples:-

Figure 3. The Apse Mosaic in the church of St Pudenziana Rome dating from 401-417 This is as it may be seen today with the lower part of the mosaic hidden behind a Baroque reredos. It has been extensively restored. (Unattributed Post Card)

---

[10] Davis 1989 p. 85
[11] Mancinelli p.62 (117)

Figure 4. This is a 16th century drawing, before church redecoration obscured the lower part of the mosaic. Note the lamb at the bottom connected to the icon of Jesus.[12]*(Osborne et al 1997)*

Figure 5. The church of Sts Cosmas and Damian off the Forum in Rome 6th century.

[12] Osborne 1997

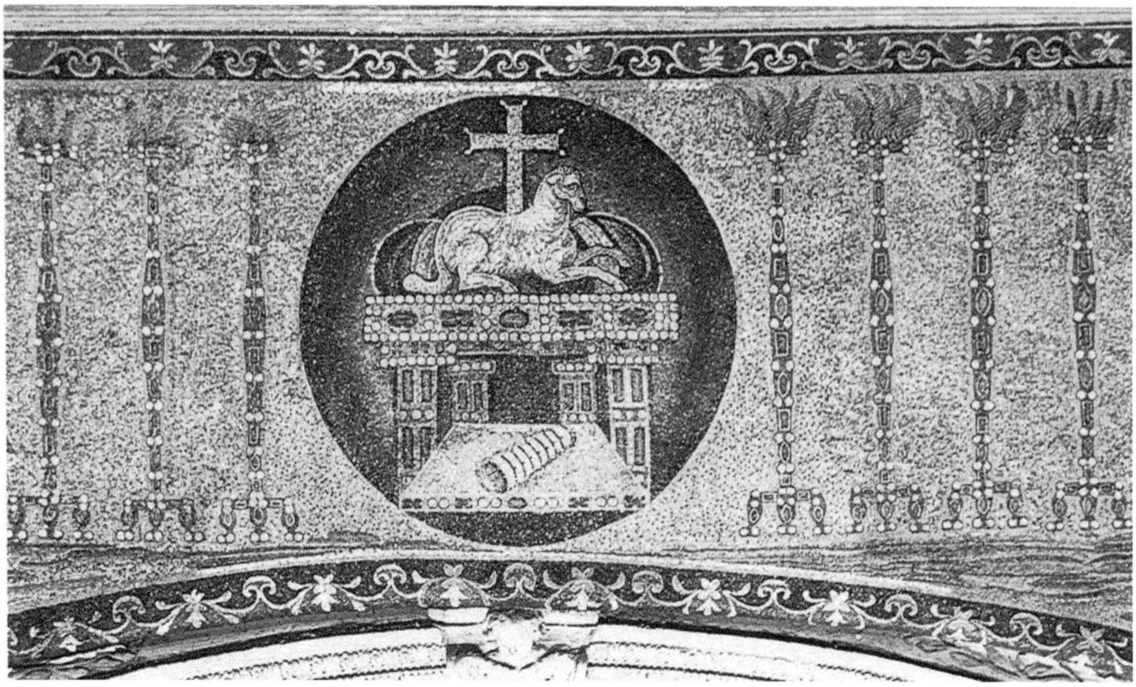

Figure 6. Sts Cosmas and Damian church, (527 – 530) Rome with the Lamb from the Book of Revelation above the triumphal arch. It is said that this icon was placed in this position by Pope Sergios himself. Figure 5 & 6 Bruno Fiorina in Conley et all

Figure 7 16th century drawing of the eastern end of Sts Cosmas and Damian church. Note the procession of Lambs/sheep emerging in the lower band coming from left and right moving from Bethlehem and Jerusalem towards the Divine Lamb. (Osborne 1997))

This type of procession is to be seen often in churches before and after Sergios, right through to the 13th century. Decoration of churches in this way was, it seems, almost universal. Many of these mosaics are now lost but fortunately many were drawn in the 16th century.

Figure 8. 16th century drawing of the mosaic in the apse of St Peter's basilica in Rome dating from the 4th century. Note again the procession of lambs and Christ depicted as a lamb in the centre.(Osborne 1997)

Should Pope Sergios have accepted the canon 82 it would have implied a wholesale re-decoration of many, perhaps even all the working churches in Rome. It is hardly surprising therefore if he dismissed Canon 82 as an "erroneous novelty".
Apart from the mosaic in Cosmas and Damian he also introduced a sentence into the Mass which is used to this day: Agnus dei qui per tollis peccata mundi, Miserere nobis" "Lamb of God who takes away the sin of the world have mercy upon us".
This is a classic reaction to ecclesiastical error – to stress the opposite.[13]

There is possibly a numismatic point here. During Justinian's first reign Constantinople was the only working mint in the East (see footnote 2 above). There were however, several in the West: Carthage, Sardinia, Sicily, Naples, Ravenna and Rome. Although we now connect Sardinia with Italy, at that time it was administered with North Africa. There is a crudely engraved coin from Justinian's reign with the first "Christ" icon,[14] but none of the Italian mints struck solidi or any other gold coins with the first icon.

It needs to be said at this point that Pope Sergios was not the only person who objected to Justinian's coins. The Arabs disliked them, but I am not convinced that they were iconoclasts at this point (687). There were also churchmen in Constantinople who objected on the grounds that Christ was made to look too much like Zeus[15].

---

[13] For instance Nestorianism which rejected the term 'Theotokos' (Mother of God), brought about the reaction of hugely increased Marian devotion. Iconoclasm had similar results.

[14] illustrated in D'Andrea 2017 p.309.

[15] When icons were restored in 843 under Michael II and Theodora, solidi were struck with icons of Christ similar to the first design of Justinian II after which, the type became universal.

When Pope Sergios died he was succeeded first by John VI (701-705) a Greek, and then by another Greek, John VII (705 – 707). Justinian returned during the latter's reign and sent the Acts of the Quinisext Council for his approval. He avoided the issue and sent them back un-amended. Interestingly he built and had decorated the church of St Maria Antiqua off the Forum. The frescoes he arranged are still in existence, but there are no lambs.

It was in his time (John VII) that the second icon of Christ appeared on Justinian's coins and the mints in Rome[16] and Ravenna[17] started to produce iconographic coins. Why then was this iconographic representation acceptable when the first one was not?

My hypothesis is predicated on the notion that at the time it was generally agreed that the second icon type was more authentic than the first type. In which case what grounds are there for them thinking this?

My suggestion would be that that they may well have thought there was an icon made-without-hands "Acheiropoieta" in Greek, that was authentic and provided the model for the new coins. The most obvious example of such an icon was the Mandylion, which was brought from Edessa to Constantinople in 944 and was believed to have been sent by Christ to Abgar, King of Edessa before his crucifixion.[18] This icon was kept in Constantinople and disappeared in 1204 after the 4th crusade. I cannot discount the possibility that copies of this icon were used as a pattern for both the coins in Constantinople and Italy.

Figure 9. Modern icon of the Holy Mandylion. Copies of the Mandylion are universal in Orthodox churches. Internet picture.

However, in 752 the LP records, in response to trouble with the Lombards as follows:-
"*On a certain day with great humility he (*Pope Stephen*) held a procession and litany in the usual way with the holy image of our Lord and God and Saviour Jesus Christ called the acheiropoieta..... with the rest of the sacerdotes the holy pope bore that holy image on his own shoulder.... "*[19]
This is the first reference to an *acheiropoieta* existing in Rome, but it is only forty odd years after Justinian.

[16] D'Andrea 2017 ps 399 & 400
[17] ibid p. 403
[18] Schott 2019 p.74
[19] Davis 1992 p.57

Is this a copy of the Mandylion? Or is it another, different *acheiropoieta?*
On balance the first seems to be most likely. However, there is an alternative possibility. In the town of Manoppello close to the Ionian sea in Italy there is a cloth known as the Holy Veil of Manoppello. It is believed to be an *acheiropoieta.* The curious thing about this is that it is believed, in Manoppello, to have been brought to Rome by the deposed and blinded Patriarch of Constantinople Kallinikos in 705. Theophanes records (AD 705/6) *"He blinded the patriarch Kallinikos and banished him to Rome:"*[20]
While Nikephoros records *"Thereafter, he sent the Patriarch Kallinikos to Rome, after blinding him for his slanders during the proclamation of Leontios."*[21]

Is it possible that Justinian spared Kallinikos his life if he took an icon with him as a proof of the pattern of icon he was now using on his coins? If he did was this actually an *acheiropoieta?* Or was it a copy? Did he bring the Veil of Manoppello, or is this another icon which has been attached to a legend?

I cannot answer any of these questions, and I doubt if they are answerable by anyone, but it does seem to me that we are faced with a very curious coincidence, and there may be the makings of an explanation for why Justinian had two quite different patterns of the depiction of Christ on his coins.

Finally is there any evidence that Christ was depicted as a lamb in any general or frequent way at the time of the Quinisext Council. There are three difficulties.
First many of the ancient churches in the East have been demolished often by earthquakes, but also by invading armies and Muslims. Second one must assume that Canon 82 was obeyed to some extent, so the lambs would have been removed. Third any that were left would almost certainly have been removed or altered during the period of Iconoclasm 726 to 843. However, outside the Great church of Agia Sophia amongst ruins and archaeological remains are two very interesting carved stones which do indeed feature lambs. Whether they were part of the present structure or come from a previous manifestation of the church is not clear. See Figures 10 and 11 below.

There is another possibility that just may be of relevance. This is the apse mosaic in the Monastery of St Catherine on Mt Sinai said to be circa 565 but possibly altered at a later date. This monastery was not troubled with iconoclasm, either Roman or Muslim. In the apse there is a mosaic with a depiction of the Transfiguration. Below is a curious band showing the heads of various saints and prophets. Was this originally a band showing lambs but changed subsequent to the Quinisext Council canon 82? (See figure 12).

[20] Mango 1997 p.523
[21] Tobias 1989 p.31

Figure 10. Stone carving amongst archaeological excavations at the Western end of Agia Sophia, Constantinople. (Author)

Figure 11. Stone carving amongst archaeological excavations at the Western end of Agia Sophia, Constantinople. Notice that the two sets of lambs are facing in different directions suggesting that they were both travelling towards the "Lamb of God" as seen in Roman churches. (Author)

Figure 12. Apse Mosaic of the Transfiguration in the church of the Monastery of St Catherine on Mt. Sinai. Could the band of heads below the main icon reflect Canon 82 of the Quinisext Council by being altered or designed to avoid lambs? (Internet Picture)

Bibliography

Primary Sources

Davis Raymond (Translator) ***The Book of Pontiffs (Liber Pontificalis)*** (to AD 715)1989, Liverpool University Press

Davis Raymond (Translator) ***The Lives of Eighth-Century Popes (Liber Pontificalis)*** 1992, Liverpool University Press

Tobias Norman & **Santoro** Anthony R. (Translators) ***An Eyewitness to History: The Short History of Nikephoros Patriarch of Constantinople*** 1989, Hellenic College Press Brookline

Mango Cyril & **Scott** Roger (Translators) ***The Chronicle of Theophanes the Confessor*** 1997, Oxford University Press

Schott Jeremy M. (Translator) ***Eusebius of Caesarea: The History of the Church*** 2019, University of California Press

Other Works Consulted

Badde Paul ***The Holy Veil of Manoppello*** 2018 Sophia Institute Press, Manchester New Hampshire

Breckenridge James D. ***The Numismatic Iconography of Justinian II*** 1959, The American Numismatic Society, New York

Conley Seraphin ***Basilica Santi Cosma E Damiano***, no date, Soprintendenza Archeologica di Roma

Crawford ***Peter Justinian II*** 2021, Pen and Sword Books Ltd., Barnsley
D'Andrea Alberto & **Ginnasi** Andrea Torno ***Byzantine Coinage in Italy Volume II*** 2017 edizioni d'andrea.
De Young Stephen ***The Religion of the Apostles*** 2021, Ancient Faith Publishing, Indiana
Head Constance ***Justinian II of Byzantium*** 1972, The University of Wisconsin Press
Osborne John & **Claridge** Amanda ***Early Christian and Medieval Antiquities Volume One Mosaics and Wall Paintings in Roman Churches*** 1997, Harvey Miller Publishers, 2300 Turnhout, Belgium
Paschalis Blandina ***Jesus Christ: The Lamb and Beautiful Shepherd (A Face to Face with the Veil of Manoppello)*** 2018, Johannes Wiemann Verlag, Nurnberg, Germany
Richards Jeffrey ***The Popes and the Papacy in the Early Middle Ages, 476-752*** 1979, Routledge & Kegan Paul, London
Sear David R. ***Byzantine Coins and their Values*** (Second Edition) 1987, Spink & Son Ltd., London.
Wroth Warwick ***Imperial Byzantine Coins in the British Museum*** (two volumes in One) MCMLXVI (1966) Argonaut, Inc., Publishers, Chicago.
Whitting P.D. ***Byzantine Coins*** 1973, Barrie & Jenkins, England

Coin Circulation in Carthage and its Hinterland

Tasha Vorderstrasse[1]

Introduction

The city of Carthage has been of considerable interest to archaeologists and travellers due to its historical significance as a Punic city destroyed by the Romans. In addition, however, there has been considerable work done on the Byzantine city which has helped us to better understand how Carthage and North Africa fit into the Late Roman, Vandal, and Byzantine worlds. There has also been recent work that examines the transition from Byzantine to Early Islamic North Africa and the implications for the region. The coins in particular have been examined in considerable detail by Morrisson (see for instance 1988b, 2003, 2012, 2022) and have allowed us to refine our understanding not only of coinage produced at Carthage in the Vandal and Byzantine periods, but also coin circulation based on hoards and excavation finds. Nevertheless, since Morrisson's initial article, comparative coin numbers have not been published for the bronze coins, though there has been considerable publication of excavation coins from the site of Carthage and to a lesser extent, elsewhere in Tunisia. Therefore, this article seeks to provide an overview of coins from different excavations at Carthage to better understand coin circulation in the period of the Byzantine reconquest in the 5th century CE.

Coin Collecting and Carthage

Excavations at the site of Carthage began under the French (Charles Beulé in 1859) and English (Nathan Davis in 1859-1860). There were also later excavations by Daux (1868), de Sainte-Marie (1874), and Saloman Reinach and Ernest Babelon (1884) and others (Reinach and Babelon 1886: 10; Laporte 1999; Fantar 2000; Freed 2008; Fumadó Ortega 2009: 62-90; Gutron 2010: 110-117; Freed 2011: 13-16; Fumadó Ortega 2013: 57). The publication of Reinach and Babelon (1886) discusses stelae, lamps, marble sculpture, bone and ivory objects, and terracottas, but only one coin is mentioned (Reinach and Babelon 1886: 32, no. 190). There is little information about coin finds prior to the 1880s even though coin finds are known to have occurred. Many of these are still unpublished, in part because they could not be identified due to the fact that they could be not cleaned (Visonà 1994: 118; Visonà 2016: 112, 115-117; Fumadó Ortega 2021: 58-59). At least one hoard was found in this period, discovered by Humbert in the 1820s, that consisted of 29 Late Roman, Vandal, and Byzantine coins (Visonà 2016: 115, no. 33. Visonà is planning to publish the hoard). Only a small number of bronze coin hoards have been attested in North Africa in general (Lafaurie 1959: 127-128).

In addition to coins found in excavations, already in the 1840s visitors to the site were collecting large numbers of coins from Carthage, including 777 in the British Museum and 483 now in the Hunter Coin Cabinet of the University of Glasgow (Bateson, Campbell, and Visonà 1990: 145-146, no. 6). Bateson et al argued that the group was likely purchased from local dealer(s) at the site as coins were commonly

[1] Oriental Institute, University of Chicago. Email: tkvorder@uchicago.edu. Thanks to Brian Muhs for his comments and suggestions and Harrison Morin for helping put together the map.

purchased by visitors. The fact that most of the bronze coins were legible and that very small denomination coins were missing though they are present in excavations from the site, in addition to the presence of precious metal coins, suggested to them that the coins were not found immediately before they were purchased, but rather had been sorted (Bateson, Campbell, and Visonà 1990: 148, 151). The British Museum group remains unpublished. Another group of coins which includes a large number of Punic coins as well as Byzantine coins minted in Carthage were obtained by Dr. Michael Mannheimer (1844-1891), who amassed a large collection of coins of different types before his death, which were then donated to the University of Chicago when his wife died in 1909. Eventually these coins were donated to the Oriental Institute. (N. A. 1891, reprinted in 1927: 659; N. A. 1909: 764; Goodspeed 1915: 492 Archer 1954: 220-221). There is no information about where or when Mannheimer purchased his coins.

Starting in the early 1970s, the UNESCO initiative "Pour Sauver Carthage" led to a large number of international teams excavating at Carthage. It is in this period that the excavations began to produce coins that have since been published. Coins have been found at sites throughout the city, although not all the material has yet been published. The coins considered here are listed by their general location. In the center of the city was the Byrsa Hill. Just on the northern side of the Byrsa Hill is where the Swedish team conducted their excavations from 1979-1983 (coins by Nilsson 2017), and further north were the Circular Monument on the Odeon Hill excavated by the Canadian team from 1974-1984 (coins published by Guimond 1979; Guimond 1981) and the joint Tunisian-French project at the Odeon of 1987-2000 (published by Brenot 2012). The Austrian excavations at the Basilica of Damous el-Karita in 1996 and 1997 (coins published by Baldus 2001) were located to the north outside the city walls. To the northeast was the Dermech area where the University of Michigan conducted excavations in 1975 and 1978 (published by Buttrey 1976; Buttrey and Hitchner 1978; Metcalf and Hitchner 1980; Metcalf 1982). In the northwest there was a Vandal Cemetery excavated in 1987-1989 (coins published by Visonà 2009), and 1 km outside the city to the northwest was the Bir Ftouha Church, which was excavated in 1994-1999 by Randolph College (coins published by Houghtalin and Mac Isaac 2005). To the east was the Decumanus Maximus site where the Germans excavated in 1986-1995 (coins published by Baldus 2007).

In the southwest there were the Roman Circus and Byzantine cemetery excavated in 1982-1983, 1985, and 1987 (some coins published by Metcalf 1988 and Visonà 1988 but not all the coins from this site were published). Further to the west was the Yasmina Cemetery excavated by the University of Georgia in 1992-1995 and 1997 (coins published by Houghtalin and Mac Isaac 2020). To the southeast was the Bir Massouada Basilica (coins published by Krmnicek 2019), while further to the southeast were the British excavations at Avenue Bourguiba, Circular Harbor, and Amirauté Island (coins published by Reece 1984,1994, and 2012[2]), and the Roman commercial port and Tophet excavated by the Punic Excavations at Carthage (Tunisia) conducted by the American Schools of Oriental Research (ASOR),

[2] Reece 1984 and Reece 1994 publish the coins only with references to their coin catalogue publication parallels, without denomination or indication of mint. Reece 2012 gives a chart of the 1984, 1994 (both single finds and the so-called hoard coins) and 2012 coins with enough information that makes it easier to determine denomination without having to look at the original publications of 1984 and 1994 where the coins are published by strata, but it should be noted that the chart has errors. First, while in this instance Reece lists the mints of the coins, after the reign of Justinian, the mint of Carthage does not appear. This turns out to be an error where coins listed as minted in Constantinople are actually minted in Carthage when one consults the coin catalogue entries. He also does not include the mint when he cites Hahn's Carthage coins that Bellinger would have assigned to the "Constantine in Numidia" mint, despite giving Constantine in Numidia as mint for other coins. In other cases, the catalogue reference is also wrong. In the Heraclius Revolt coinage, the mint of Constantinople is listed not only as the mint, but also in the catalogue references. However, since this does not exist, it has been corrected to what appears to be the correct mint: Carthage. In at least one instance, the information about the denomination of the coin is also wrong. This has been corrected as well as possible for this article.

Harvard University, and the University of Chicago in 1975-1980 (coins published in Betlyon 2008). To the south was the Bir Knissia Church (coins published by Visonà 1993).

In addition, coin finds are mentioned but not published from the southeast Bir Massouada excavations by the Tunisian Institut National du Patrimoine in collaboration first with the University of Amsterdam and then Ghent University in 2000-2005 (Docter et al 2006), and from the Canadian excavations in the northern part of Carthage along the Late Roman wall (Blockley 1978; Ellis 1985). Blockley discusses the coins generally but does not publish them. He also reports not finding any Byzantine coins at the site at all (Blockley 1978: 11; Ellis 1985). In the Bir Massouada publications there was mention of a "hoard" of 215 Byzantine and Vandal coins, which came from a disturbed context and given that they were of same types of coins (which are not specified in the report) were likely to come from an actual hoard (Docter et al 2006: 79). Only two coins have been published from these excavations (Docter et al 2006: 76, 85, no. 244).

Coin Circulation

Gold, silver, and bronze coins have provided evidence from hoards and excavations for a monetized economy in the initial Late Roman, Vandal, and 6th/7th century Byzantine period (Morrisson 2016: 175-178; Morrisson 2022: 417). Assessing the actual coin circulation at Carthage, however, has proved to be challenging. One of the difficulties with the coins has been their condition. There are reports of the poor condition of the coins found in the excavations which needed extensive cleaning, which echoes the observations on those found in the 19th century (Reece 1984: 171; Docter et al 2006: 79; Betlyon 2008: 322 and Reece 2012: 265-266, Table 1, both of whom note that many coins disintegrated on cleaning; Nilsson 2017: 138). At Carthage itself, most of the Vandal and Byzantine coins were struck in the city, with Constantinople being the second largest mint but in much smaller numbers (Metcalf 1987: 78; Morrisson 2003: 81; Betlyon 2008: 328). It has been suggested that coins minted in the style of Carthage but with a Constantinople mintmark were actually minted at "Constantine in Numidia," but this has been questioned and Carthage is now generally thought to be the mint. Nevertheless, in the charts here, these coins are designated as Constantine in Numidia in order to make them distinct from the regular coins minted at Carthage.

While Morrisson discusses both the hoard and excavation evidence (Morrisson 2016: 177, 179), one still needs to go back to the original reports to get the actual coin numbers. It is also evident that some scholars do not see these comparisons as particularly helpful. Reece suggests that comparing the British excavations at Carthage with other Carthage excavations and other sites in the Byzantine world as "at best incomplete, at worst, totally misleading" (Reece 2012: 272). He feels that many of the publications of the coins include no stratigraphic detail and is "sceptical of the use of comparing data published by many different people at many different times and in many different ways" (Reece 2012: 272). Rather, he advocates that all the coins should be returned to Carthage itself and one person or group should go through all the coins (Reece 2012: 272).

The coins were compared in detail by Morrisson in 1988, when she noted that there were comparisons that could be made. She observed that the University of Michigan Dermech site located to the northeast of the center of the city produced far more coins in the 7th century than the southwest site of the Circus and the southeast site of Avenue Bourguiba, which were similar to one another and where most of the coins were earlier. She suggests that perhaps these sites were abandoned earlier than Dermech, which continued into the Islamic period. She also noted that there were large numbers of 5th century nummi, which she suggested were a result of the University of Michigan sifting their finds (Morrisson 1988b:

428, 431, 434. See also Buttrey 1976: 165; Ellis 1985: 38). Others have argued there is likely to be a different reason for this - namely it appears that the population at Carthage did not use large denomination bronze coins (Buttrey and Hitchner 1978: 101-103; Metcalf 1978: 78-79). In the Canadian excavations, Ellis notes that under a 6th-7th century floor they found 100 nummi (Ellis 1985: 32, he does not indicate if they were Vandal or Justinian), which again points to large numbers of small denomination coins in circulation. There is a small number of coins from the reigns of Justin II, Tiberius, and Maurice, which Betlyon has suggested is a result of the fact that the emperors were concentrating their efforts in regions that were not North Africa (Betlyon 2008: 326). While the coin numbers increase in the 7th century in the Dermech site, few Constantine IV and Justinian II were found, suggesting that they did not mint very many coins at Carthage (Humphrey 1980: 89). Another reason why there may be fewer coins is that the Byzantines already had enough coins and so did not need to mint more (Morrisson 1988b: 436). Indeed, it has been argued that Roman and Vandal coins continued to circulate into the Byzantine period (Buttrey 1976: 165; Humphrey 1980: 89) and this is backed up by hoard evidence (Metcalf 1984: 65; Hurst 1994: 257-260). Other sites are also said to be similar. Brenot in the study of the Odeon suggests that those coins resemble those of the coins found at Avenue Bourguiba which are called a "hoard" (Brenot 2012: 729), while Krmnicek (2019: 221) compares his coin numbers with those of recent excavations including Baldus, Betlyon, and Docter, and states that they are similar. Since the work of Docter is unpublished (see above), however, this is not easy to confirm. Betlyon also compares his finds with other UNESCO excavations at Carthage in the 1970s (Betlyon 2008: 329).

If one looks at the overall coin numbers, it is possible to make a number of statements about these excavations. It is clear that some sites produced a large number of coins, namely the Dermech site in particular (Buttrey 1976; Buttrey and Hitchner 1978; Metcalf and Hitchner 1980; Metcalf 1982), as well as at the Byrsa (Nilsson 2017), Bir Ftouha (Houghtalin and Mac Isaac 2005), the Circus (Metcalf 1988; Visonà 1988), the British Museum excavations (Reece 1984; Reece 1994; Reece 2012), the Commercial Port and Tophet (Betlyon 2008), and Bir el-Knissia (Visonà 1993). The number of coins found of the earlier Byzantine rulers prior to the re-conquest of Carthage by Justinian in 533 is not large. There is only one coin of Zeno attested, with a small number of coins of Anastasius and Justin I. The coins are almost all minted in Constantinople, with Nicomedia and Antioch also represented. The coins are all found in either the center (Nilsson 2017) or southern part of the city (Reece 1984; Betlyon 2008; Houghtalin and Mac Isaac 2020) (see Chart Two). As has been observed elsewhere, coin numbers greatly increased under Justinian, primarily in the small denominations. Large numbers are attested particularly in the Dermech area excavated by the University of Michigan (Buttrey 1976; Buttrey and Hitchner 1978; Metcalf and Hitchner 1980; Metcalf 1982), but also at the Bir el-Knissia church (Visonà 1993). Numbers drop considerably after that, with a much smaller number of coins of Justin II, and start to rise in some parts of the city under Maurice, namely at the Dermech (Buttrey and Hitchner 1978; Metcalf and Hitchner 1980; Metcalf 1982) and the central Byrsa hill (Nilsson 2017). These sites continue to be well represented under Phocas, Heraclius, and Constans II. Numbers of coins were also rising under Phocas and Heraclius at Bir Ftouha (Houghtalin and Mac Isaac 2005), and in the southeast in the Commercial Harbor and Tophet (Betlyon 2008), also rising under Heraclius in the British Museum excavations (Reece 1984; Reece 1994; Reece 2012). After that coin numbers drop considerably and only sites in the central Byrsa (Nilsson 2017) and the Dermech (Buttrey 1976; Buttrey and Hitchner 1978; Metcalf and Hitchner 1980; Metcalf 1982) have coins of Constantine IV and Justinian II. It is interesting that Bir Ftouha has large numbers of coins despite being quite a way outside of the city.

Silver coins are also attested in excavations, indicating that they were minted by Carthage and used by its population (Morrisson 2016: 182). Silver coins were used throughout the Byzantine period in different parts of the site. The majority of the coins are small denomination copper coins, with a number of groups of coins being classified as hoards, although not everyone agrees (see Brenot 2012: 729). There were coin groups found by the British Museum excavations that were classified as hoards, but Nilsson suggests that these should be referred to as "groups of coins" or small hoards that were worn and found together (Nilsson 2017: 141). At the site of Leptiminus Magna, the excavators reported finding coin-filled layers that they describe as "dumping layers" that were connected with later occupants of the site removing earlier levels in search of spolia and coins (Stirling, Ben Lazreg, and Moore 2021: 13). These hoards have not been examined here because of the uncertainty of their status as hoards or parcels or single finds that happen to be associated with each other.

Coins have been published from other sites in the region, although less attention has been given to inland rural sites (Morrisson 2022: 420). In countryside of Carthage the presence of small numbers of Vandal bronze and Byzantine silver coins-minted at Carthage is attested (Abram 2019: 332-334, 337). Along the coast, Metcalf (1992, 2001) has published coins from the port site of Leptiminus Magna, which is located 180 km southeast of Carthage. The number of coins found at the site is much smaller than those at Carthage. It does fit into the picture that we see at Carthage, however, with the mint of Carthage dominating the coins that were found. They did find a single coin from the mint of Antioch, which they described as being a rather unexpected find (Metcalf 2001: 460). There are more signs of monetization elsewhere, however. At Uchi Maius, excavators found a hoard of 32 silver coins in addition to a few Byzantine bronze coins (Baldassari 2007a; Baldassari 2007b: 290). Further to the west of Carthage, at Bulla Regia, excavators reported finding a small hoard of 9 coins of Justin II along with "low value" coins of the 4th and 5th centuries CE. Although they claim the hoard is made up of "nummi" (Chaouali, Fenwick, and Booms 2018: 195), the photograph clearly shows that 7 of the coins are 5-nummi coins and appear to be from the Carthage mint (Chaouali et al 2017: 26, 35, Fig. 35). But the coin numbers are much smaller than at Carthage suggesting that while the countryside and smaller towns were monetized, they were not using coins with such intensity.

Conclusion

If we compare coins from excavations at Carthage, we can see that they follow a fairly consistent pattern. While Reece may be quite gloomy about the utility of doing this type of study one can see trends and patterns in the coins, as Morrisson's work has already shown (1988b). This study supports her work on the subject and even though the evidence has considerably expanded since her publication, one can nevertheless see that the Dermech is an area where there was considerable use of coins throughout the Byzantine period. Other parts of the site see drops in the number of coins particularly after Justinian, but in the northern (and even far northern) and southern parts of the city, particularly around the harbor area. one sees the use of coins later in the 7th century. This does not necessarily prove that the other sites were abandoned in this period, as coins continued in use, but it does point to active use of 7th century coins only in certain parts of the site. As more sites are published, it is hoped that this picture can be further refined and studied.

Bibliography

Abram, S., 2019. "Monete." In *Rus Africum IV. La fattoria Bizantina di Aïn Wassel (Alto Tell, Tunisia). Lo scavo stratigrafico e i materiali*, eds by M. de Vos Raaijmakers and B. Maurina, 330–338. Oxford: Archaeopress.

Archer, H. R. 1954. *Some Aspects of the Acquisition Program at the University of Chicago Library, 1892-1928.* Unpublished PhD dissertation, University of Chicago.

Baldassari, M. 2007a. "2007. "Gruzzolo di monete d'argento di Eraclio." In *Uchi Maius 3, I frantoi. Miscellanea*, ed. C. Vismara, 164-181. Sassari.
2007b. "Reperti numismatici dalle aree dei frantoi (2.200, 22.000, 24.000 e 25.000)." In *Uchi Maius 3, I frantoi. Miscellanea*, ed. C. Vismara, 289–302. Sassari.

Baldus, H. R. 2001. "Die Fundmünzen." In *Damous-el-Karita. Die österreichisch-tunesischen Ausgrabungen der Jahre 1996 und 1997 im Saalbau und der Memoria des Pilgerheiligtumes Damous-el-Karita in Karthago,* H. Dolenz, 121-125. Österreichisches Arhäologisches Institut Sonderschriften Band 35: Vienna: E. Becvar GmbH.
2007. "Die Fundmünzen." In *Karthago: Die Ergebnisse der hamburger Grabung unter dem Decumanus Maximus,* H. G. Niemyer, R. F. Docter, K. Schmidt, and B. Bethold, 821-840. Hamburger Forschungen zur Archäologie Band 2. Mainz: Philipp von Zabern.

Bateson, D., I. Campbell, and P. Visonà. "The Early Nineteenth-Century Jackson Collection of Coins from Carthage." *Numismatic Chronicle* 150 (1990): 145-177.

Berndt, G. M. and R. Steinacher. 2008. "Minting in Vandal North Africa: coins of the Vandal period in the Coin Cabinet of Vienna's Kunsthistorisches Museum." *Early Medieval Europe* 16: 252-298.

Betlyon John Wilson. 2008. "The Coins from the 1975-1978 Seasons in the Punic Port and Tophet of Carthage, Tunisia." *Revue numismatique* 6th series 194: 321-353.

Blockley, R. C. 1978. "Appendix II: Coins from the 1976 Excavations." *Echoes du Monde Classique* 22: 11-12.

Brenot, C. 2012. "Dépôt monétaire et catalogue des monnaies de fouilles" and "Les monnaies." In *Carthage, colline de l'Odeon: maison de la rotonde et du cryptoportique: (recherches 1987–2000), Volume 2,* ed. by C. Balmelle et al., 561–596 and 719–730 Coll. de l'Ecole francaise de Rome 457. Rome.

Buttrey, T. V. 1976. "The Coins – 1975." In *Excavations at Carthage 1975.Conducted by the University of Michigan I,* 157-197. Tunis.

Buttrey, T. V. and B. R. Hitchner. 1978. "The Coins – 1976." In *Excavations at Carthage 1976. Conducted by the University of Michigan IV*, 99-163. Tunis.

Chaouali, M., C. Fenwick, and D. Booms. 2018. "Bulla Regia 1: A New Church and Christian Cemetery." *Libyan Studies* 49: 187-197.

M. Chaouali, C. Fenwick, D. Booms, G. Carpentiero, S. Cox, G. Hopkinson, G. Jorayev, E. Nikita, M. Brinsi and A. Ten Harkel. 2017. *The Bulla Regia Archaeological Project 2017: End of Season Report September 7th-22nd.* https://www.bilnas.org/wp-content/uploads/2019/04/End-of-season-report_The-Bulla-Regia-Archaeological-Project-2017.compressed-1.pdf?ref=slsrebranded

Docter, R. F., F. Chelbi, B. M. Telmini, B. Bechtold, H. B. Romdhane, V. Declercq, T. De Schacht, E. Deweirdt, A. De Wulf, L. Fersi, S. Frey-Kupper, S. Garsallah, I. Joosten, H. Koens, J. Mabrouk, T.

Redisssi, S. R. Chebbi, K. Ryckbosch, K. Schmidt, B. Taverniers, J. Van Kerckhove, and L. Verdonck. 2006. "Carthage Bir Massouda: Second preliminary report on the bilateral excavations of Ghent University and the Institut National du Patrimoine (2003-2004)." *BABesch* 81: 37-89.

Ellis, S. 1985. "Carthage in the Seventh Century: An Expanding Population?" *Cahiers des etudes anciennes* 17: 30-42.

Fantar, M. H. 2000. "Pionniers d'archéologique punique." In *La Tunisie mosaïque,* edtied by P. Cabanel and J. Alexandropolos, 510-512. Toulouse.

Freed, J. 2008. "Le père Alfred-Louis Delattre (1850-1932) et les fouilles archéologiques de Carthage." *Histoire et missions chrétiennes* 4: 67-100.
2011. *Bringing Carthage Home: The Excavations of Nathan Davis, 1856-1859.* University of British Columbia Studies in the Ancient World. Vol. 2. Oxford and Oakville: Oxbow Books.

Fumadó Ortega, I. 2009. *Cartago: Historia de la investigación.* Madrid.
2013. "Colonial Representations and Carthaginian Archaeology." *Oxford Journal of Archaeology* 32: 53-72.
2021. "Carthaginiancoinfinds: una base de datos sobre hallazgos numismáticos geolocalizados." *Revista Numismatica Hecate* 8: 53 – 67.

Goodspeed, T. W. 1916. *A History of the University of Chicago Founded by John D Rockefeller. The First Quarter-Century.* Chicago: University of Chicago Press.

Guimond, L. 1979. "Monnaies des campagnes 1976 et 1978." *Cahiers des études anciennes* 10: 25-50.
1981. "Monnaies des campagnes 1978 et 1979." *Cahiers des études anciennes* 13: 55-72.

Gutron, C. 2010. *L'archéologie en Tunisie (XIXe-XXe siècles): Jeux généalogiques sur l'Antiquité.* Paris: Karthala.

Houghtalin, L. and J. D. Mac Isaac. 2005. "The Coins." In *Bir Ftouha: A Pilgrimage Church Complex at Carthage,* ed. S. T. Stevens, A. V. Kalinowski, and H. van der Leest, 181-208. JRA Supplementary Series No. 59. Portsmouth, RI.
2020. "The numismatic finds from the Yasmina cemetery." In *For the Love of Carthage: Cemeteries, a Bath and the Circus in the Southwest Part of the City; Pottery, Brickstamps and Lamps from Several sites; the Presence of saints, & Urban development in the Pertica region,* ed. By J. H. Humphrey. 115-162. JRA Supplementary Series Number 9. Portsmouth, RI.

Humphrey, J. H. 1980. "Vandal and Byzantine Carthage: Some New Archaeological Evidence." In *New Light on Ancient Carthage,* ed. By J. G. Pedley, 85-120. Ann Arbor: University of Michigan Press.

Hurst, H. R. *Excavations at Carthage. The British Mission (Vol. II, 1: The Circular Harbour, North Side),* ed. H. R. Hurst. Oxford.

Krmnicek, S. 2019. "The Coins." In *Bir Messaouda Basilica: Pilgrimage and Transformation of a Landscape in Sixth Century AD Carthage*, R. Miles and S. Greenslade, 221-236. Oxford and Philadelphia: Oxbow Books.

Lafaurie, J. 1959. "Trésor de monnaies de cuivre trouvé à Sidi-Aïch (Tunisie)." *Revue numismatique* 6th series, Vol. 2: 113-130.

Laporte Jean-Pierre. Carthage : les stèles Sainte-Marie. In: Bulletin de la Société Nationale des Antiquaires de France, 1999, 2002. pp. 133-146.

Metcalf, W. E. 1982. "The Coins – 1978." *In Excavations at Carthage 1987. Conducted by the University of Michigan VII,* ed. J. H. Humphrey, 63-168. Michigan.
1987. "The Michigan Finds at Carthage, 1975-1979: An Analysis." *American Numismatic Society Museum Notes* 32: 61-84.
1988. "The Coins – 1982." In *The Circus and a Byzantine Cemetery at Carthage*, ed. J. Humphrey, 337-382. Ann Arbor: University of Michigan Press.
1992. "Coin Finds." In *Leptiminus (Lamta): A Roman Port City in Tunisia Report no. 1,* N. Ben Lazreg and D. J. Mattingly, 264-266. JRA Supplementary Series No. 4. Portsmouth, RI.
2001. "Coins from the 1992 and 1994 Seasons." In *Leptiminus (Lamta) Report No. 2: The East Baths, Cemeteries, Kilns, Venus Mosaic, Site Museum, and Other Studies,* L. M. Stirling, D. J. Mattingly, and N. Ben Lazreg. 460-464. JRA Supplementeary Series No. 41. Portsmouth, RI: JRA.

Metcalf, W. E. and R. B. Hitchner. 1980. "The Coins." In *Excavations at Carthage 1977. Conducted by the University of Michigan V*, ed. J. H. Humphrey, 185-270. New Delhi.

Morrisson, C. 1988a. "Carthage, production et circulation du bronze à l'époque byzantine d'après les trouvailles et les fouilles." *Bulletin de la Société Nationale des Antiquaires de France*: 239-253.
1988b. "Coin Finds in Vandal and Byzantine Carthage. A Provisional Assessment." In *The Circus and a Byzantine Cemetery at Carthage*, ed. J. Humphrey, 423-436. Ann Arbor.
2001. "Caratteristiche ed uso della moneta protovandalica e vandalica." In *Le invasioni barbariche nel meridione dell'impero: Visigoti, Vandali, Ostrogoti. Atti del Convegno svoltosi alla Casa delle Culture di Cosenza dal 24 al 26 luglio 1998,* ed. P. Delogu, 151-180. Rubbettino.
2003. "L'atelier de Carthage et la diffusion de la monnaie frappée dans l'Afrique vandale et byzantine (439-695)." *Antiquité Tardive* 11: 65-84.
2016. "'Regio dives in omnibus bonis ornata' African economy from the Vandals to the Arab conquest in the light of coin evidence." In *North Africa under Byzantium and Early Islam*, eds. S. Stevens and J. Conant, 173–198. Washington D. C.
2022. "Late Roman, Vandal, and Byzantine Coinage in North Africa." In *A Companion to North Africa in Antiquity*, edited by R. B. Hitchner. John Wiley & Sons, Inc.

N. A. 1891 (reprinted in 1927). "August, 1891." *The Reform Advocate* LXXIII: 659.
1909. "Bequests to Charity by the Late Mrs. A. Mannheimer." *The Reform Advocate*: 764.

Nilsson, H. 2017. "Coins from the Swedish Excavations at Carthage." In *Carthage II: The Swedish Mission to Carthage Part of the UNESCO Project "Pour Sauver Carthage,"* J. Lund, R. Larje, and H. Nilsson, 138-230. Sjrifter Utgivna av Svenska Institutet I Rom 4, 54: 2. Stockholm.

Reece, R. 1984. "Coins." 171-181. In *Excavations at Carthage. The British Mission (Vol. I, 1: The Avenue du President Habib Bourguiba, Salammbo. The Site and Finds other than Pottery),* H. R. Hurst and S. P. Roskams, 249-256.
1994. "Coins." In *Excavations at Carthage. The British Mission (Vol. II, 1: The Circular Harbour, North Side),* ed. H. R. Hurst, 249-256. Oxford.

2012. "Coins from the British Excavations at Carthage: Date of Minting and Date of Deposit." *The Archaeological Journal of Numismatics* 2: 265-280.

Reinach, S. and E. Babelon. 1886. "Recherches archéologiques en Tunisie (1883-1884)." *BA/BCTH*: 4-40.

Stirling, L. M., N. Ben Lazreg, and J. P. Moore. 2021. "The Leptiminus Archaeological Project and the East Cemetery: An Introduction," ed. N. Ben Lazreg, L. M. Stirling, and J. P. Moore, 9-15. JRA Supplementary Series 110. Portsmouth, RI.

Visonà, P. 1988. "The Coins." In *The Circus and a Byzantine Cemetery at Carthage*, ed. J. Humphrey, 383-422. Ann Arbor: University of Michigan Press.
1993. "The Coins -1990." In *Bir el Knissia at Carthage: A Rediscovered Cemetery Church* Report No. 1, S. T. Stevens, 201-224. JRA Supplementary Series no. 7. Ann Arbor.
1994. "Carthage. A Numismatic Bibliography." *Studi di Egittologia e di Antichità Puniche* 13: 117–231.
2009. "The Coins." In *A Cemetery of Vandalic Date at Carthage*, S. T. Stevens, M. B. Garrison, and J. Freed, 173-206. Journal of Roman Archaeology Supplementary Series 75. Portsmouth, RI.
2016. "More Greek Coins from Carthage and Elsewhere in Tunisia." *Numismatic Chronicle* 176: 111-133.

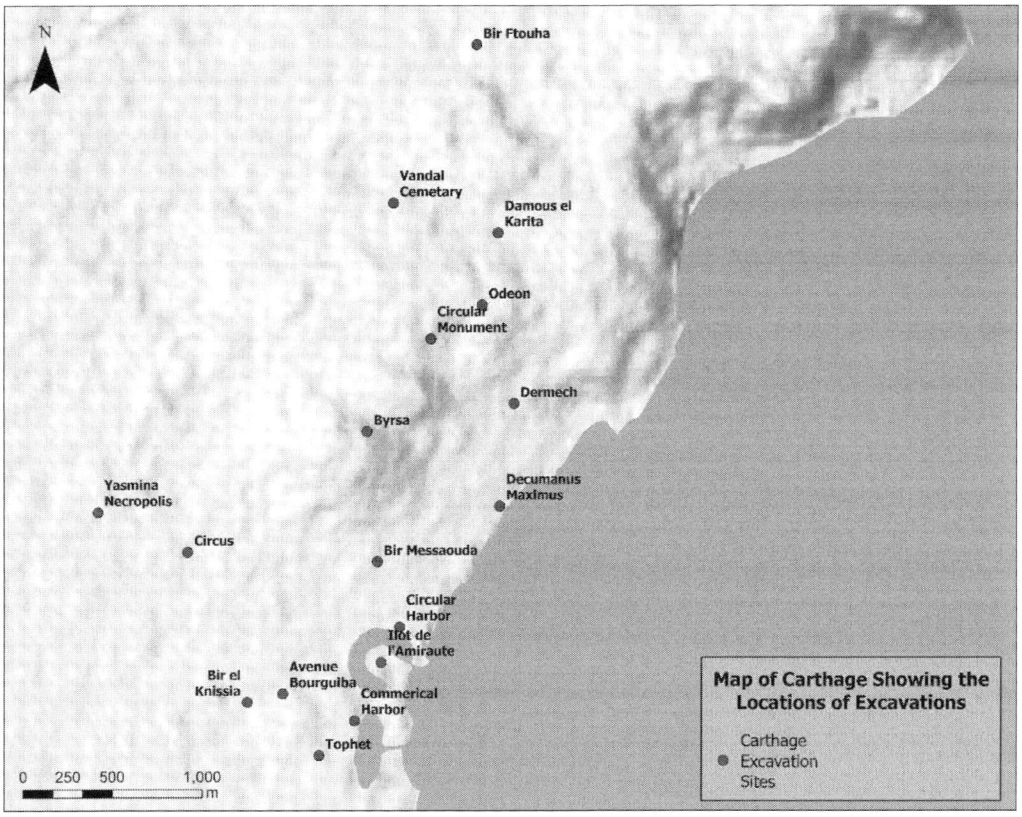

Map of Carthage showing location of excavations. Courtesy H. Morin (CAMEL, University of Chicago)

Name	Author
Ilot de l'Amiraute	Reece 2012
Circular Harbor	Reece 1994
Avenue Bourguiba	Reece 1984
Commerical Harbor	Betlyon 2008
Tophet	Betlyon 2008
Byrsa	Nilsson 2017
Odeon	Brenot 2012
Circular Monument	Guimond 1979 & 1981
Vandal Cemetary	Visona 2009
Damous el Karita	Baldus 2001
Decumanus Maximus	Baldus 2007
Dermech	Buttrey 1976; Buttrey & Hitchner 1978; Metcalf & Hitchner 1980; Metcalf 1982
Bir Ftouha	Houghtalin & Mac Isaac 2005
Circus	Metcalf 1988; Visona 1988
Yasmina Necropolis	Houghtalin & Mac Isaac 2020
Bir Messaouda	Krmnicek 2019
Bir el Knissia	Visona 1993

Chart One: Total Coin Numbers

Loc	Aut	Z	A	JI	A-Jst	Jst	J?	J.J	JII	TII	M	T/M	M?	Ph	HRv	H	P/H	CII	CIV	JII	Tot
Cen	Nil 2017		2	5		54			4		22			40	4	25		33	1		190
NE	But 1976					39			1		2	1		1		6		32		3	85
	But. & Hit					121			2		11			20	7	42		88	6	2	299
	Met & Hit					223			6		23			16	11	53		39	3	3	377
	Met 1982					343			13		42		1	21	7	56	15	52	7	4	561
N	Gui 1978					24			2	1	1				1	8		5		2	44
	Gui 1981					11			0												11

	Bre 2012					8	1		1		2			1		1		1			15
N out	Bal 2001					1			1		3			1	1	2					9
N W	Vis 2009					5			1							1					7
Far N	Hou &Mac 2005					64			1		8			18	4	21		34			150
E	Bal 2007					3			1					1		2		2			9
S W	Met 1988					88		1			5			5		5	1	9			114
	Vis 1988					49					6			1		3		2			61
S W	Hou & Mac 2020	1	1			5															7
SE	Krm 2019				1	39			1		1				2	5	1	2	1		53
	Ree 1984		1	1		51			1		19			2		12		3			90
	Ree 1994					28					15			9	2	26		23	1		104
	Ree 2012					40			1		6			8	5	20		18	1		99
	Bet 2008		1			47			8	1	13			16	1	13		37	2		139
	Vis 1993					100			1		5				5	8	1	12			132

Chart Two: Coin Numbers Zeno-Justin I

Location	Publication	Zeno	Mint		4-nummi	
Further west southwest	Houghtalin 2020 and Mac Isaac		Con		1	
	Publication	**Anastasius**	**Mint**	**Nummus**	**4-nummi**	**5-nummi**
Center	Nilsson 2017		Con	1		
			Ant			1
Southeast	Reece 1984		Con	1		
	Betlyon 2008		Con	1		
Further west southwest	Houghtalin and Mac Isaac 2020		Con?		1	
	Publication	**Justin I**		**Nummus**		**5-nummi**
Center	Nilsson 2017		Con	2		
			Nic			3
Southeast	Reece 1984		Nic			1

Chart Three: Coin Numbers of Justinian I

Location	Publication	Mint	N	1.5 N?	2-N	2.5-N	4-N	5-N	10-N	12-N	Fol	Den	Sil	?
Cen	Nils 2017	Car	43	1	7			1	1		1			
NE	But 1976	Car					37	2						
NE	But/Hit 1978	Car	119					1					1	
NE	Met/ Hit 1980	Alex								1				
		Con Num							1					
		Car	215		1			5						
NE	Met 1984	Car	320		17			4	2					
N	Gui 1978	Car	24											
N	Gui 1981	Car	11					1						
N	Bre 2012	Car?							1					
		Car	6					1						
N Walls	Bal 2001	Car	1											
NW	Vis 2009	Car	3		1			1						

Far N	Hou/ Mac 2005	Car	64											
E	Bal 2007	Car	3											
SW	Met 1988	Car	79		2			1						
SW	Vis 1988	Car	49											
Far SW	Hou/Mac 2020	Car	3											2
		?												
SE	Krm 2019	Car	29		1				2		1			
		Rom										1		
		Rav							2			3		
SE	Ree 1984	Car	42					3	2					
		Tes			1									
		?	2											
		Con Num							1					
SE	Ree 1994	Car	19					2	3		1			
		Tes			1									
		?						2						
SE	Ree 2012	Car	29						3		1			
		Tes			3									
		Ant						1						
		?	2							1				
SE	Bet 2008	Car	28		2			1	4					
		Rom	8											
		Rav	1			1								
		Sic							1					
		Tes					1							
SE	Vis 1993	Car	99											
		Rom	1											

Chart Four: Coin Numbers of Justin II and Tiberius II

Location	Publication	Justin II	Mint	5-nummi	10-nummi	half-folles	folles
Center	Nilsson 2017		Carthage	1	3		
NE	Buttrey 1976		Tes			1	
NE	But/ Hit 1978		Carthage	1	1		
NE	Met/Hit 1980		Carthage	2	4		
NE	Metcalf 1982		Carthage	4	7	2	1
N	Gui1978		Carthage	1	1		
N	Brenot 2012		Carthage			1	
N over wall	Baldus 2001		Carthage		1		
NW	Visonà 2009		Carthage			1	
Far N	Hou/Mac 2005		Carthage		1		
E	Baldus 2007		Carthage	1			
SE	Krm 2019		Carthage		1		
SE	Reece 1994		Carthage		1		
	Reece 2012		?		1		
	Betlyon 2008		Carthage		6	1	
			Con			1	
			?	1			
SE	Visona 1993		Carthage		1		
Location	**Publication**	**Tiberius II**	**Mint**			**half-folles**	**folles**
N	Gui 1978		Nicomedia				1
SE	Betylon 2008		CON			1	

Chart Five: Coin Numbers of Maurice

Location	Publication	Mint	N	2-N	2.5-N	5-N	10-N	20-N	folles	0.5 sil	ill
Center	Nil 2017	Con Num					3				
		Car		2		5	11	1			
NE	But1976	Car					2				
NE	But/Hit	Car				1	6	2			
NE		Con Num				1	1				
NE	Met/Hit 1980	Car				2	3	4			
NE		Con						1			
NE		Con Num				7	2	2			
NE		?		1	1	2					
NE	Met 1982	Car		5	2	11	7	4			
NE		Con Num				12	1				
N	Gui 1978	Con					1				
N	Brenot 2012	Car	1				1				
N outside	Baldus 2001	Car				3					
Far N	Hou & and Mac 2005	Car					7	1			
SW	Met 1988	Con Num						1			
		Car				4					
SW	Visona 1988	Car				2	3	1			
SE	Krm 2019	Car				1					
SE	Reece 1984	Ant					1				
		Car					2	1			
		Con Num				10		1			
		Con						1	2		
		?									1
SE	Reece 1994	Car		1		3	4				
		Con Num				3	1				
		Con							1		
		?						1			1

SE	Reece 2012	Car				1	3				
		Con Num				1					
		?						1			
SE	Betl 2008	Car				8	2				
		Mil Im					1				
		Nic									
		Ant						1			
		Con						1			
SE	Visona 1993	Car			1	1	1			1	
		Con Num				1					

Chart Six: Coin Numbers of Phocas

Location	Publication	Mint	2-N	5-N	10-N	12-N	Half-folles	folles	AV 200-N?	?
Center	Nil 2017	Con/Cyz						1		
		Car			8	13	18			
NE	But 1976	Car					1			
NE	But and Hit 1978	Alexandria				1				
		Carthage		8	2		8		1	
NE	Met and Hit 1980	Carthage		9	3		4			
NE	Met 1988	Carthage		9	6		6			
N	Brenot 2012	Carthage					1			
N outside	Baldus 2001	Carthage					1			
Far N	Hou & Mac 2005	Carthage		2	2		14			
E	Baldus 2007	Carthage			1					
SW	Met 1988	Carthage		3			1	1		
SW	Visona 1988	Carthage		1						
SE	Reece 1984	Carthage		1			1			
SE	Reece 1994	Carthage					4			
		?			1		2			2
SE	Reece 2012	Carthage		1	1		5			

		?	1							1
SE	Bet 2008	Carthage		7	3		5			
		Cyzicus					1			

Chart Seven: Coin Numbers of Heraclius Revolt

Location	Publication	Mint	2-nummi	5-nummi	10 nummi	Half-folles
Center	Nil 2017	Carthage	1	1	2	
NE	But & Hit 1978	Carthage	1	6		
NE	Met / Hit 1980	Carthage	8	3		
NE	Metcalf 1982	Carthage	4	1	2	
NE	Gui 1978	Carthage			1	
N out	Baldus 2001	Carthage			1	
Far N	Hou & and Mac 2005	Carthage		4		
SE	Krm 2019	Carthage				2
SE	Reece 1984	Carthage	1		1	
SE	Reece 2012	Carthage	1	3	1	
SE	Bet 2008	Carthage		1		
SE	Visona 1993	Carthage	4	1		

Chart Eight: Heraclius Coinage

Location	Publication	Mint	5-N	6-N	10-N	20-N	0.5 sil	AV 200-N?	Sil	?
Center	Nil 2017	Tes			1					
		Car	3		6	15				
NE	But 1976	Car	1		1	4				
NE	But & Hit 1978	Car				34		7		
		Cat				1				
NE	Met & Hit 1980	Car	8		17	17		2		
		Alex		1						
NE	Met 1982	Car				53		3		
N	Gui 1978	Car			1	7				
N	Bre 2012	Car				1				
N out	Bal 2001	Car				2				
NW	Vis 2009	Car	1							
Far N	Hou &Mac 2005	Car	1		8	12				
E	Bal 2007	Car			1	1				
SW	Met 1988	Car	3		2					
SW	Vis 1988	Car			3	1				
SE	Krm 2019	Car			2	3				
SE	Ree 1984	Car	5		5	1				
		?								1
SE	Ree 1994	Car	3			16				
		Alex		1						
		?								6
SE	Ree 2012	Car	2		4	10	1			
		Alex		1						
		?								2
SE	Betl 2008	Car	1		2	8				
		Nic	2							
SE	Vis 1993	Carthage			4	4				

Chart Nine: Coins of Constans II

Location	Publicaiton	Mint	5-N	10-N	20-N	folles	Sil	0.5 Sil	AV
Center	Nil 2017	Car		2	28	1			
		Syr				2			
NE	But 1976	Car		1	30	1			
NE	But & Hit 1978	Con				1			
		Car		5	71	8	3		
NE	Met & Hit 1980	Car		5	30	2			1
		Con				1			
NE	Met 1982	Car		6	43	1			2
NE	Gui1978	Car			5				
NE	Brenot 2012	Car			1				
Far N	Hou & Mac 2005	Car	1	26	6	1			
E	Baldus 2007	Car			1	1			
SW	Met 1988	Car		1	6	2			
SW	Visona 1988	Car			1	1			
SE	Krmnicek 2019	Car			2				
SE	Reece 1984	Car			3				
	Reece 1994	Car			22				
		Rom			1				
SE	Reece 2012	Car	4		14				
SE	Betlyon 2008	Car		2	32	1		2	
SE	Visona 1993	Car			12				

Chart Ten: Coins of Constantine IV and Justinian II, first reign

Location	Publicaiton	C IV	Mint	20-N	folles	silver
Center	Nilsson		**Carthage**	1		
NE	Buttrey and Hitchner 1976		Carthage	2	4	
NE	Metcalf and Hitchner 1980		Carthage	2	1	
NE	Metcalf 1982		Carthage	2	3	2
SE	Krmnicek		Carthage		1	
SE	Reece 1994		Syracuse		1	
SE	Reece 2012		Carthage	1		
			Illegible	1		
SE	Betlyon 2008		Carthage		2	
Location	**Publication**	**J II, first reign**	**Mint**	**20-N**	**folles**	
NE	Buttrey 1976		Carthage		3	
NE	Buttrey and Hitchner 1976		Carthage		2	
NE	Metcalf and Hitchner 1980		Carthage		3	
NE	Metcalf 1982		Carthage		4	
NE	Gui 1978		Carthage	1	1	

More on a very peculiar group of early Pseudo-Byzantine coins

Tony Goodwin[1]

At the 2019 Round Table I described a small group of Pseudo-Byzantine coins which exhibited two unusual features.[2] Firstly there was a great variety of both obverse and reverse types, probably unique for a small Arab-Byzantine 'mint', and secondly the die engraving of the obverse dies was highly imaginative, although somewhat crude. At the time three obverse and four reverse dies were known, all die-linked as shown in Fig. 1 below.

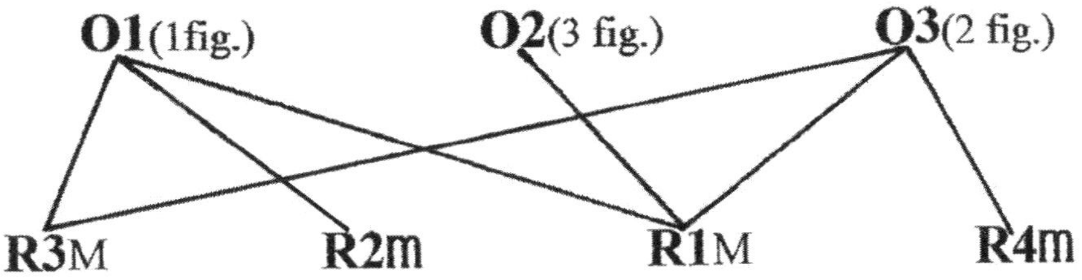

Figure 1. Die-links within the group as reported in 2020

Since then a number of new dies have been discovered, so that the group now comprises nine obverse and six reverse dies as shown in Fig. 2. All known dies and die combinations are illustrated in the catalogue at the end of this article.

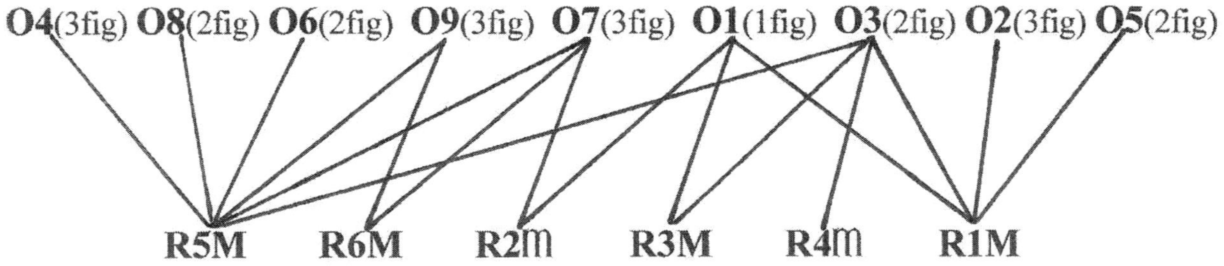

Figure 2. All die-links including recent discoveries

The obverse images (See Fig. 3)

As noted in the 2020 article, the three dies then known are probably the work of the same die engraver (die engraver 1) and two of them (dies O1 and O2) have remarkable obverse images. O1 shows a standing figure wearing a flared tunic and perhaps a scabbard, one hand rests on his hip and the other holds a long cross, whilst his hair or headdress is shown as two large diagonal elements with spikes on top. O2 shows three figures and the left-hand figure appears to be walking towards the other two,

---

[1] Tony Goodwin is an independent scholar a.goodwin2@btopenworld.com. I would like to thank Hugh Williams, David Woods and Piotr Tomczyk for bringing examples of this group of coins to my notice.

[2] Goodwin, T., 2020 'A very peculiar group of early Pseudo-Byzantine coins' in ***Coinage and History in the Seventh Century Near East*** 6 (ed. T. Goodwin), pp 97-100.

perhaps offering them a cross. He wears what appears to be a chlamys with spikes on the top, similar to those on O1. Die O3 is more conventional; it is loosely based on a Class 5 follis of Heraclius, but with the addition of a long cross-on-globe between the two figures, perhaps a recollection of the common Antioch folles of Justin II. New examples have revealed another odd feature not noted in 2020 – an additional cross below the long cross. A new die (O5) is also probably the work of this die engraver and is only known from a single example, so not all details are clear, but it could be based on almost any 6th or early 7th century two-figure Byzantine prototype. Figure 3 groups together the four dies by die engraver 1 and shows the common stylistic traits e.g. relatively deep die cutting, a fairly neat elliptical hatched border, feet pointing to the right, isolated crosses and elongated globus crucigers, pellets etc. Despite this stylistic similarity, each design is very different.

Die engraver 1

O1 **O2** **O3** **O5**

Die engraver 2 *Die engraver 3* *Die engraver 4*

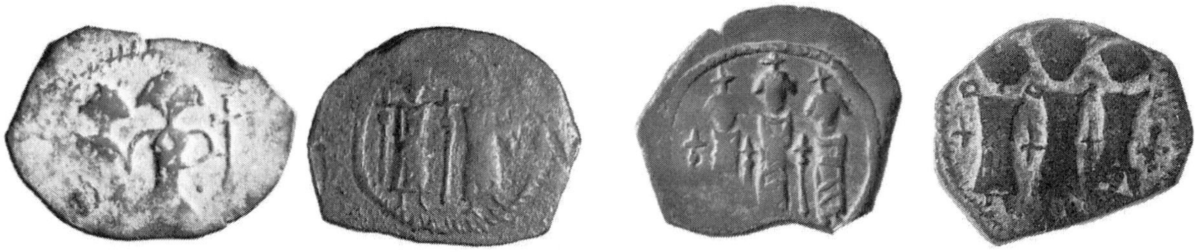

O6 **O8** **O4** **O9**

Figure 3: obverse dies (not to scale).

The new obverse dies include two which are clearly the work of a different hand (die engraver 2, O6 and O8, see Fig. 3). The workmanship is cruder with rather shallow engraving and an untidily hatched border, but again both designs are quite imaginative. O6 is loosely based on a Class 5 follis of Heraclius, but with the two figures transposed and an elongated detached globus cruciger to the right. Uniquely the two figures appear to be holding hands. O8 is more conventional and is presumably based loosely on a Class 2 Heraclius follis, or possibly on two out of three figures from a Class 3 or 4 follis.

The three other new obverse dies both imitate Class 3 or 4 folles of Heraclius, but the styles are very different. O4 is something of a surprise as it is a neatly engraved, reasonably close copy of the prototype and clearly the work of a third, more competent but less imaginative, die engraver. In fact it is a perfectly normal, but better than average, example of the common SICA Type B Pseudo-Byzantine follis. O7 and O9 are also a fairly typical examples of the cruder sort of Type B coin and clearly not the work of the work of die engraver 3. O9 appears to be the work of a fourth die engraver, but O7(see Cats. 13, 14 and 15) could conceivably be the work of die engraver 1 or, more probably, of a fifth die engraver.

The reverse images (See Fig. 4)

The 6 reverse dies are perhaps less unusual than the obverses, but exhibit considerable variety. Each die is shown in Fig. 4 along with a note of the probable Byzantine prototype, although it is almost certain that all these dies were cut from memory. Die R1 has a clear CON mintmark and so must have been inspired by the recollection of an uncertain Constantinople follis; dies R3 and R6 have a tall narrow M and what appears to be a blundered Cyprus mintmark, whilst R5 has a date numeral XЧII, so all three probably derive from the Cyprus folles of Heraclius issued in years 17 to 19. Die R2 has a cursive m reverse and is clearly in the style of a Constans II follis. R4 also has a cursive m reverse, but could be based on a 6th century follis rather than one of Constans II.

Figure 4: Reverse dies (not to scale). Possible prototypes noted in italics.

None of the reverse dies is close to the suggested prototype and there are a number of stylistic peculiarities which have no precedent in regular Byzantine coinage, for example the O officina letter and the additional cross next to the date numeral on R1, the extra large officina letter on R5 and the imaginative date numerals on R1, R2 and R6. There is no clear stylistic similarity between any of the dies to enable us to confidently assign them to the same die engraver and it is even possible that they are the work of 6 different engravers.[3]

Metrology

With weights now known for 22 examples it is possible to give a rather more reliable estimate of the average weight for the group; the mean weight is 4.86g and the median 4.66g, i.e. typical of the general population of Type B Pseudo-Byzantine coins.

Conclusions

The examples discovered since 2020 tell us nothing more about provenance or date and the best guess remains as northern Syria, probably late 640s or early 650s, but I should emphasise that this is no more than an educated guess. However, the new chart of die links shown in Fig. 2 does provide some useful new information as it demonstrates that the 'mint' did not follow the chronological sequence of Byzantine prototypes. It appears that single, two and three figure obverses were chosen apparently at random, as were reverses based on prototypes of Heraclius and Constans II. The 'mint' appears to have deliberately varied both obverse and reverse designs in a way that is only paralleled, in the Arab-Byzantine series, by the much larger Pseudo-Damascus mint. But there can be no connection between the two as the Pseudo-Damascus mint was located in Jund al-Urdunn and was active at least 30 years later. In the case of the 'peculiar' group under consideration here it is difficult to suggest a logical reason for this extreme variety and it may have been no more than a whim of the die engravers. Another interesting feature of Fig. 2 is that the four dies by die engraver 1(O1, O2, O3 and O5) are grouped together as are the two dies by die engraver 2 (O6 and O8), suggesting that perhaps only one die engraver was employed at any one time. As drawn the die chain suggests that the mint started with the conventional die O4 and then had to employ less skilled die engravers. This is an attractive possibility, but it should be noted that any of the dies O2, O5, O6 or O8 could be the first or last die used.

It seems highly probable that more new dies from this 'mint' will be identified in the future and it is possible that most of these will be relatively normal three-figure types, in which case the unusual dies described in this article may represent just a short eccentric episode in the life of a relatively large mint. But, whether or not 'peculiar' designs were the norm for the 'mint', we can only speculate about the motivation behind them. We can, however, hope that some better evidence emerges about the location of the mint and perhaps even some more precise dating evidence.

[3] I am slightly tempted to suggest that R1 and R2 could be the work of obverse die engraver 1. They both show a similar crude, but bold die cutting technique and both show the same imaginative approach to design.

Catalogue (all coins shown approximately1.5x actual size)[4]

1. O1/R1. 4.23g 6h
Obv: Standing figure holding long cross, detached gl. cr. to r.
Rev: M with cross above, ANNO - Ϛ (retrograde) + either side, **o** officina, CON in exergue.
(Author's collection)

2. O1/R2. 6.28g
Obv: as last.
Rev: m with cross above, AИИO - XIIIO either side, KOC retrograde in exergue. (Leu Numismatik web auction 24.2.19 lot 1650)

3. O1/R3 4.65g 5h
Obv: as last, double struck.
Rev: M with cross above, AИИ. - III III either side, Γ officina, KVII in exergue. (Author's collection)

4. O2/R1 4.10g 12h
Obv: three standing figures holding crosses.
Rev: M with cross above, ANNO - Ч (retrograde) + either side, **o** officina, CON in exergue.
(Author's collection)

5. O3/R1 weight unknown 12h
Obv: two standing figures, rh figure holds cross, long cross on globe between with additional cross below (see Cat. 8 below).
Rev: as last. (Trade 2018)

6.O3/R4 4.78g 12h
Obv: as last.
Rev: m with ANNO – XIII either side, other details unclear.
(Williams collection)

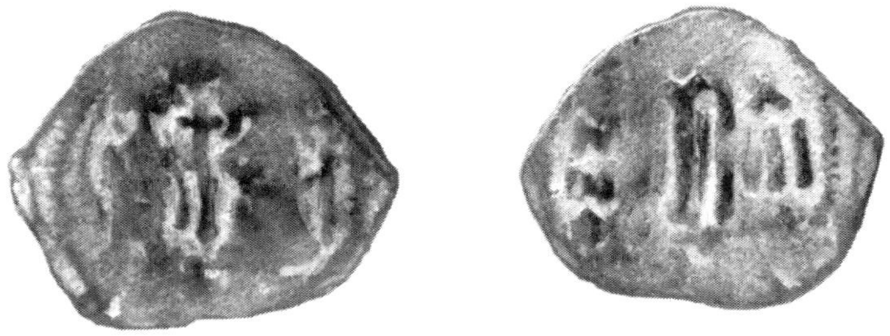

[4] Die duplicates not included in catalogue: O1/R1 5.16g 5h (private collection), O1/R2 4.62g 7h (author's collection), O7/R5 7.41g zeno #210904, O7/R6 4.5g Charachmoba Gym on vcoins 12.22.

7. O3/R3 4.81g 7h
Obv: as last.
Rev: as Cat. 3 above.
(Leu web auction 11, 23.2.20 lot 2296)

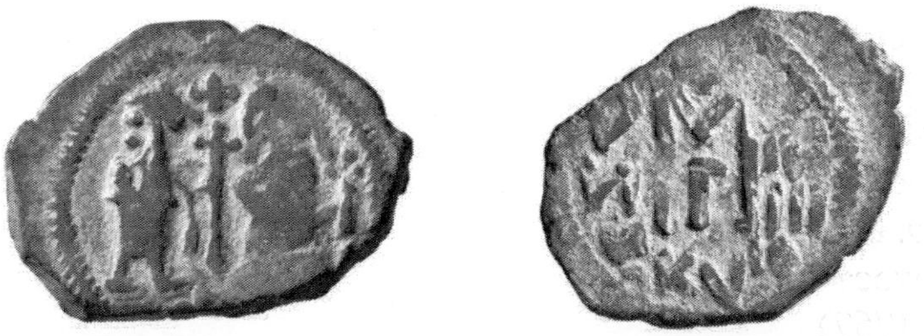

8. O3/R5 4.37g
Obv: as last.
Rev: **M** with **ANN - XЧII** either side and **B** officina, small circle and crescent either side of **B**.
(Ares auction 7 21.2.20 lot 885)

9. O5/R1 5.20g 1h
Obv: two standing figures with crosses either side and between.
Rev: **M** with cross above, **ANNO** - **Ч** (retrograde) + either side, **o** officina, **CON** in exergue.
(Author's collection)

10. O4/R5 3.76g 2h
Obv: three standing figures holding globus crucigers.
Rev: as Cat. 8 above.
(Leu web auction 23.2.20 lot 2693 part)

11. O6/R5 4.69g 6h
Obv: two standing figures (rh figure in military dress) with large elongated globus cruciger to r.
Rev: as last.
(Leu web auction 14, 13.12.20 lot 1782)

12. O8/R5 5.73g 12h
Obv: two standing figures holding globus crucigers.
Rev: as last. Die starting to break up. (Author's collection)

13. O7/R5 6.66g
Obv: three standing figures, outer figures holding crosses (double struck).
Rev: as last.
(Savoca 94 Blue auction 31.1.21 lot 1757)

14. O7/R2 4.80g 2h
Obv: as last.
Rev: as Cat. 2. Die staring to break up.
(Author's collection)

15. O7/R6 4.24g 12h
Obv: as Cat. 13. Thick patination.
Rev: M with ANN – X= either side and uncertain officina, K..? in exergue.
(Author's collection)

16. O9/R6 5.19g 12h
Obv: three standing figures holding crosses, additional cross to right.
Rev: as last.
(Author's collection)

17. O9/R5 3.95g
Obv: as last.
Rev: as Cat. 8 above.
(Ares 1,130.8.20, Lot 867)

Two Seventh Century Coins from Udhruh Jordan

Michael den Hartog & Mark Driessen[1]

Introduction

Since 2011 a joint team of archaeologists from Jordan (Al Hussein bin Talal University) and the Netherlands (Leiden University) has been researching the town of Udhruh and its surroundings. Udhruh, approximately 15 km east of Petra, is the location of a Roman legionary fort and lies on the route from the Hejaz to the Mediterranean. The town is said to have prospered in Byzantine times and had an historic role in the early Islamic era, especially in the 7th century AD or first century AH. During surveys and fieldwork a large array of coins from Nabatean times to the Ottoman empire and other finds have been collected. In this paper the focus will be on some small finds from the early Islamic period, including a crucifix and especially two 7th century Arab-Byzantine coins. First a short description of the site will be given. This is followed by some details on the significance of the site for the early Islamic period. Then a short overview is given of the small finds, after which the two 7th century coins will be discussed and some final conclusions are made.

The site

The site is dominated by a Roman legionary fort (*castra*), but was already inhabited by the Nabateans. During the reign of emperor Trajan the eastern border of the Roman empire was strengthened and the *Via Nova Traiana* was built between the southern coastal town of Aila ('Aqaba) and Bostra in northern Jordan. Like Petra also Udhruh came under Roman rule in AD 106. From a votive stone it is known that the legionary *castra* was (re-)constructed in AD 303-304 by the legion VI Ferrata, a military unit with a long history in the Levant.[2] As it is absent from the late 4th century *Notitia Dignitatum,* one can assume that the legion did not exist anymore at the end of the 4th century.[3] This was not the case with the town. As Augustopolis, Udhruh prospered under the Byzantines. Moreover, it had been an important bishopric since late Roman times. The Beersheba tax edict (AD 536) mentions the town paying the highest taxes of *Palaestina Tertia* in the form of an annual payment of 65 gold Solidi.[4] At some time a Byzantine church was built within the walled enclosure of the fort. With the diminishing power of the central Byzantine government the town came under the influence of their regional *foederati*, the Ghassanids. The historian Hamza Al-Isfahani credits the Ghassanid

---

[1] Michael den Hartog: Archaeologist at the Province of Noord-Brabant heritage programme and independent researcher in Middle East history.
Mark Driessen: Project director of the Udhruh project and lecturer in archaeology at Leiden University

[2] Falahat, H. & D. Kennedy, 2008: Castra Legionis VI Ferratae: A Building Inscription for the Legionary Fortress at Udhruh near Petra. ***Journal of Roman Archaeology***, 21 (1), pp.150-169.

[3] Berry, J. & N. Pollard, 2016: ***The Complete Roman Legions***, London, p.155.

[4] Killick, A, 1987: History of Udhruh, in A. Killick, A. (ed.), ***Udhruh: Caravan City and Desert Oasis: A Guide to Udhruh and its Surroundings***, Romsey, p.6. Abudanh, F., Falahat, H. & al-Salameen, Z. 2011: New Arabic-Christian Inscriptions from Udhruh, in: ***Arabian Archaeology and Epigraphy***, vol 22, p.233.

ruler Al-Harith Ibn Jabalah (AD 528-569) with the reconstruction of Udhruh.[5] This fits in with Justinian's reorganisation of the *Limes Orientalis*. This frontier region was divided up into an Armenian sector north of the Euphrates and a southern sector, the *Limes Arabicus* with a unified command of the Arab *foederati* under Al-Harith Ibn Jabalah.[6]

Early Islamic period

The town had some historical importance during the early Islamic period. The Muslim army probably passed through Udhruh during their AD 629 expedition that ended in the lost Battle of Mu'tah (11 km south of Karak, Jordan) with Byzantine forces. The tombs of the fallen Muslim commanders are still present at the Makam Mu'tah near the battlefield. From the Byzantine side the battle had a tribal character as it was partly fought by its Arab tribal allies.[7] By then Udhruh was part of a border zone where control depended maybe more on alliances than on effective military presence. When the prophet Muhammad and his army marched on Tabuk (260 km southeast of Udhruh) in AD 630 in order to block an expected Byzantine force, the Muslim forces managed to bring southern Jordan under their jurisdiction by concluding special agreements with the inhabitants of Aila ('Aqaba), Al-Jarba, Ma'an and Udhruh. Effective control meant that the new government would levy the *Jizya* (poll tax) on the Christian population of these towns.[8]

The town is well-known for the peace conferences convened there in AD 658 and AD 661 between the factions of Mohammed's son-in-law Ali and of the first Umayyad ruler Mu'awiya.[9] Archaeological research has shown that the church within the enclosure of the Roman fortifications was used in the medieval period. In a later era the Ottomans turned the church into a mosque and built a small fort on the remains of its Roman predecessor.[10]

The small finds

Among the finds collected at Udhruh there are 73 coins, which come from different campaigns, n.b. 2011; 2012; 2016 and 2018. They date from the 1st century AD to the early 20th century. Based on the period of minting and relating historical and cultural contexts the coin finds have been classified in six categories; A) Nabatean (4); B) Roman Provincial 2nd and 3rd century (6); C) Roman/ Byzantine 4th and 5th century (48); D) 7th century Pseudo-Byzantine (2); E) Islamic medieval and Ottoman (7); and F) unknown because of their state of preservation (4).

---

[5] Abudanh, F., Falahat, H. & al-Salameen, Z. 2011: New Arabic-Christian Inscriptions from Udhruh, in: ***Arabian Archaeology and Epigraphy***, vol 22, p.233.

[6] Arce, S., 2015: Severan *Castra*, Tetrarchic *Quadriburgia*, Justinian *Coenobia*, and Ghassanid *Diyarat*: Patters of transformation of Limes Arabicus forts during late antiquity, in: R. Collins, M. Symonds & M. Weber (eds.), ***Roman Military Architecture on the Frontiers, Armies and Their Architecture in Late Antiquity***, Oxford, 103. Shahid, I., 2002: ***Byzantium and the Arabs in the Sixth Century. vol. 2, Part 1: Toponymy, Monuments, Historical Geography, and Frontier Studies***, Washington DC, Dumbarton Oaks, p.21.

[7] Kaegi, W.,1995: ***Byzantium and the early Islamic conquests*** (paperback edition), Cambridge, p.68

[8] Ibid, p.82. Abudanh, F., 2004: The Archaeological Survey for the Region of Udhruh, 2003 (Preliminary Report), ***Annual of the Department of Antiquities of Jordan***, vol 48, p.57.

[9] Killick, A, 1987: History of Udhruh, in A. Killick, A. (ed.), ***Udhruh: Caravan City and Desert Oasis: A Guide to Udhruh and its Surroundings***, Romsey, p.6.

[10] Abudanh, F., Falahat, H. & al-Salameen, Z. 2011: New Arabic-Christian Inscriptions from Udhruh, in: ***Arabian Archaeology and Epigraphy***, vol 22, pp.232-242.

The 2018 campaign yielded the two 7th century Pseudo-Byzantine coins and also a 4 cm bronze Byzantine crucifix. This find may be dated to the 5th to 7th century AD period and belongs to one of the most common types of early Byzantine crosses found in the *Bilad al-Sham* region.[11]

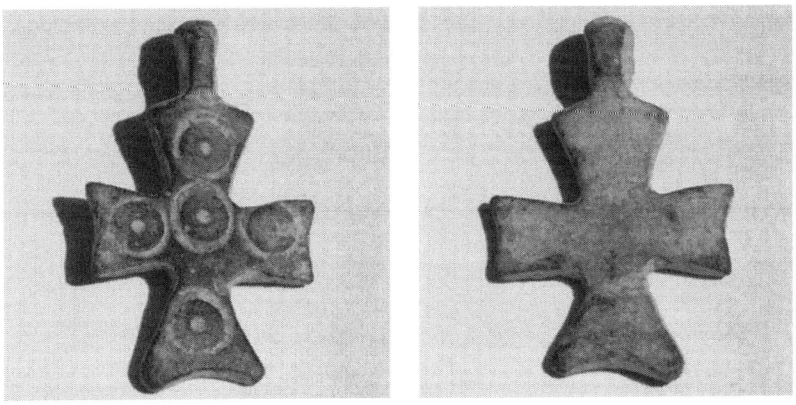

Fig.1: 5th-7th century crucifix from Udhruh. (Photo: Udhruh Project, Leiden University)

Two seventh century coins

The two 7th century Pseudo-Byzantine specimens are early Islamic *fulus*. They fill in the gap in the coin finds from the early Islamic times at Udhruh as well as from previous research on Roman forts of the *Limes Arabicus*. In the 1980s a British team conducted excavations in Udhruh. During their work some 150 coins were found dating from Nabatean times to the 14th century AD. These included three 6th century Byzantine coins, but no specimens from the early Islamic period.[12] For the Limes Arabicus project Betlyon list two early Islamic coins from the forts at el-Lejjun and Qasr Bashir. These coins are younger than the two coins found at Udhruh and belong to the Umayyad period and date roughly to AD 700-750.[13]

The first coin from Udhruh is a Pseudo-Byzantine copy of a Constans II follis. Byzantine copper coinage from Constans II (AD 641-668) was widely used in the Levant.[14] But at the same time Arab rulers saw the need to mint their own small change. Byzantine minting had already ceased in the Bilad al-Sham by AD 610 when the mint in Antioch was closed.[15] This led to the minting of copies close to the Byzantine originals. The Pseudo-Byzantine coin can be identified as a SICA type E. The type E is the most common type of the Pseudo-Byzantine issues.[16] The obverse shows a standing emperor with long hair holding a long cross in his right hand and a globus cruciger in his left hand. To the left

[11] Löw, A., S. Baumann, et al. (eds.), 2001: ***Byzanz, Das Licht aus dem Osten. Kult und Alltag im Byzantinischen Reich vom 4. Bis 15. Jahrhunder***t, Mainz, pp.304-305.
[12] Bowsher, A., 1987: Coins, in: A. Killick (ed.), ***Udhruh: Caravan City and Desert Oasis: A Guide to Udhruh and its Surroundings***, Romsey, pp.12-13.
[13] Betlyon, J.W., 2006: The Coins, in: S. Th. Parker (ed.), ***The Roman Frontier in Central Jordan, Final Report on the Limes Arabicus Project 1980-1989***, Volume II, Washington D.C., pp.437-438.
[14] Goodwin, T. 2005: ***Arab-Byzantine Coinage*** (Studies in the Khalili Collection Volume IV), London, p.14.
[15] Goussous, N.G., 1996: ***Umayyad Coinage of Bilad al-Sham***, Amman, p.57.
[16] Goodwin, T. 2005: ***Arab-Byzantine Coinage*** (Studies in the Khalili Collection Volume IV), London, p.16. Goodwin, T. & R. Gyselen, 2015: ***Arab Byzantine Coins from the Irbid Hoard. Including a new introduction to the series and a study of the Pseudo-Damascus mint***, Royal Numismatic Society Special Publication no. 53, London, pp.14-15.

of the standing figure, or in Goussous' words "imperial image", there is some blundered lettering which is a characteristic for this type of coins.[17]

Fig. 2: Type E Pseudo-Byzantine falls from Udhruh. Obverse and reverse.(Photo: Udhruh Project, Leiden University)

The reverse shows a cursive **m**. The cross above the **m** is blurred. On the left there are the letters NNO, which on the Byzantine original would stand for ANNO or year. On the right from the **m** there may be a star. On the exergue the letters showing a mint are absent. The coin, however, has a feature in which it differs from the SICA type E issues found in Syria and Lebanon.[18] Between the uprights of the reversed **m** there are two small pellets. These pellets occur frequently on coins found in Jordan. Similar coins from Jordan have been described by Goussous.[19] From Jordan even coins with more detail, explicit Christian symbols and pellets between the uprights are known.[20] From this, one may assume that adding the pellets to the die was not done for extra decoration on a simplified reverse image, but more as an identifier for a region, mint or minting authority. As for the date, the coin was probably struck sometime around AD 670.[21]

The second coin can be dated somewhat later and is an issue from the so-called Pseudo-Damascus mint. The imagery is farther away from the original Byzantine examples than the Pseudo-Byzantine coinage and likewise more blurred. The obverse shows a standing emperor with long hair holding a long cross in his right hand and a tall globus cruciger in his left hand. Besides this, the figure has a diagonal band across his robe and a cross-shaped object underneath his left arm, maybe hanging from the waste. The obverse has been identified as belonging to the catalogued die O48. The Pseudo-Damascus obverse O48 has a die chain with the reverse dies R118B, R120B and R62.[22]

---

[17] Goussous, N,G, 2004: ***Rare and Inedited Umayyad Copper Coins. The Goussous Collection in the Jordan National Bank Numismatic Museum***, Amman, p.241. Goodwin 2005, ***Arab-Byzantine Coinage***, p.16.
[18] Correspondence Tony Goodwin October 7th 2022.
[19] Goussous 2004: ***Rare and Inedited Umayyad Copper Coins. The Goussous Collection in the Jordan National Bank Numismatic Museum***, pp.252-258.
[20] Ibid, p.254.
[21] Correspondence Tony Goodwin October 7th 2022.
[22] Goodwin, T. & R. Gyselen, 2015: ***Arab Byzantine Coins from the Irbid Hoard. Including a new introduction to the series and a study of the Pseudo-Damascus mint***, Royal Numismatic Society Special Publication no. 53, London, pp.100-101, p.166.

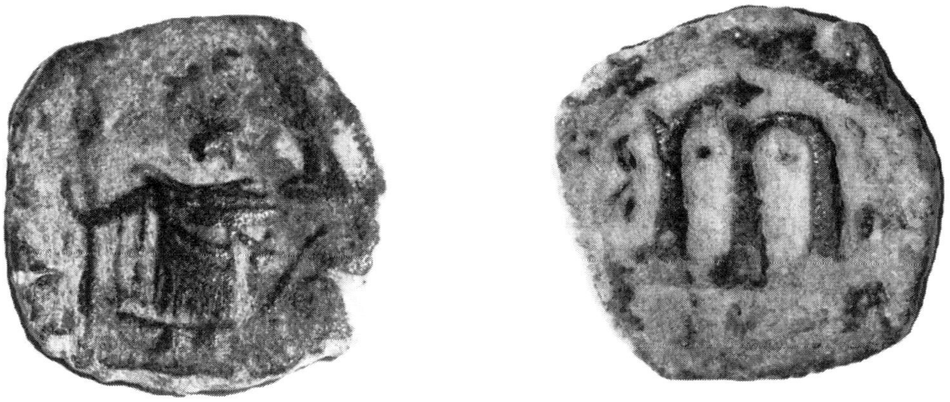

Fig. 3: Pseudo-Damascus falls O48/R62 from Udhruh. Obverse and reverse. (Photo: Udhruh Project, Leiden University)

On the reverse a cursive **m** occurs. On the left the word ANNO has become blundered. Between the upright stems of the **m** two pellets are visible. The exergue shows some worn off lettering. The reverse of the coin from Udhruh resembles the known reverse die R62B. Pseudo-Damascus issues mainly have cursive **m** reverses of which type B is the most common. This type has marks between the uprights of the **m**. These can be two to four pellets or two stars.[23] When a readable mint name is present, this normally is a blurred version of the Greek lettering ΔAM (abbreviation for Damascus).[24] On the R62B reverse issues as published by Kirkbride the lettering on the exergue resembles +PY.[25] Foss seems to date Pseudo-Damascus coinage to the AD 660-680 period, which was dominated by Mu'awiya's rule.[26] However, in Goodwin's view the date for the coin from Udhruh may lie sometime in the AD 680s.[27]

The location where the Pseudo-Damascus coinage was minted remains unknown. Foss suggests that they were an official issue and probably produced in northern Palestine or Jordan.[28] This area is generally identified as the Jund Al-Urdunn military district of Bilad al-Sham.[29] The presence of such coins in for instance the Irbid hoard from northern Jordan seems to confirm this. Likewise, the coins described by Kirkbride and Goussous were found in northern Jordan.[30] Both coins seem to have originated from the Jund al-Urdunn district while Udhruh itself fell under the governance of the large Jund Dimashq (Damascus) district.[31] This may look somewhat puzzling, but an explanation can be found in that towns in Jund al-Urdunn were not only geographically closer than Damascus but also that the existing road infrastructure made them more accessible for travel and trade from southern Jordan.

---

[23] Ibid, pp.75-78.
[24] Ibid, p.75.
[25] Kirkbride, H., 1948: Coins of the Byzantine-Arab Transition Period, ***Quarterly of the Department of Antiquities of Palestine*** 13, p.60, plate xxiv.
[26] Foss, C., 2008: ***Arab-Byzantine Coins, an Introduction, with a Catalogue of the Dumbarton Oaks Collection***, Dumbarton Oaks Byzantine Collection Publications 12, Dumbarton Oaks, pp.47-48.
[27] Correspondence Tony Goodwin October 7th 2022.
[28] Foss, C., 2008: ***Arab-Byzantine Coins, an Introduction, with a Catalogue of the Dumbarton Oaks Collection***, Dumbarton Oaks Byzantine Collection Publications 12, Dumbarton Oaks, p.47.
[29] Goussous, N.G., 1996***: Umayyad Coinage of Bilad al-Sham***, Amman. p.67.
[30] Correspondence Tony Goodwin October 7th 2022.
[31] Goussous, N.G., 1996: ***Umayyad Coinage of Bilad al-Sham***, Amman, p.83.

Conclusions

The Udhruh site has yielded a great number of coins, of which only two can be attributed to the 7th century AD. Despite their small number they fill in a gap in the coinage from this site and also in that from the large inventory of the Limes Arabicus project of the 1980s. Moreover, because of Udhruh's role in the 7th century one would also expect finds from that period. Originating in Jund Al-Urdunn the two coins would be common finds in northern Jordan. For Udhruh they are more than that as they provide information that contacts existed between the town and northern Jordan in the early Islamic era. The number of coins is however too small to put them into a context of the political dynamics in the Bilad al-Sham area during last quarter of the 7th century.

Bibliography

Abudanh, F., 2004: The Archaeological Survey for the Region of Udhruh, 2003 (Preliminary Report), ***Annual of the Department of Antiquities of Jordan***, vol 48, pp.51-69.

Abudanh, F., Falahat, H. & al-Salameen, Z. 2011: New Arabic-Christian Inscriptions from Udhruh, in: ***Arabian Archaeology and Epigraphy***, vol 22, pp.232-242.

Abudanah, F. & M. Driessen, 2018: The Udhruh region: A green desert in the hinterland od ancient Petra. In: Zhuang, Y. & M. Altaweel, ***Water Societies and the Technologies from the Past and Present***, London, pp.127-157.

Arce, S., 2015: Severan *Castra*, Tetrarchic *Quadriburgia*, Justinian *Coenobia*, and Ghassanid *Diyarat*: Patters of transformation of Limes Arabicus forts during late antiquity, in: R. Collins, M. Symonds & M. Weber (eds.), ***Roman Military Architecture on the Frontiers, Armies and Their Architecture in Late Antiquity***, Oxford, pp.98-122.

Berry, J. & N. Pollard, 2016: ***The Complete Roman Legions***. London.

Betlyon, J.W., 2006: The Coins, in: S. Th. Parker (ed.), ***The Roman Frontier in Central Jordan, Final Report on the Limes Arabicus Project 1980-1989***, Volume II, Washington D.C., pp.413-444.

Bowsher, A., 1987: Coins, in: A. Killick (ed.), ***Udhruh: Caravan City and Desert Oasis: A Guide to Udhruh and its Surroundings***, Romsey, pp.12-13.

Falahat, H. & D. Kennedy, 2008: Castra Legionis VI Ferratae: A Building Inscription for the Legionary Fortress at Udhruh near Petra. ***Journal of Roman Archaeology***, 21 (1), pp.150-169.

Foss, C., 2008: ***Arab-Byzantine Coins, an Introduction, with a Catalogue of the Dumbarton Oaks Collection***, Dumbarton Oaks Byzantine Collection Publications 12, Dumbarton Oaks.

Goodwin, T. 2005: ***Arab-Byzantine Coinage*** (Studies in the Khalili Collection Volume IV), London.

Goodwin, T. & R. Gyselen, 2015: ***Arab Byzantine Coins from the Irbid Hoard. Including a new introduction to the series and a study of the Pseudo-Damascus mint***, Royal Numismatic Society Special Publication no. 53, London.

The seven obverse Lazy Z dies are very similar to those paired with a lazy B reverse except that none are yet known with a triangle (possibly a letter Δ) below the *globus cruciger*. Four of them have pendilia suspended from the crown instead of hair.

The ten Lazy Z reverse dies are distinguished by having either **S S** or **S S S** above the **m**. In the exergue, the **IIIIIn** of the Lazy B reverses is usually replaced by **IIIh** or **IIId**

Related to the Lazy Z group are coins with either **S+S** or **O+S** above the **m**. Seven obverse dies and six reverse dies are known; the die links are indicated in figure 3 and the dies and die links are illustrated in figure 7. This group is die linked to the lazy B coins via obverse die 13.

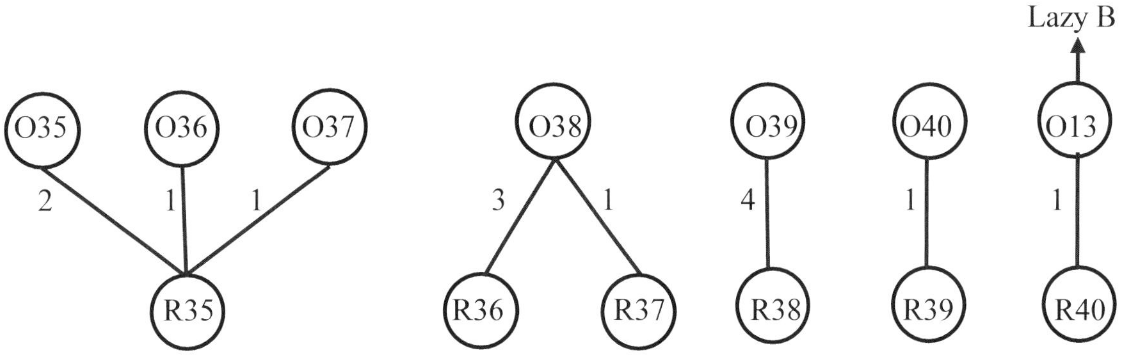

Figure 3. Die links for Lazy Z coins with **+** *above the* **m**

There can be no doubt that these three groups of coins are the product of a single establishment which can conveniently be known as the Lazy BZ Workshop. The word 'workshop', rather than 'mint', is used to describe a place for the production of coins which were clearly not made under the control of the central government. It is generally assumed that the Byzantine-Arab Phase 1 coinage was produced in towns all over Greater Syria under the auspices of local magnates, be they rich landowners, magistrates or bishops.

In addition to the three groups of coins already described, seven coins have been identified (struck from five pairs of dies) where the reverse dies show some features in common with the reverses of the Lazy BZ coins. All have a six (or more) pointed star above the **m** and two have the symbol **S** to the right of the ✱ and one has this symbol to the left. One reverse die has **IIIh** in the exergue. There are also lettering peculiarities that possibly connect them with the Lazy BZ dies, in particular the form of the letter Ā on two dies. These coins are illustrated in figure 8 without further comment pending the discovery of other specimens which may strengthen – or otherwise – the association with the Lazy BZ workshop.

Finally one coin has been noted with a letter Z (or recumbent N) over the **m** but which has two standing figures on the obverse. There is very little stylistically to connect it to the Lazy BZ workshop but an image is presented here as a basis for further research.

Figure 4. ebay January 2018
3.75g 22mm

Figure 5. Lazy B dies.

a. O1/R1 2.73g 12.00h P1	b. O1/R2 2.85g 6.30h P1	c. O1/R2 3.21g 6.00h P2	d. O2/R2 3.59g 1.30h P1	e. O2/R2 3.54g 7.00h R3[7]	f. O2/R3 3.31g 6.00h P3

g. O3/R4 3.12g 7.00h R1	h. O3/R4 3.08g 6.00h P1	i O3/R4 2.35g 1.00h P1	j. O4/R4 Trade	k. O5/R4 3.21g 5.00h [8]	l. O5/R4 ebay

m. O5/R5 3.77g 11.00h P1	n. O6/R6 3.62g 6.00h P3	o. O6/R6 2.79g 7.30h P1	p. O7/R7 3.17g 8.00h P1	q. O8/R7 5.17g ebay	r. O9/R7 3.46g 6.00h[9]

Figure 5. Lazy B dies. *continued below*

P1 = Oddy P2 = Schulze P3 = Goodwin P4 = Private UK P5 = Phillips P6 = Mansfield

[7] M Phillips and T Goodwin, A Seventh-Century Syrian Hoard of Byzantine and Imitative Copper Coins, ***Numismatic Chronicle*** **157** (1997) 61-87, no. C22.

[8] Westfäliches Landesmuseum, Münster.

[9] M Phillips and T Goodwin, A Seventh-Century Syrian Hoard of Byzantine and Imitative Copper Coins, ***Numismatic Chronicle*** **157** (1997) 61-87, no. C7.

Figure 5 continued. Lazy B dies.

s. O10/R8 2.57g 4.00h R1	t. O11/R9 2.01g 6.00h P3	u. O12/R9 2.17g 6.30h P1	v. O13/R10 3.11g 6.00h P2	w. O13/R11 2.99g 6.00h R3	x. O14/R12 3.50g 6.00h[10]

Figure 5 continued. Lazy B dies.

Figure 6. Lazy Z dies

a. O22/R22 2.04g 12.00h P1	b. O22/R22 2.24g 5.00h P1	c. O22/R22 2.31g 12.00h P1	d. O22/R23 3.34g VCoins	e. O23/R24 2.58g 7.00h P1	f. O23/R24 2.70g 5.00h P3

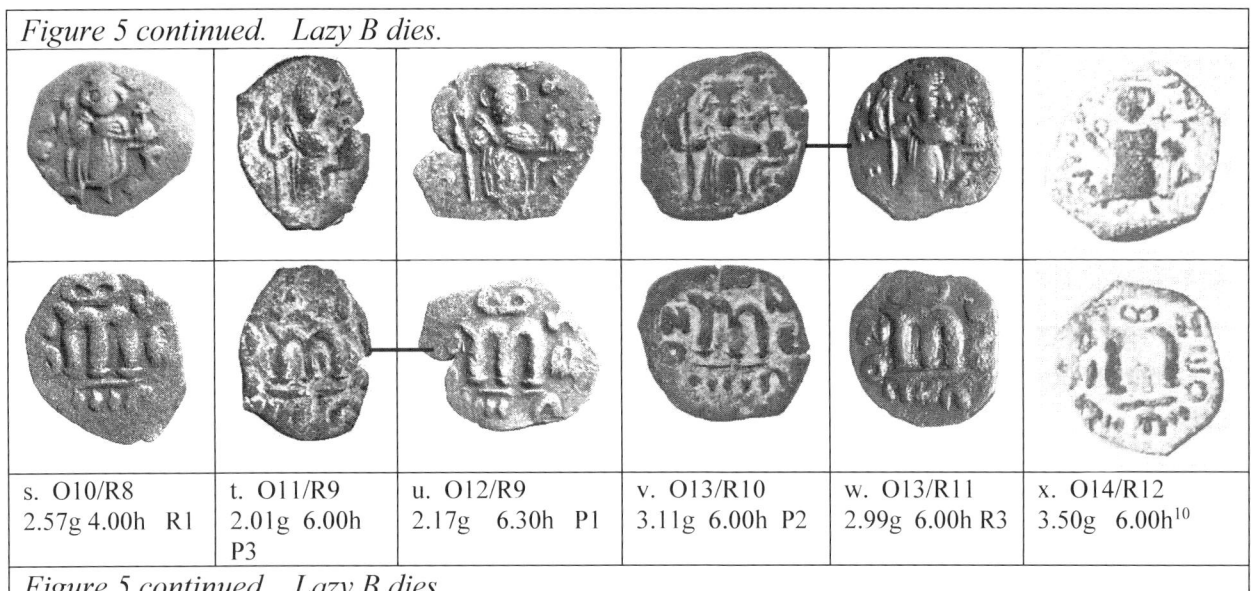

g. O23/R25 3.7g VCoins	h. O23/R26 2.66g 5.00h P1	i. O23/R26 2.29g 6.00h P1	j. O23/R27 2.97g 6.00h P2	k. O23/R27 3.28g 12.00h P1	l. O24/R28 3.13g 12.00h P1

Figure 6. Lazy Z dies continued below

[10] T Goodwin, 7th Century Arab Imitations of Byzantine Folles, ***Numismatic Circular*** **CIII** (1995) 336-7, no. 6.

Figure 6 Lazy Z dies continued

m. O24/R28 3.03g 6.00h P2	n. O25/R28 4.08g 6.00h [11]	o. O3/R28 2.69g ebay	p. O3/R29 3.76g 7.00h P1	q. O26/R30 2.17g 6.00h P2	r. O27/R31 2.29g 12.00h P1

Figure 6. Lazy Z dies continued

Figure 7. Lazy Z dies with a **+** *above the* m

a. O35/R35 3.71g 6.00h[12]	b. O35/R35 3.76g 12.00h[13]	c. O36/R35 3.84g 12.00h P2	d. O37/R35 trade	e. O38/R36 3.24g ebay	f. O38/R36 2.8g VCoins

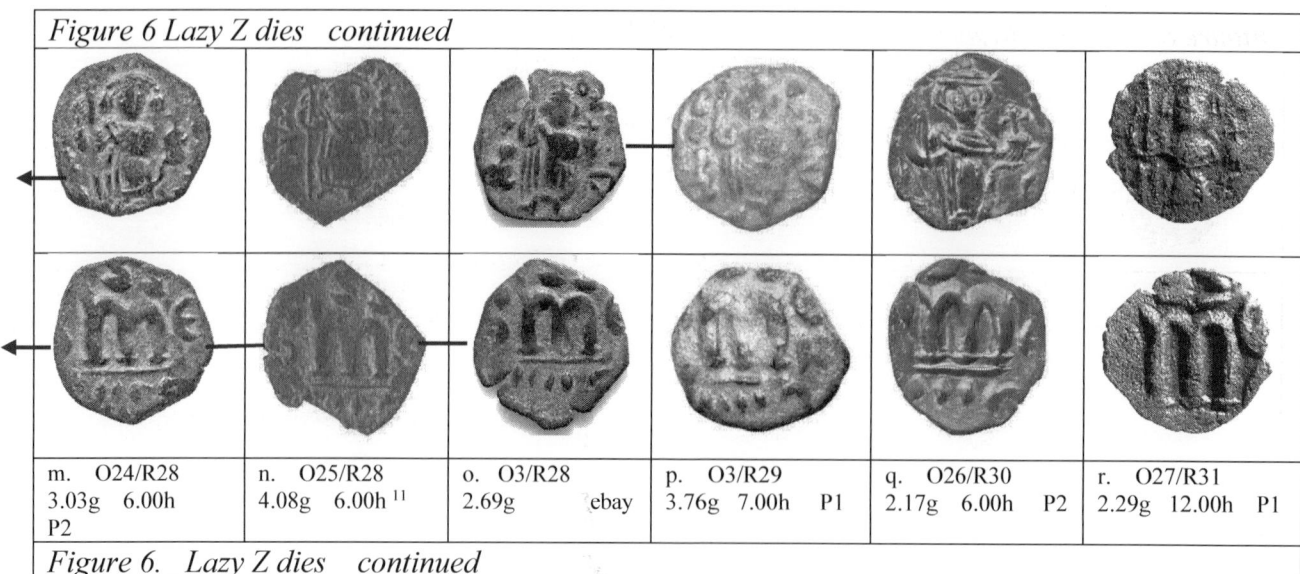

g. O38/R36 2.69g 12.00h P1	h. O38/R37 3.70g 10.30h P1	i. O39/R38 3.71g 12.00h P3	j. O39/R38 2.99g 6.00h P1	k. O40/R39 3.98g 6.00h P2	l. O13/R40 3.71g ebay

Figure 7. Lazy Z dies with a **+** *above the* m

---

[11] M Phillips and T Goodwin, A Seventh-Century Syrian Hoard of Byzantine and Imitative Copper Coins, ***Numismatic Chronicle*** **157** (1997) 61-87, no. C35.

[12] M Phillips and T Goodwin, *op. cit,* no. C61.

[13] T Goodwin and R Gyselen, ***Arab Byzantine Coins from the Irbid Hoard***, Royal Numismatic Society Special Publication no.53, London, 2015, p.44, no. 5.

Figure 8. Coins with some features similar to those of Lazy BZ coins

a. O41/R41 2.65g 4.30h P4	b. O42/R42 2.39g 6.00h P4	c. O43/R43 ebay	d. O43/R43 2.64g 5.00h P1	e. O44/R44 2.24g 9.00h P2	f. O44/R44 3.20g ebay

Figure 8. Coins with some features similar to those of Lazy BZ coins

Where the weights of the coins are known, they are plotted in figure 9 for the Lazy B coins and in figure 10 for the Lazy Z coins (both with and without a **+** over the **m**).

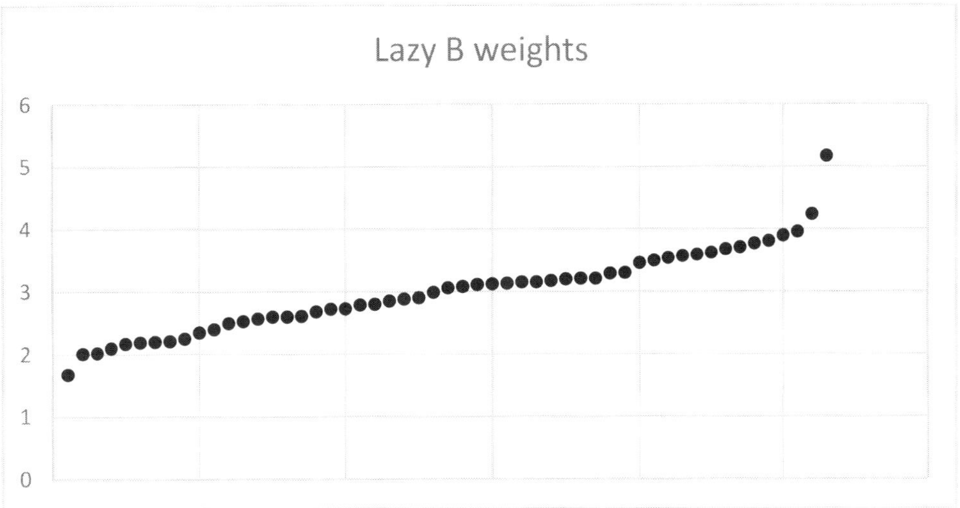

Figure 9. Weights of Lazy B coins in grams

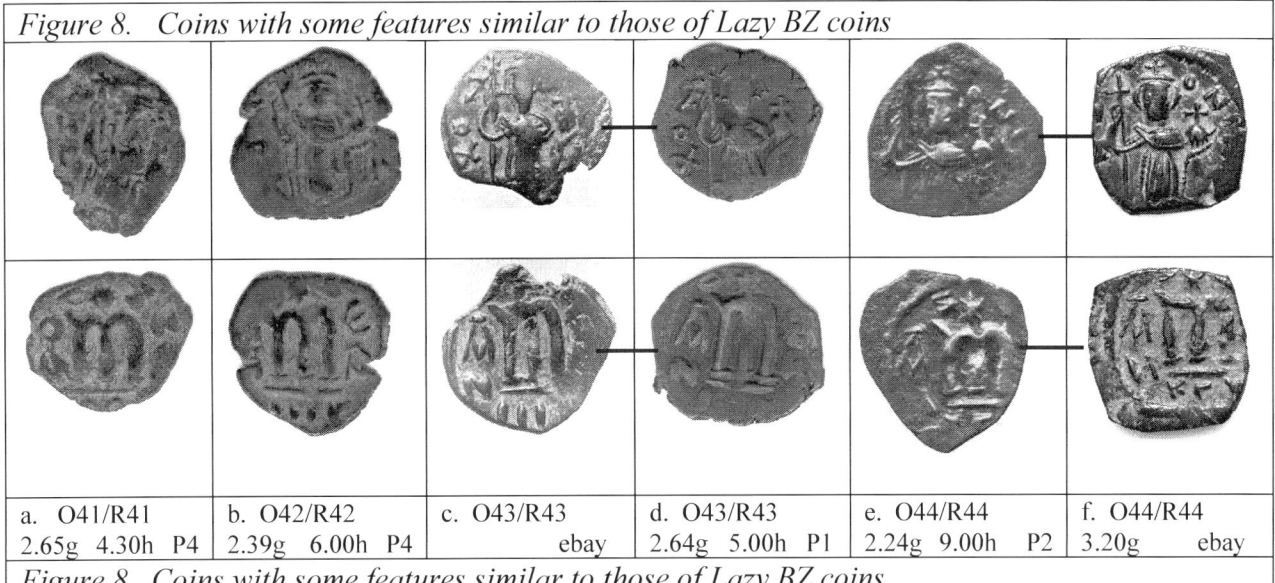

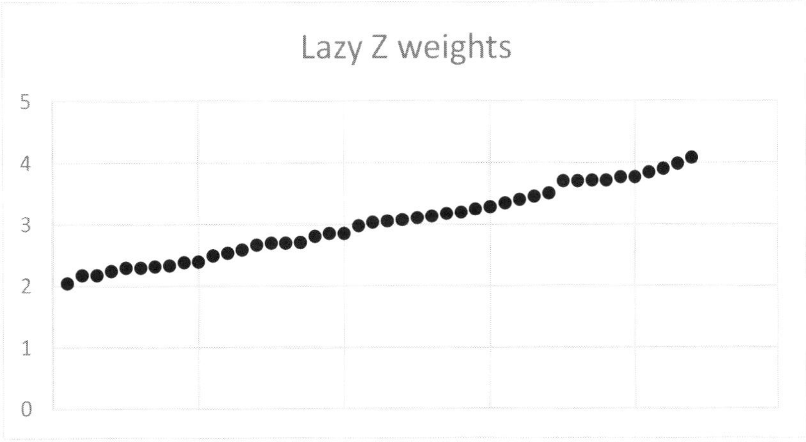

Figure 10. Weights of Lazy Z coins in grams

These results are very unusual in not showing any clustering around a preferred weight. The weights of virtually all the Lazy BZ coins lie between 2 and 4g and are evenly spread over the range. It is difficult to explain this weight distribution. The only control seems to be that the coins should weigh more than 2g and less than 4g. But the manufacture of blanks within this range ought to give rise to a Gaussian distribution of weights as those making the blanks would know roughly the weight of a 3g piece of bronze, and pieces of approximately this weight would predominate.

The known die axes for the Lazy B dies are plotted in figure 11 and those for the Lazy Z coins (both with and without a **+** over the **m**) are plotted in figure 12

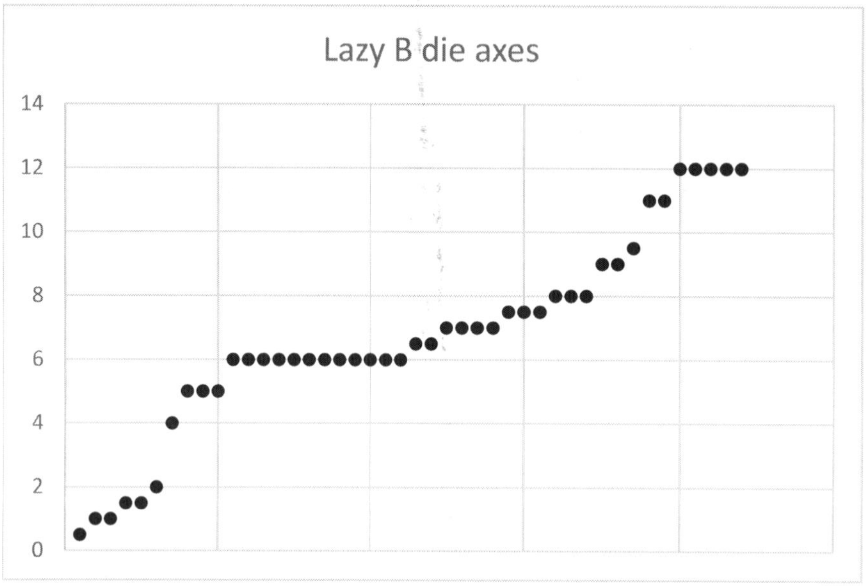

Figure 11. Die axes of Lazy B coins using the hour notation (whereby 6h indicates vertically opposed axes).

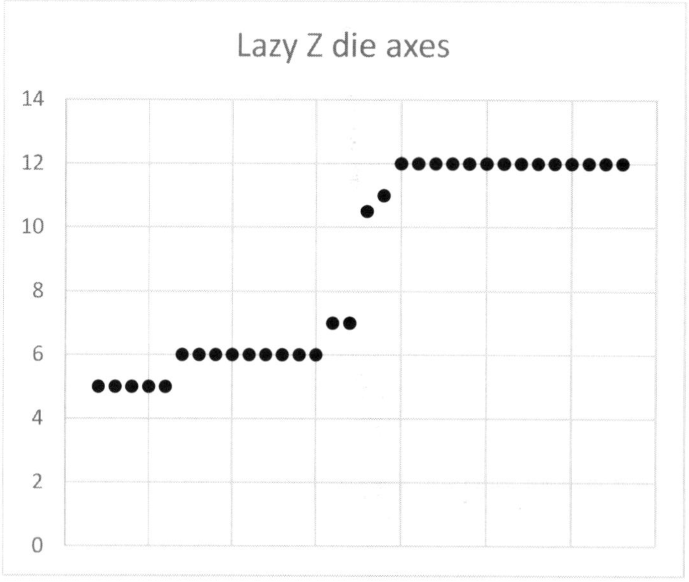

Figure 12. Die axes of Lazy Z coins using the hour notation (whereby 6h indicates vertically opposed axes).

These figures indicate that the preferred axes were either 6h or 12h. Interestingly, a greater degree of control was applied to the Lazy Z coins then to the Lazy B coins. Does this mean they were made in two separate workshops or that the issues are consecutive with the degree of control increasing (or decreasing) according to whether Lazy B coins preceded or succeeded the Lazy Z coins?

Finally, there are the questions of when and where the coins were struck. One lazy Z coin has been reported as a surface find at the Nesher-Ramla salvage excavation in Israel [14] and four Lazy BZ coins were included in the so-called 'Hama' hoard [15] However, one provenanced coin cannot be used to locate the mint as it has been shown that Phase 1 coins could travel a long way from their postulated place of origin.[16]

As far as the dates of the coins are concerned, the main designs of a standing facing figure on the obverse and a lower case **m** on the reverse are derived from the coinage of Constans II struck at Constantinople between 641 and 648. It seems very likely, therefore, that the Lazy BZ workshop was operating from the mid to late 640s. In 651, Constans replaced the **m** on the reverse with an **M** and it might have been a reasonable assumption that the Lazy BZ workshop ceased operation before 651 or very soon after. However, the Hama hoard, buried after 657, contained four Lazy BZ coins which appear from the published photographs not to be extensively worn. This suggests the Lazy BZ workshop may not have closed before Constans changed the reverse of the regular Byzantine coinage in 651. A probable conclusion is that the Lazy BZ workshoip was in operation from the mid 640s to the early 650s.

The OHO workshop

This is another workshop whose first identification was also due to Tony Goodwin. Some die links between coins with a single standing figure and a facing bust were first noted in the ground-breaking article published as an occasional paper by the Oriental Numismatic Society in 1993,[17] (coins 1 and 3). These die links were expanded in 1995 with links noted between coin numbers 7 and 8, 10 and 11, and 11 and 12.[18] Then, more than a decade later, Pottier, Schulze and Schulze [19] confirmed that the die linking included not only a facing bust and a standing facing figure but also two standing facing figures. What was known by 2020 was brought together in a review paper by Oddy.[20]

Recent searches of sale catalogues and private collections has now revealed a corpus of 76 OHO workshop coins struck from six obverse dies and seven reverse dies. One of the obverse dies has two standing figures, another has one standing figure, and four others have a facing bust. Five of the

---

[14] Y Farhi, The Coins, in S Kol-Ya'akov, ***Salvage Excavations at Nesher-Ramla Quarry***, Zinmann Institute of Archaeology at Haifa University, 2010.

[15] M Phillips and T Goodwin, A Seventh-Century Syrian Hoard of Byzantine and Imitative Copper Coins, ***Numismatic Chronicle*** **157** (1997) 61-87, nos. C7, C22, C35 and C61. Hama, the putative find spot, is that reported by the trader handling the hoard in the UK. How secure this is must remain speculative as traders have a habit of telling purchasers what they want to hear and also of hiding the sources of their stock to preserve their supply. Hama is a city on the banks of the Orontes River in west-central Syria. It is located 213 km (132 miles) north of Damascus and 46 kilometres (29 miles) north of Homs.

[16] A Oddy, The Lazy S Workshop: Coin Production in Early Arab Syria, in T Goodwin (ed.), ***Coinage and History in the Seventh Century Near East 6***, London, 2020 pp. 77-96.

[17] T Goodwin, ***Imitations of the Folles of Constans II***, Oriental Numismatic Society Occasional Paper no. 28, April 1993.

[18] T Goodwin, 7th Century Arab Imitations of Byzantine Folles, ***Numismatic Circular*** **CIII** (9) (November 1995) 336-7.

[19] H Pottier, I Schulze and W Schulze, Pseudo-Byzantine Coinage in Syria under Arab Rule (638-c.670) Classification and Dating, ***Revue Belge de Numismatique*** **CLIV** (2008) 87-155, pl. X.

[20] A Oddy, An Overview of the Phase 1 Byzantine-Arab Coinage, in T Goodwin (ed.), ***Coinage and History in the Seventh Century Near East 6,*** London, 2020, 47-76, esp. Appendix 1 on p. 73.

reverse dies have **M** on the reverse and two have an ᗰ. The die links are illustrated in figure 13 and the dies and die links in figure 16.

The coins with die O8 show two standing facing figures but all the examples known are either very corroded or very worn or badly struck and details of the clothing are indistinct. The figures wear crowns with a cross above and the hair is barely delineated. Both figures hold a long cross in their right hands. There is another cross in the obverse field between the two crowns. There is no trace of a legend.

The coins with die O6 show a standing facing figure holding a long cross in the right hand and a *globus cruciger* in the left hand. The figure wears a crown with a cross and a long robe and has hair hanging on both sides of the head. There are traces of lettering on both sides of the figure but it has not been possible to decipher the legend which is probably meaningless.

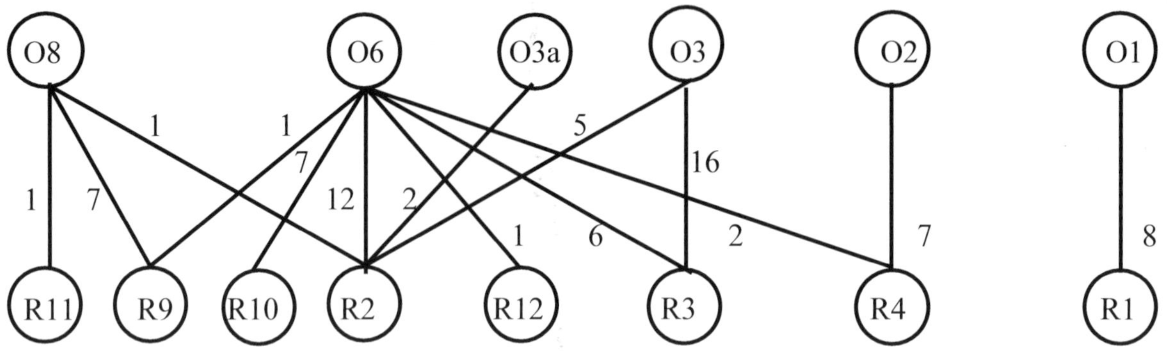

Figure 13. Die links for coins of the OHO *workshop*

Dies O1, O2, O3 and O3a all show a facing bust with a crown surmounted by a cross and with hair bunched at either side of the head. On O1, O2, O3 and O3a there is a *globus cruciger* in the right hand of the facing bust and indistinct traces of lettering to the right and left of the figure. Die O3a is very close indeed to die O3 but the *globus cruciger* is not present and instead there is an **O** surmounted by **II** in the left field. Detailed examination shows that the **O** on die O3a coincides with the *globus* on die O3 and it is almost certain that die O3a has been re-cut from Die O3 by replacing the cross of the *globus cruciger* with **II.** This is difficult to explain as if it was a deliberate de-Christianisation it might be expected that the cross on the Crown would also be eliminated. These dies have no meaningful legend but occasional crescents in the fields right and left.

Two reverse dies (R10 and R11) have a lower case **m** on the reverse but depicted thus ᗰ. There is a **+** above and meaningless letters to the right and left of the ᗰ and in the exergue.

The other five reverse dies (R1, R2, R3, R4, and R9) all have an upper case **M** with a **+** above and an ∩ or an Ʌ below. Various letters are arranged to the right and left of the **M** and in the exergue where, in one case, the legend reads **OHO** and this has given the workshop its name.

This suggested obverse die arrangement of two standing figures followed by one standing figure followed by a facing bust follows the chronology of the designs of the Imperial coinage. In the latter years of his reign (c.634-640) Heraclius struck small folles with two Imperial figures on the obverse, Heraclius wearing military apparel and holding a long cross in his right hand and Heraclius Constantine wearing civil dress and holding a *globus cruciger* in his right hand. There is no obverse legend. The reverse has an **M** with A/N/N/O to the left and the regnal year to the right.

On his accession in 641, Constans II struck folles with a standing facing figure holding a long cross and a *globus cruciger* on the obverse and a letter **m** on the reverse. The obverse legend reads ЄNTϒTO NIKA However, in year three (643-4), Constans also struck an unusual follis with a facing crowned bust holding a *globus cruciger* in the right hand on the obverse. The obverse legend reads InPЄR COhST. Although presumed to be struck in Constantinople, the vast majority of these coins are found in the northern part of greater Syria and it has been postulated that they were struck in Constantinople and exported to the conquered territories of the Levant as a form of propaganda which announced to the population, now living under Arab rule, that Constans was the 'legitimate' ruler.[21]

When this paper was presented at the Round Table in September 2022, Tony Goodwin speculated on the possibility that the InPЄR COhST coins were actually struck in Greater Syria. However, the issue is clearly regular Imperial, even if badly struck and frequently overstruck, and it is impossible to believe that a 'regular Byzantine mint' could operate in an area controlled by the Arabs, as some or most of Greater Syria was by 640 according to the modern received wisdom. However, in 2019, Stephen Maxfield, on the basis of a detailed examination of the coinage, concluded that:

> ... for the first five years of Constans II reign the Empire was conducting a war throughout Syrian territory and that these coins [22] were struck in order to finance this war. That such a war took place is not particularly difficult to envisage and it may be that its course could be approximated by mapping coin hoards.[23]

Maxfield has here postulated a scenario by which the IhPЄR COhST coinage could have been struck in Syria if it is regarded as a Military production. However, it is not only the year 3 IhPЄR COhST coins that Maxfield thinks were struck as part of the war-effort and it is difficult to believe that any of the 'standing facing figure' coins of Constans' first five years were not struck in Constantinople. It remains most likely then that the IhPЄR COhST issue of year 3 were struck in Constantinople but that they were destined for wholesale export to Greater Syria.

The weights of the coins are plotted in figure 14 where die O8 is placed at the beginning of the series as coins with this die usually weigh more than 4g. The coins with a standing figure (obverse die O6) are placed next in the sequence as they are die linked to O8. The four dies with a facing bust are assumed to represent the major output of the workshop.

The die axes of the OHO coins are plotted in figure 15 from which it can be seen that the preferred die axis was either 6.00h or 12.00h, but the fact that other die axes between these two extremes have been recorded indicates that the dies themselves were probably not constrained in a square collar.

Finally there is the question of place and date of issue. No excavation reports are known which list finds of OHO coins, but those on the market come mostly from modern Lebanon and northern Syria. Eventually, no doubt, OHO coins will be discovered in situ and if a concentration of find spots can be established then the possible location for the workshop can be postulated.

The coins with two standing figures on the obverse and the letter **M** on the reverse are derived from the folles of Heraclius struck at Constantinople between 631 and 640 and it is suggested that the first

---

[21] A Oddy, An Overview of the Phase 1 Byzantine-Arab Coinage, in T Goodwin (ed.*), **Coinage and History in the Seventh Century Near East 6***, London, 2020, 47-76, see fn. 86 on p. 66.

[22] ie the coins struck by Constans in his first five regnal years.

[23] S Maxfield, Using the iconography and inscriptions on Heraclean Dynasty coins to construct an historical narrative of the 7th century Byzantine Empire, in T Goodwin (ed.) ***Coinage and History in the Seventh Century Near East 6***, London, 2020, P. 24.

OHO coins with obverse O8 were produced in the very late 630s. These were almost certainly followed by the coins with obverse O6 having a standing facing figure based on the earliest coins of Constans II. In year 3, Constans struck coins with a facing bust (mentioned above) and the OHO coins with these obverses must postdate 643. This suggests that the OHO coins were produced from the late 630s until the mid to late 640s

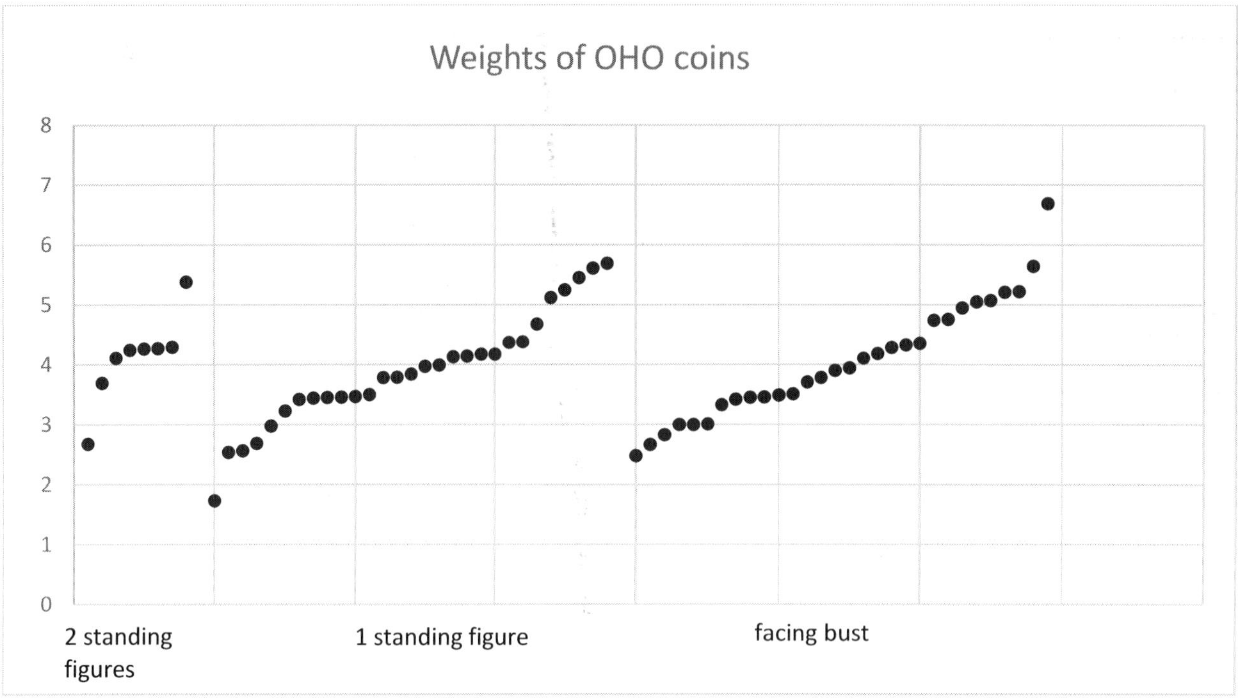

Figure 14. Weights of OHO coins in grams

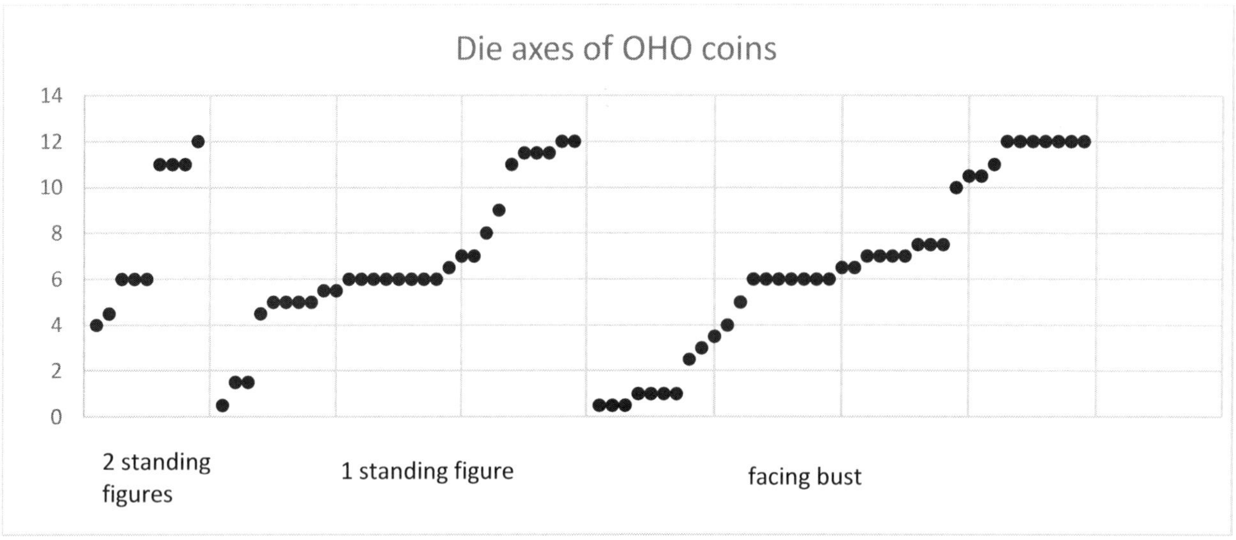

Figure 15. Die axes of OHO coins using the hour notation (whereby 6h indicates vertically opposed axes).

Figure 16 OHO dies

a. O8/R11 5.38g 6.00h P3	b. O8/R9 2.68g 4.00h P3	c. O8/R9 4.11g 11.00h P1	d. O8/R2 4.26g 11.00h P3	e. O6/R2 2.54g 1.30h[24]

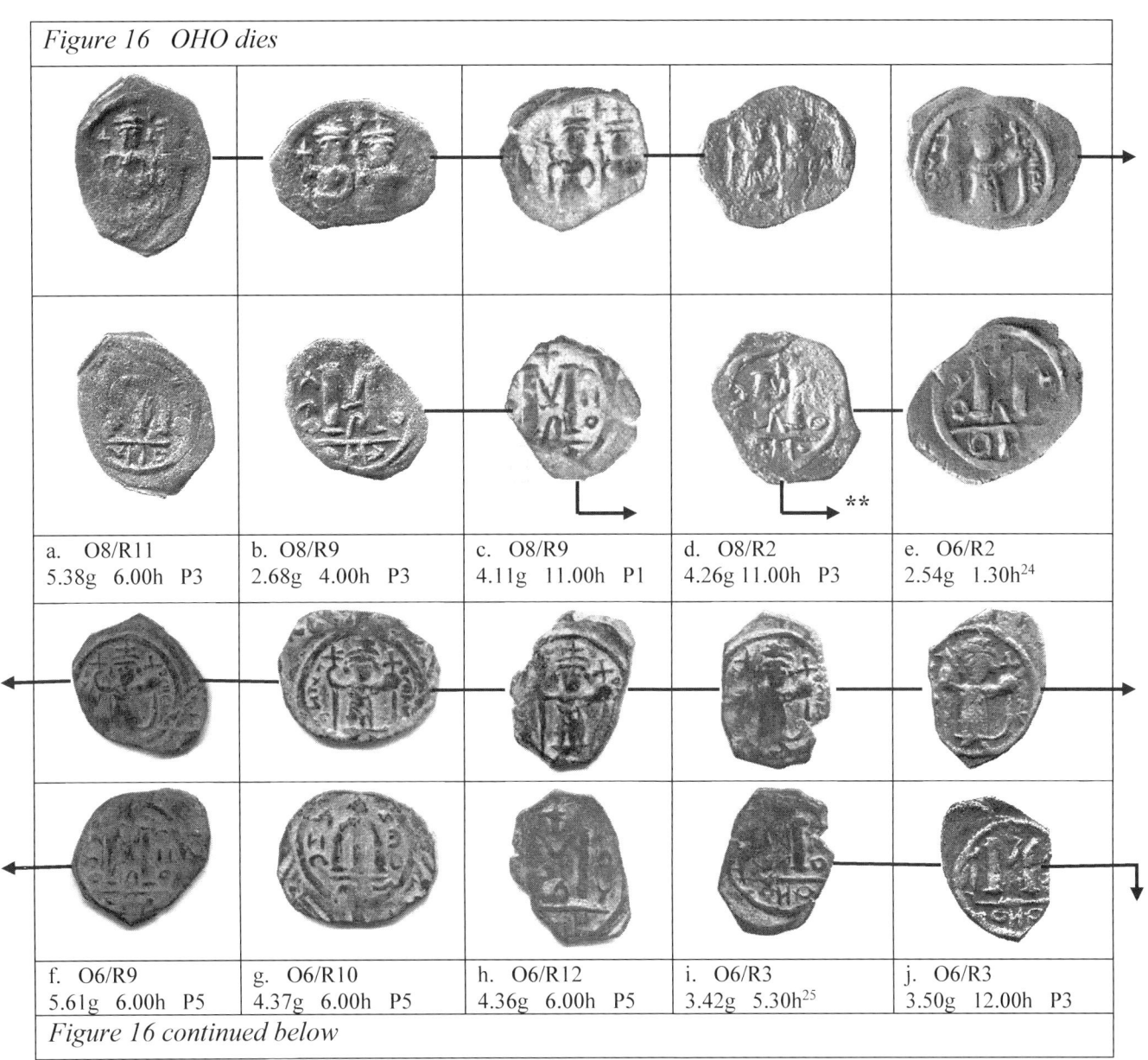

f. O6/R9 5.61g 6.00h P5	g. O6/R10 4.37g 6.00h P5	h. O6/R12 4.36g 6.00h P5	i. O6/R3 3.42g 5.30h[25]	j. O6/R3 3.50g 12.00h P3

Figure 16 continued below

[24] T Goodwin, ***Imitations of the Folles of Constans II***, Oriental Numismatic Society Occasional Paper no. 28, April 1993, no. 1; T Goodwin, 7th Century Arab Imitations of Byzantine Folles, ***Numismatic Circular*** CIII (9) (1995) 336-7, no. 11.

[25] H Pottier, I Schulze and W Schulze, Pseudo-Byzantine Coinage in Syria under Arab Rule (638-c.670) Classification and Dating, ***Revue Belge de Numismatique*** **CLIV** (2008) 87-155, pl. X..4.

Figure 16   OHO dies continued

k. O6/R4 5.12g 5.00h P2	l. O2/R4 3.46g 7.30h P1	m. O2/R4 3.36g 6.30h P5	n. O3/R2 2.67g 10.30h P3[26]	o. O3/R3 4.36tg 6.30h P6

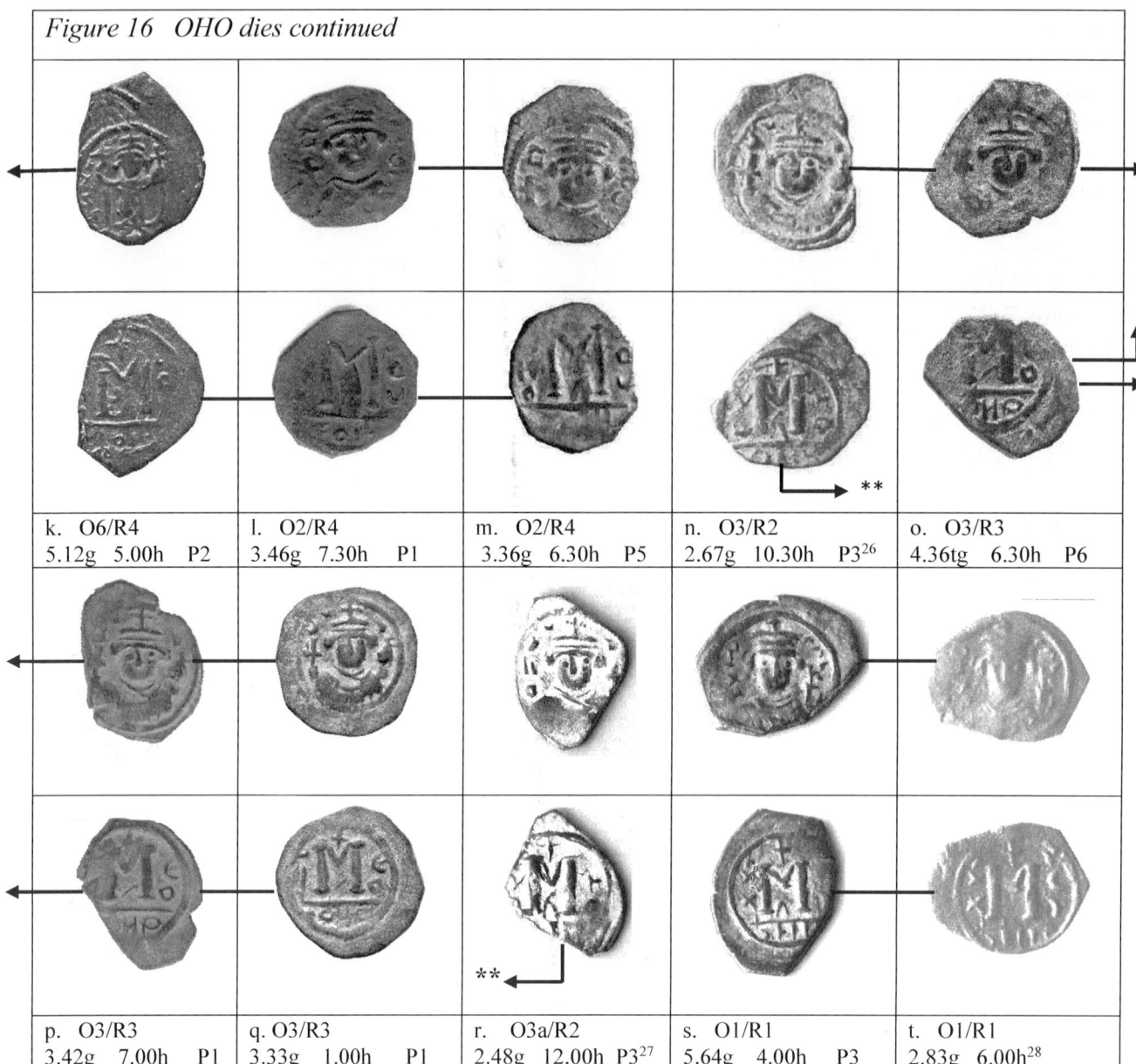

p. O3/R3 3.42g 7.00h P1	q. O3/R3 3.33g 1.00h P1	r. O3a/R2 2.48g 12.00h P3[27]	s. O1/R1 5.64g 4.00h P3	t. O1/R1 2.83g 6.00h[28]

Conclusion

This paper fully publishes two of the eleven Phase 1 workshops listed by Oddy [29] and illustrates in the appendices several other groups of coins which need further investigation but are probably further workshops. In addition, the coins of Phase 1 with three standing figures on the obverse can be shown to have several groups of die linked coins that also deserve further investigation. The number of workshops that are now known to have been active in Greater Syria from the completion of the Arab Conquest until the start of the Phase 2 coinage under Muʿāwiya demonstrates that there was a widespread demand for small change to facilitate local trade. This is an indication that the conquest did not seriously disrupt life in the towns and villages of this part of the former Byzantine Empire.

---

[26] T Goodwin, ***Imitations of the Folles of Constans II***, Oriental Numismatic Society Occasional Paper no. 28, April 1993, no. 28; H Pottier, I Schulze and W Schulze, Pseudo—Byzantine Coinage in Syria under Arab Rule (638-c.670) Classification and Dating, ***Revue Belge de Numismatique*** **CLIV** (2008) 87-155, pl. X.2.

[27] T Goodwin, 7th Century Arab Imitations of Byzantine Folles, ***Numismatic Circular*** CIII (9) (1995) 336-7, no.12.

[28] Jena 303-D07

[29] A Oddy, An Overview of the Phase 1 Byzantine-Arab Coinage, in T Goodwin (ed.), ***Coinage and History in the Seventh Century Near East 6***, London, 2020, 47-76, see p. 76.

Appendices

This paper and others like it over the past 30 years have shown that organised workshops were not uncommon in greater Syria in the years following the Arab conquest. The identification of mints involves searching through large numbers of images of Phase 1 coins in order to identify die links. Very often, as is the cases above, the full publication of a workshop may result from building on the initial work of others. In the following appendices, die links are presented which have been derived from a database of over 400 Phase 1 coins with a facing bust on the obverse and a similar number with three figures on the obverse. The even larger corpus of coins with a single standing figure have not been included in the search. In the following appendices groups of coins are illustrated where there are die links between at least two obverses or two reverses. These are presented here as the basis for future research at trying to enlarge the die chains and thus postulate more workshops.

Appendix 1

The obverses of this group are close to obverse O3 of the OHO workshop illustrated above. No die link has been found and for the moment it must be assumed that this group is a separate workshop. Seven examples are known which appear to be from the same pair of dies. See figure 17.

3.51g 12.00h P1	3.96g 12.00h P5	3.69g 12.00h P6	3.23g 11.00h P1

Figure 17

This group of coins all have a crude Heraclean monogram over the **M**. which first appears on regular folles of Heraclius class 5 struck in regnal year 24 (634/5). This monogram becomes the norm on folles of class 6 struck in regnal years 30-32 from which the reverses of the coins illustrated in Figure 17 are probably derived. The obverses, with a facing bust, are clearly derived from the IhPER COhST coins of Constans years 3 (643).

Other coins are known with a very similar style of bust but with no die linking and with a **+** over the **M** (see fig. 18).

2.91g 12.00h P1	3.37g 6.00h P1	4.93g 12.00h P1	3.23g 11.00h P1

Figure 18

Appendix 2

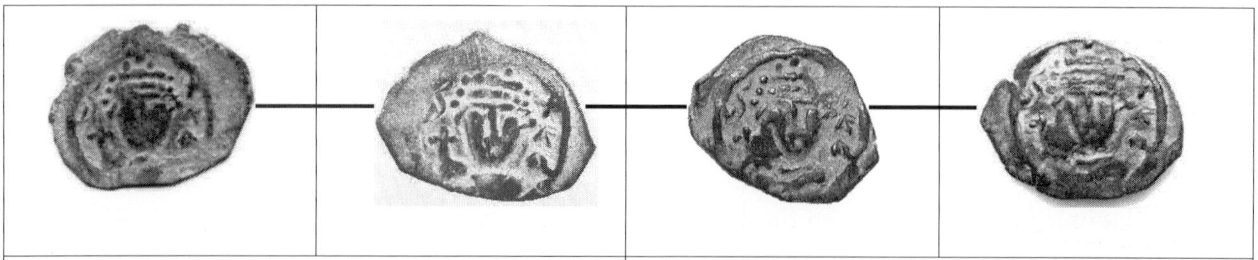

3 examples		2 examples	

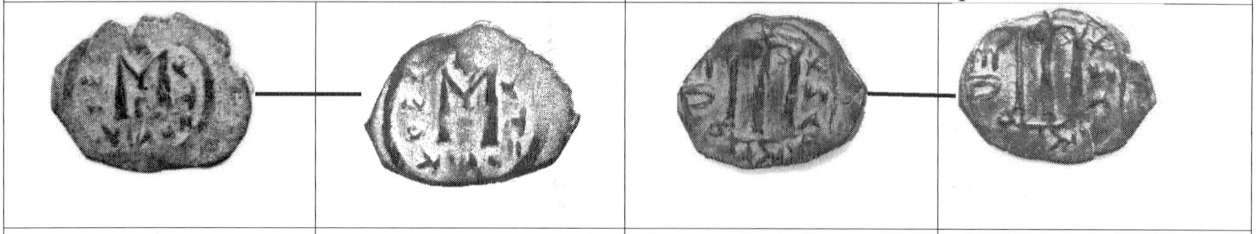

5.65g 12.00h P6	4.75g 12.00h P1	4442g 11.00h eBay October 2018	4.93g 12.00h eBay May 2020
Figure 19			

The die link in figure 19 is interesting because one reverse has an **M** and the other a more crudely drawn **m**.

Appendix 3

This workshop has, so far, two obverse dies and four reverse dies. The most common die pairing has 22 examples, one of which was found in the excavations at Antioch.[30] Several others have appeared in auction sales in recent years and two have been published in academic sources.[31]

7 examples	22 examples		1 example	1 example

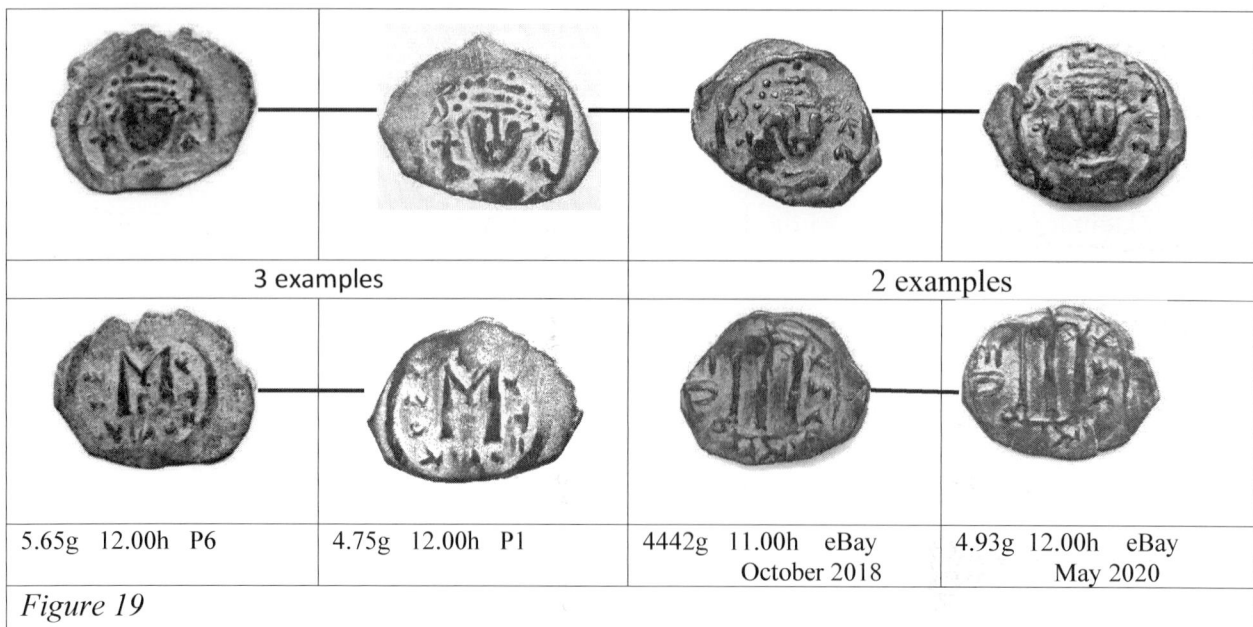

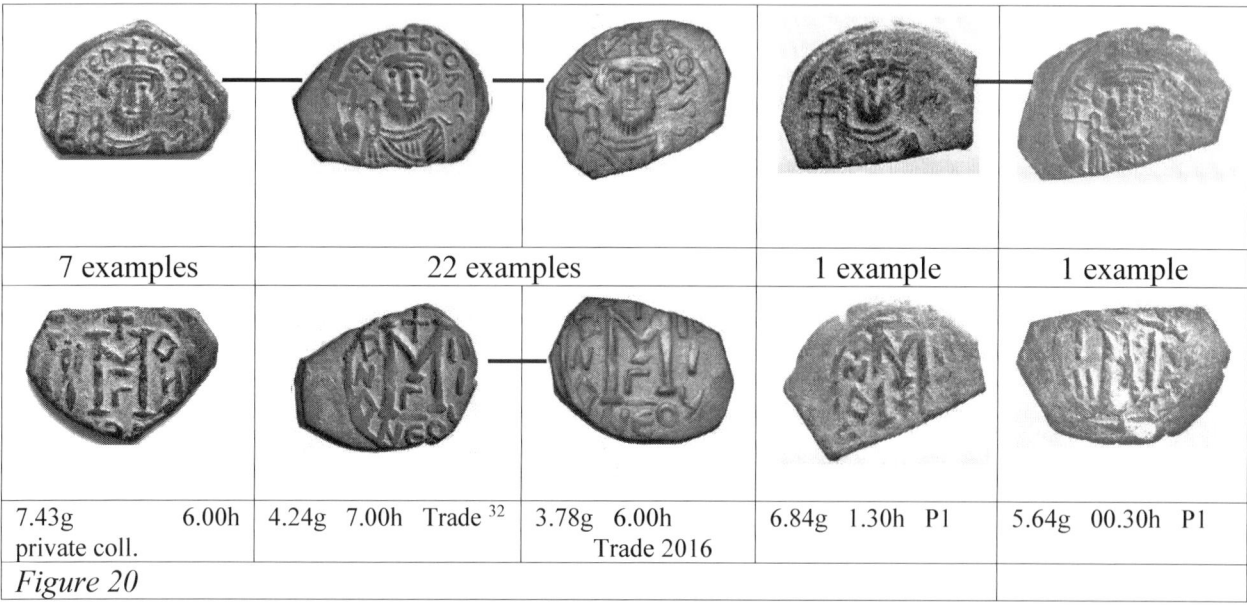

7.43g 6.00h private coll.	4.24g 7.00h Trade [32]	3.78g 6.00h Trade 2016	6.84g 1.30h P1	5.64g 00.30h P1
Figure 20				

[30] D B Waage, ***Antioch on the Orontes, IV, Part 2, Greek, Roman, Byzantine and Crusader Coins***, Princeton, 1952, no. 2255

[31] T Goodwin, Some Interesting Arab-Byzantine Coins from the Barber Institute Collection, ***Numismatic Circular*** (August 2003) 196-198, fig. 2; W Hahn, ***Moneta Imperii Byzantini: Band 3 - Von Heraclius bis Leo III. / Alleinregierung (610-720)***, Vienna, 1981, pl. 29, no. X18

[32] Leu Web Auction 5 (23.9 .2018) lot 1376

Various coins have been identified which are similar to the above but not yet die linked with them. However four of them are die linked with the same obverse but four different reverse dies (see figure 21). One of the reverse dies has a debased Heraclian monogram  over the **M** (see comments in appendix 1.

1 example	1 example	1 example	2 examples	3 examples

4.50g 6.00h P1	4.63g 11.00h trade [33]	4.61g 6.00h eBay 2019	3.13g 1.00h P1	4.48g 12.00h P1
Figure 21				

Appendix 4

The next group consists of 22 coins which have some stylistic distinctions but very few die pairings or die links. The condition of the coins is often poor and details of the design are difficult to distinguish when attempting die comparisons.

The obverse usually has no indication of a right arm; this design is also true for the coins in appendices 1-3, but it is more marked in this group. There is a brooch on the right shoulder with three 'streamers' hanging vertically downwards. To the left of this is a *globus cruciger* (Figure 22).

The reverse has an **M** on which the serifs usually consist of oval–shaped 'globules' which are often barely attached to the **M** itself (Figure 22).

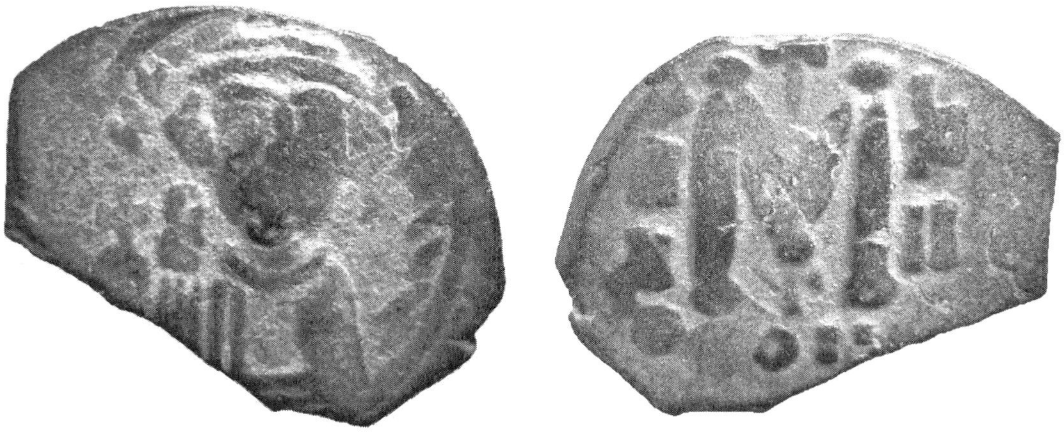

Figure 22. 4.50g 12.00h Oddy

[33] Professus on ebay January 2020

Five of these coins are illustrated in figure 23 in which the similarities can be discerned. Like all these groups, the weights are very variable. The 12 weights recorded vary between 2.99g and 6.06g and the average is 4.45g. The die axis is usually 12.00h.

4.42g 3.00h P1	Trade	Private collection	4.61g 12.00h Trade [34]	4.88g 11.00h P1

Figure 23

Appendix 5

There is no doubt that the facing bust obverse on the coins in these appendices is derived from the IhPЄR COhST coinage of Constans II which, as mentioned above, is most frequently found in Greater Syria and was probably struck in Constantinople and then shipped in bulk for use in the Levant.[35] Traces of this legend appear on the coins of Appendix 3. The coins presented here in Appendix 5 are more obviously derived from the IhPЄR COhST coinage.

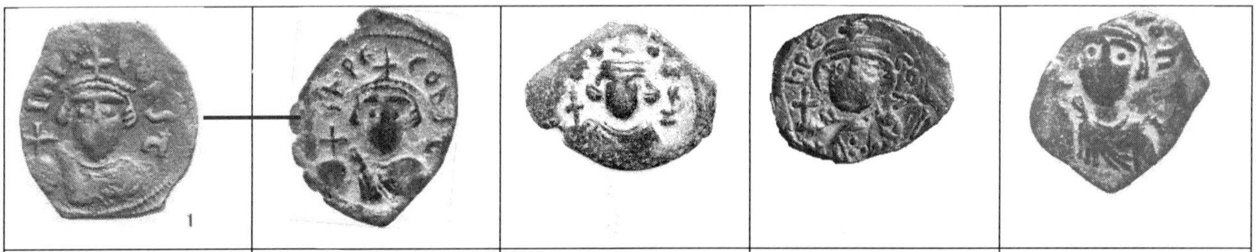

2 examples	2 examples			

4.22g 6.00h [36]	3.84g 1.00h P6	3.35g 12.00h P1	4.31g 6.00h P5	3.11g 6.00h P1

Figure 24

---

[34] CNG 288 (10 October 2012) lot 628

[35] A Oddy, An Overview of the Phase 1 Byzantine-Arab Coinage, in T Goodwin (ed.), ***Coinage and History in the Seventh Century Near East 6***, London, 2020, 47-76, see fn. 86 on p. 66

[36] H Pottier, I Schulze and W Schulze, Pseudo—Byzantine Coinage in Syria under Arab Rule (638-c.670) Classification and Dating, ***Revue Belge de Numismatique*** **CLIV** (2008) 87-155, pl.VII no. 1.

Large numbers of Phase 1 coins with a facing bust and traces of the IhPER COhST legend have survived but there are very few die links given the number of coins that have been examined. One die-linked pair is illustrated here together with three similar, but not die linked, coins to give an indication of what was being produced in the 640s.

Acknowledgements

My debt to those who have attended the ***Seventh Century Syria Numismatic Round Table*** over the past 30+ years is inestimable. Knowledge and photographs and opinions have been shared freely and gentle criticism has been given and received. My greatest debts in preparing this paper are to Tony Goodwin, Stephen Mansfield, Marcus Phillips, Ingrid Schulze, Wolfgang Schulze and Susan Tyler-Smith, but, above all, to the late Dr Nayef Goussous who was generous with his time and with access to his collection on several visits to Amman. It is with admiration that I dedicate this paper to his memory.

Dr Nayef G Goussous

2002 St. Joseph University (Beirut): Ph.D. thesis: ***Rare and Inedited Umayyad Copper Coins from the Goussous Collection in the Jordan National Bank Numismatic Museum.*** .

1995 Yarmouk University: M.A. in Archaeology and Anthropology thesis: ***Umayyad Coinage of Bilad al-Sham : an Analytical and chemical Study***. Winner of the Shamma Prize for Islamic Numismatics in 1998.

1961 Cairo University: D.D.S. (Doctor of Dental Surgery). Nayef Goussous spent his working life as a dentist.

Honours :
Certificate of Honor, Amman Rotary Club (1995).
Commendation, Fohais Orthodox Club (2013).
Commendation, Mota University (1993).
Commendation, Amman Armenian Club (1992).

Publications:

2014 N G Goussous, H A Alzuod and A M Naghawy ***Inedited and Rare Ancient, Classical and Byzantine Coins***, Amman (Published by Jordan Ahli Bank Numismatic Museum).

2014 N G Goussous, H A Alzuod and A M Naghawy, ***Inedited and Rare Islamic Coins***, Amman (Published by Jordan Ahli Bank Numismatic Museum).

2014 N G Goussous, O Al-Ghul, H Al-Zuod and A Naghawy,(eds.) ***'Azza Mithluhu, Studies in Memory of Samir Shama*** , Amman (Published by Yarmouk University).

2014 N G Goussous (ed.) ***Memoirs of Dr Jean al-Goussous al-Halasa (1885-1953).***
A letter of thanks was received from the Royal court in appreciation of this publication (27 April 2014).

2009 N G Goussous (ed.) ***Memoirs of Odeh al-Goussous al-Halasa (1877-1943)*** supplemented by three volumes of Jordanian documents and records related to the memoirs.
A letter of thanks from His Majesty King Abdullah II was received by the editor appreciating his efforts in collecting and publishing such important national documents (2nd of July 2012).

2004 N G Goussous, ***Rare and Inedited Umayyad Copper Coins: The Goussous Collection in the Jordan National Bank Numismatic Museum***, Amman (Published by The Jordan National Bank).

1996 N G Goussous, ***Umayyad Coinage of Bilad al-Sham***, Amman (Published by The Arab bank).

1991: N G Goussous.and K F Tarawneh, ***Coinage of the Ancient and Islamic World***, Amman (Published by The Arab Bank).

1984-1995: Fifteen Numismatic articles in: ***Studies in the History and Archaeology of Jordan***, and in ***Yarmouk Numismatics,*** and in ***Rayat Mutah*** Journals.

The author is indebted to Dr Hasan Zyoud of the Jordan Ahli Bank Numismatic Museum for providing the biographical data about Dr Nayef Goussous.

Byzantine Solidi in 7th century Syria, Arab-Byzantine imitations and the transition to the post-reform dinar.

Dietrich Schnädelbach[1]

Introduction

When the Arabs conquered Syria, the Byzantine solidus was in use (figure 1). The Arabs continued the use of the Byzantine solidus until the Reign of Constantine IV. His type 2 (figure 2) is the last type occurring in hoards in significant numbers. Since this type was struck until 681 CE, the hoards suggest that in the early 680s the solidi were hidden and disappeared from circulation.

Figure 1: Solidus of Heraclius struck at the time of the Arab conquest of Syria[2]

Figure 2: Solidus of Constantine IV[3]

When the Byzantine solidi disappeared from circulation, Arab-Byzantine solidi were used. These include copies of Byzantine solidi (figure 3) and solidi which were designed by the Arabs using Byzantine patterns. Arab-Byzantine solidi were used until the introduction of the strictly epigraphic dinar by ʻAbd al-Malik in 77 AH (696/7 CE) (figure 4).

Figure 3: Arab-Byzantine solidus[4] (copy of a solidus of Heraclius, see figure 1)

Figure 4: Dinar of ʻAbd al-Malik[5] (post-reform dinar of 78 H)

[1] Dietrich Schnädelbach is an independent scholar schnaedelbachs@arcor.de

[2] Leu Numismatik AG Web Auktion 20, Lot no. 2923

[3] Wikipedia

[4] Numismatica Genevensis SA Auction 8 (2014) lot 226

[5] https.//www.ancient.eu/image/11658/

Gold hoards from 7th century Syria

A major number of hoards containing gold coins which were hidden in Syria and the adjacent regions in the seventh century are published. These hoards contain mainly Byzantine solidi, sometimes fractions thereof and only in one case an Arab Byzantine solidus.[6] The examination of these hoards revealed a very complex metrological situation. Therefore, and in order to focus on the principles according to which the solidi were used, this article is restricted to two mayor hoards: the hoards from Bet She'an (ancient Nysa-Scythopolis)[7] and Nikertai.[8]

The Hoards from Bet She'an and Nikertai

The hoards from Bet She'an and Nikertai cover the whole period from the Arab conquest of Syria[9] until the reign of Constantine IV. Class II solidi of Constantine IV are the last group of Byzantine solidi in the hoards from Bet She'an and Nikertai. The same is true for several other hoards which were hidden at the same time i.e. after 681 CE: "None of the hoards includes issues from the last class of this ruler (681-686 CE)."[10] Thus, probably at this time in Syria the use of Byzantine solidi came to an end.

The two hoards represent the situation in two different regions in Syria / Bilad al-Sham (figure 5). Nikertai is located north of Damascus next to Hims in Jund Hims whereas Bet She'an / Baysan is located south of Damascus in Jund al-'Urdunn. This is important, since below it will turn out that the Byzantine solidi were used in both regions according to different weight standards.

The unit of account

Fortunately both hoards are complete, allowing us to examine the total weight. The total weight of 751 solidi from Bet She'an is 3,300.44 g. This suggests that the intended weight was 3,265.92 g. This weight is 1.06 percent below the total weight. However, usually the actual weight of a complete hoard of gold or silver items is slightly above the intended weight. Probably the intention was to ascertain that everybody weighing the complete hoard would at least find the intended weight. The intended weight of 3,265.92 g represents 10 Byzantine gold pounds, 8 Bagdadī *ratl* of 408.24 g or 720 solidi of 4.536 g.

The Nikertai hoard comprises 516 solidi and 18 semisses. Unfortunately, the weight of a few solidi is not given. Consequently, the total weight of the hoard has to be estimated. Using the average weight of the solidi we arrive at a total weight of 2,298.45 g. The intended weight was probably

---

[6] According to Bijovsky (p. 181) only one hoard (Daphne) "includes a transitional solidus". Gabriela Bijovsky, 'A Hoard of Byzantine solidi from Bet She'an in the Umayyad Period', ***Revue numismatique,*** 6e série – Tome 158, année 2002 pp. 161-227.

[7] Bijovsky as footnote 6

[8] Cecile Morrisson, 'Le Trésor Byzantin de Nikertai', ***Revue belge de numismatique et de sigillographie***, CXVIII – 1972, pp. 29-91, pl. II-VIII

[9] The hoards from Bet She'an and Nikertai also contain solidi from the time before the Arab conquest: solidi of Maurice (Nikertai) and Phocas (Bet She'an and Nikertai). These are not discussed here, since this text is focussed on the period after the Arab conquest until the introduction of the post-reform dinar.

[10] Bijovsky as footnote 6, p. 181

2,268 g. In this case the intended weight is 1 $^{1}/_{3}$ per cent below the estimated total weight. This difference is in line with the one of the Bet She'an hoard. The intended weight represents 500 solidi of 4.536 g.

The hoards from Bet She'an and Nikertai demonstrate that in Syria in the early 680s the unit of account was 4.536 g. This is the same unit of account which was used in the Byzantine Empire. This is perfectly in line with a report from the Nessana papyri according to which ***"taxes were still calculated in Byzantine gold nomismata."***[11]

Figure 5: Bilad al-Sham[12]

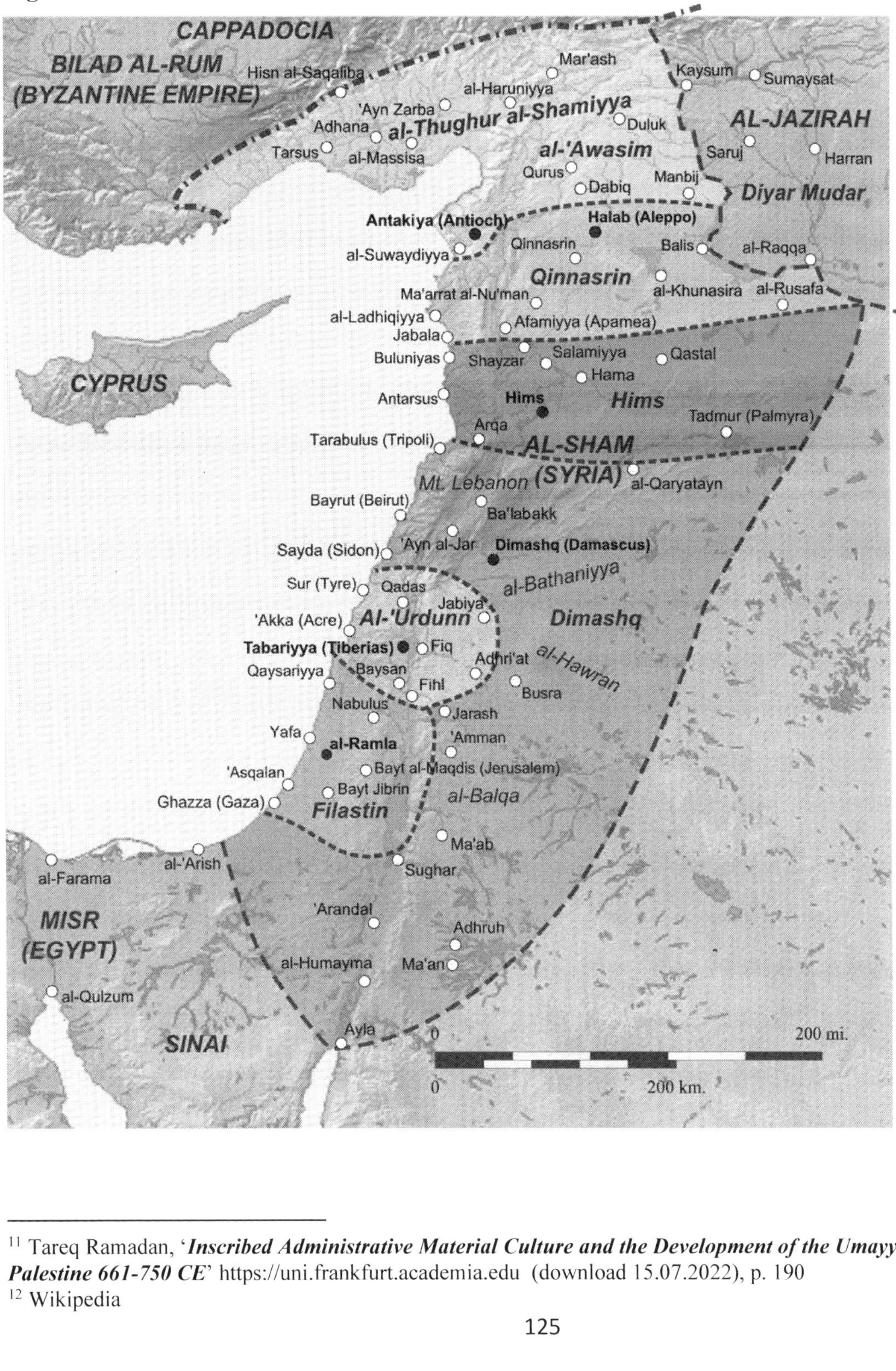

---

[11] Tareq Ramadan, '***Inscribed Administrative Material Culture and the Development of the Umayyad State in Syria-Palestine 661-750 CE***' https://uni.frankfurt.academia.edu (download 15.07.2022), p. 190

[12] Wikipedia

Precision of weighing

Balances of the type used in antiquity are still used (figure 6). A typical set of weights usually ranges from pieces of 1 mg to pieces of 100 g. Once this type of balances is used, according to the experience of the author, differences of 5 mg will certainly be very clearly indicated.

Figure 6[13]

Flinders Petrie examined the precision of Egyptian glass weights. "The dinar averages on six examples (725-840 CE) 65.30 grains, mean error 0.10.",[14] i. e. 4.23144 g +/- 6.48 mg.[15] Compared to the precision of modern balances of the type used in the 7th century, the finding of Flinders Petrie looks realistic. However, we need to keep in mind that the precision applied at the production and standardisation of coin weights certainly was the utmost which could be achieved at the time. Consequently, we need to assume that in the everyday business the precision of weighing was not that high. Nevertheless, we can expect that even in everyday business the precision of weighing allowed detecting differences in the magnitude of 0.01296 g (2 x 6.48 mg) or 1/5 grain. Consequently, it is realistic to assume that even weight standards defined by half grains could be used.

The nominal weight of the solidus at Bet She'an and Nikertai

Once we examine the upper end of the weight distribution of the solidi contained in the two hoards (table 1) we see that it is at Bet She'an 4.55 g and at Nikertai 4.49 g.[16] The weight of 4.55 g is usually found once major groups of solidi are examined.[17] However, the nominal weight of the solidus was 4.536 g and this was usually the upper limit of the specification.[18] Nevertheless, the

[13] Wikipedia

[14] Sir W. M. Flinders Petrie, ***Glass Stamps and Weights***, The British School of Archaeology in Egypt 1926, Reprint Guildford 1974, p. 11

[15] The calculated weight of the Egyptian dinar is 4.2336 g. The weight of 4.23164 g is a light version thereof.

[16] In the case of Nikertai three single solidi above the main group are disregarded.

[17] This may be the reason why in publications the weight of the solidus is usually given as 4.55 g.

[18] The discussion on the true weight of the solidus and the Roman (gold) pound is described by Grierson and Mays. It illustrates the confusion created by the lacking differentiation of weight standards. Philip Grierson and Melinda Mays,

weight of 4.55 g is not really surprising. Before striking, the weight of the flans was controlled by the mint. If the flans were too heavy their weight was adjusted. Obviously, the flans were weighed to a precision of +/- ¼ grain/*habba* (1/16 *keration*). In light of the precision of weighing which was possible at the time (see above) this is realistic. If the nominal weight of 4.536 g is taken as 96 grains of 0.04725 g we get as the upper end of the possible individual weights 4.5478125 g (96.25 x 0.04725 g).

The solidi of the hoards from Bet She'an and Nikertai were struck at Constantinople. Consequently, it makes sense to assume that they were struck according to the same specification. From this point of view the upper end of the main group from the Nikertai hoard at 4.49 g is very surprising. Thus, in the case of the solidi from the Nikertai hoard, the upper end of the weight distribution is obviously not related to the precision of the weighing of the flans at the mint. Consequently, we can expect that it was related to the use of the solidi at Nikertai. If we assume that the precision of weighing was the same as at the mint, we get an upper end of 4.49064 g (96.25 x 0.046656 g) which is related to a nominal weight of 4.478976 g (96 x 0.046656 g). **Consequently, the nominal weight of the solidus was not everywhere identical with the unit of account i.e. 4.536 g.**

Table 1: Weight distribution of the solidi from Bet She'an and Nikertai

(g)	Bet She'an	Nikertai	comment
4.55	**2**	-	4.5478125 g (96.25 x 0.04725g)
4.54	1	-	4.536 g (96 x 0.04725 g)
4.53	1	1	
4.52	4	-	
4.51	1	1	
4.50	7	1	
4.49	12	**3**	4.49064 g (96.25 x 0.046656 g)
4.48	20	5	4.478976 g (96 x 0.046656 g)
4.47	33	4	
4.46	36	14	
4.45	40	33	
4.44	46	29	
4.43	60	39	
4.42	47	29	
4.41	37	33	
4.40	37	42	
4.39	37	32	
4.38	59	30	
4.37	46	21	
4.36	43	15	
4.35	39	29	
4.34	34	17	
4.33	24	18	
4.32	17	15	
4.31	15	14	
4.30	11	21	

Catalogue of late Roman coins in the Dumbarton Oaks Collection and in the Whittemore Collection: from Arcadius and Honorius to the accession of Anastasius, Washington D.C. 1992, pp. 29-30

(g)	Bet She'an	Nikertai	comment
4.29	7	8	
4.28	6	19	
4.27	10	10	
4.26	9	8	
4.24	1	2	
4.23	2	**6**	4.230144 g (68 x 0.062208 g)
4.22	1	3	
4.21	-	-	4.214592 g (67.75 x 0.062208 g)
4.20	2	1	4.19904 g (67.5 x 0.062208 g)
4.19	1	-	
4.16	-	1	
4.15	-	-	
4.14	-	1	
	751	512	
total	3,300.44 g	2,247.17 g	
mean	4.395 g	4.389 g	

The nominal weight and standard weight used at Bet She'an

The maximum of the solidi of Heraclius from Bet She'an (histogram 1) indicates a standard weight of 4.4064 g (68 x 0.0648 g). This standard weight was maintained until the reign of Constantine IV (histogram 2). According to Bijovsky [19] "...it seems that the Bet She'an hoard presents a considerable number of die-links. In view of the extensive output of gold solidi issued during the 7th century, this phenomenon might suggest that the hoard consists of at least a number of solidi, which were disseminated as a group or groups after leaving the mint. It is tempting to suggest that some of those gold coins reached our region together, and were concealed with the rest in the hoard pot at Bet She'an." This observation is very important since it suggests that the solidi in the Bet She'an hoard were struck at Constantinople from the time of Heraclius until Constantine IV according to specification 1. Below (see annex: Weight standard of the solidus in the time of Heraclius) it is demonstrated that this really was the case.

Histogram 1:
Solidi of Heraclius at Bet She'an

N x 0.0648 g	number of solidi
70	4
69	101
68	149
67	106
66	19
65	3

Histogram 2:
Solidi of Constantine IV. at Bet She'an

N x 0.0648 g	number of solidi
70	-
69	20
68	25
67	20
66	2
65	-

[19] Bijovsky as footnote 6, p. 171

Specification 1: Solidi stuck by Heraclius from the Bet She'an hoard

	n x 0.0648 g	grams
Nominal weight	70	4.536
Standard weight	68	4.4064
Lower limit	66	4.2768
Pass weight	65	4.212

Histogram 3: Jerusalem hoard of 610-613 CE[20]

n x 0.1296 g	number of solidi				
36	5				
35			69		
34				92	4.4064 g
33			65		
32		32			
31	1				

The standard weight of 4.4064 g was already used when Heraclius struck an emergency issue in Jerusalem in 610-613 CE (histogram 3). However, the tolerance of this emergency issue (specification 2) was twice the tolerance used at Bet She'an.[21] This makes sense, since an emergency issue needs to be manufactured very rapidly and consequently precision is of secondary importance. Nevertheless, the emergency issue was struck according to the standard weight used at Constantinople and thus underlines its importance.

Specification 2: Solidi stuck by Heraclius from the Jerusalem hoard

	n x 0.0648 g	weight (g)
Upper limit	72	4.6656
Nominal weight	70	4.536
Standard weight	68	4.4064
Lower limit	64	4.1472

Unit of account and nominal weights of the Byzantine solidus at Bet She'an and Nikertai

As in the Byzantine Empire at Bet She'an the nominal weight of the solidus was identical to the unit of account i.e. 4.536 g. At Nikertai the unit of account was also 4.536 g. However, at Nikertai the nominal weight of the solidus was 4.478976 g, i.e. well below the nominal weight at Bet She'an. Whereas the weight distribution of the solidi of the Bet She'an hoard suggests that they were struck to a specification with the nominal weight of 4.536 g and a standard weight of 4.4064 g (specification 1), the solidi of the Nikertai hoard offer a different impression. The beginning of the main group of solidi at Nikertai (4.49 g) marks the nominal weight. However, some scattered solidi above that weight demonstrate that the solidi were not struck to a corresponding specification but selected from those circulating.

[20] Gabriela Bijovssky, 'A single die solidi hoard of Heraclius from Jerusalem', ***Mélanges Cécil Morrison,*** Travaux et Mémoires 16, Paris 2010, pp. 55-92

[21] Since the tolerance is 0.2592 g (4 x 0.0648 g) the upper limit of the specification is well above the nominal weight. This demonstrates that the upper limit of a specification is not necessarily identical to the nominal weight. Consequently, it may be misleading once the upper end of the weight distribution is taken as the nominal weight.

The selection of solidi at Nikertai

The lower end of the weight distribution of the solidi from Nikertai (table 1) exhibits a small peak at 4.23 g. This represents the lower limit of the set of weight standards used at Nikerkai for the selection of solidi from circulation.

Table 2: Weight standards used for the selection of the solidi at Nikertai

	n x 0.062208 g	grams	
upper limit	72	4.478976	see above: section on the nominal weights
middle	70	4.35456	Syrian *mithqāl*
lower limit	68	4.230144	

The main series of solidi ends just above 4.214592 (67.75 x 0.062208 g). This confirms that these solidi were selected from circulation according to the weight standards given in table 2 by weighing to the precision of one quarter grain. Since these weight standards were used to select solidi it is not likely that in addition to the lower limit a pass weight was used. We need to keep in mind that the selection of solidi may have been performed using the standard weight (in this case 4.35456 g) together with a small weight representing the acceptable difference of 0.124426 g.[22]

If we disregard an isolated solidus at the top (4.53 g) and two isolated solidi at the end (4.16 g and 4.14 g) the weight of the remaining solidi reaches from 4.51 g to 4.20 g. These weights represent 4.51008 g (72.5 x 0.062208 g) and 4.19904 g (67.5 x 0.062208 g) and are +/- 0.1552 g (2.5 x 0.062208 g) of 4.35456 g (70 x 0.062208 g). Thus they confirm that the latter weight represents the middle of the weight distribution of the solidi of the Nikertai hoard.

From the above it appears that at Nikertai we find the mean of a weight distribution which looks like the standard weight of a specification. Since the solidi were struck according to specification 1 this set of weight standards was not used for their production. However, it is very remarkable to note that 4.35456 g (70 x 0.062208 g), the middle of the weight distribution, is two grains below the nominal weight of 4.478976 g (72 x 0.062208 g). This is very similar to 4.4064 g (68 x 0.0648 g), the standard weight which is related to 4.536 g (70 x 0.0648 g) in specification 1. Thus, the weight distribution in the Bet She'an and the Nikertai hoard is very similar.

As can be seen in the annex (Weight standards of the solidus in the time of Justinian) at Thessalonica a specification which is based on the nominal weight of 4.478976 g was used to strike solidi for Illyricum and Dalmatia.

Individual weight standards

If the individual weights of the solidi of Constans II from the Nikertai hoard are converted into multiples of 0.023328 g, which is ½ of 0.046656 g or $^1/_3$ of 0.069984 g, we get the histogram 5. The maximum at 4.408992 g (63 x 0.069984 g) suggests that these solidi were mainly selected from those circulating which complied with a standard weight of 4.408992 g (63 x 0.069984 g). This is

[22] The importance of the unit of 4.35456 g (24/25 of 4.536 g) is attested by a text (*P. Lond.* IV 1412) from AD 698-705 which leads "to an average deficiency of .92 carats per solidus. Departing from 4.536 g we get 4.36212 g which is just 0.00756 g above 4.35456 g. See: Nicholas Borek, ***"Specialized Personnel" The Zygostates, the Solidus, and Monetary Technology in the Later Roman Empire***, academia.edu, p. 48-49

just one *habba* of 0.069984 g below the nominal weight of 4.478976 g (64 x 0.069984 g).[23] This weight standard of 4.408992 g became later known as the Egyptian *mithqal.*[24] A secondary maximum at 4.339008 g (62 x 0.069984 g) is one *habba* of 0.069984 g below the first maximum. This suggests that these weight standards were preferred at Nikertai. Probably this happened when the solidi arrived at Nikertai i.e. during the reign of Constans II (641-668 CE) or shortly thereafter.

Histogram 5: The solidi of Constans II from Nikertai

N x 0.023328 g	number of solidi		
192	ii		4.478976 g (64 x 0.069984 g)
191	iiiii iiiii iiiii i 16		
190	iiiii iiiii iiiii iii 18		
189	iiiii iiiii iiiii iiiii iiiii iiiii iiiii	35	4.408992 g (63 x 0.069984 g)
188	iiiii iiiii iiiii ii 17		
187	iiiiii iiiii iii	13	
186	iiiii iiiii iiiii iiiii i	21	4.339008 g (62 x 0.069984 g)
185	iiiiii iiiii i	11	
184	iiiii iiii		
183	iiiiii iiiii i	11	4.269024 g (61 x 0.069984 g)
182	-		
181	iii		
180	-		4.19904 g (60 x 0.069984 g)

If we convert the individual weights of the solidi of Constantine IV from Bet She'an and Nikertai into multiples of 0.02268 we get histograms 6 and 7. Histogram 6 demonstrates that at Bet She'an, in addition to the standard weight of 4.4064 g, individual weight standards such as 4.44528 g (98 x 0.04536 g) 4.39992 g (97 x 0.04536 g) and 4.3092 g (95 x 0.04536 g) were used. These can all be related to the Syrian *mithqāl* of 4.35456 g (96 x 0.04536 g). Apart from 4.3092 g these standards appear as well at Nikertai. In addition the solidi from Nikertai show a maximum at 4.35456 g (96 x 0.04536 g, 70 x 0.062208 g). This demonstrates that at Nikertai the Syrian *mithqāl* was of special importance. In fact it represents exactly the middle between the nominal weight of 4.478976 g and the lower limit of 4.230144 g (table 1).

N x 0.02268 g	Solidi of Constantine IV Bet She'an (**histogram 6**) number of solidi		Solidi of Constantine IV Nikertai (**histogram 7**) number of solidi	
198	iii		-	
197	iii		-	
196	iiiii iii	4.44528 g	ii	4.44528 g (98 x 0.04536 g)
195	iiiii ii		i	
194	iiiii iiiii ii	4.39992 g	iiiii i	4.39992 g (97 x 0.04536 g)
193	iiiii ii		i	
192	Iiii		iiiii iii	4.35456 g (96 x 0.04536 g)
191	ii		ii	
190	iiiii ii	4.3092 g	-	4.3092 g (95 x 0.04536 g)

[23] As regards the reduction of a nominal weight by one grain see the annex: Weight standards of the solidi above the standard weight.

[24] 100 Syrian *mithqāls* are equal to 98 ¾ Egyptian *mithqāls*. Walther Hinz, ***Islamische Masse und Gewichte umgerechnet ins metrische System***, Handbuch der Orientalistik Abt. 1, Erg. Bbd. 1 Heft 1, Leiden/Köln 1970, p. 4

The weight standards used in Syria

The examination of Byzantine solidi used in 7th century Syria reveals a very complex system of weight standards. At the top we find the unit of account of 4.536 g which represents the nominal weight of the Byzantine solidus. This unit of account was used throughout the Byzantine Empire. Obviously it was also applied in regions outside the Byzantine Empire where the solidus was used. In some cases the unit of 4.536 g was also used in Syria as the nominal weight of the solidus. However, in addition we find a second nominal weight of 4.478976 g. Below the nominal weight we find the standard weight of the Byzantine solidus (4.4064 g = 34/35 of 4.536 g) and the Syrian *mihqāl* (4.35456 g = 24/25 of 4.536 g) which was an important reference weight.

In 7th century Syria a major number of solidi complying very precisely with individual weight standards appear. This suggests that these solidi were selected from those circulating and thus accumulated. Altogether people had to face a very complex system of weight standards which was difficult to handle.[25] Consequently, officials called *zygostates* were employed to assist the population.

The Zygostates

In 363 CE Julian decreed the appointment of an official weigher (*zygostates*) in each municipality to settle disputes over the weight standard of solidi.[26] In addition, the *zygostatai* deposited solidi in bags which were marked by weight and then sealed.[27] Further they collected taxes.[28] Egyptian papyri provide reports about some cases where the *zygostates* was involved. As an example the following case is presented: According to a will three payments had to be made. However, deficiencies in the weight of the solidi in question were observed: "0.93; 0.96; 0.97 carats per solidus on the Alexandrian standard." If we assume that the resulting weights are comparable to the weights of the solidi appearing in coin hoards and the weight standards reported in other papyri, it appears that the standard in question is the nominal weight of the solidus i.e. 4.536 g (24 carats of 0.189 g). This case shows that even major sums were probably weighed to the precision of one grain or even one half grain. Consequently, the weight standards of the solidi calculated from such weighing present units such as 1/100 carat.

Egyptian papyrus (575-625 CE)[29]

Deficient solidi:	Weight (g)	comment	
0.97 carat	4.35267	4.536 g – 0.18333 g (0.189 g x 0.97)	
0.96 carat	4.35456	4.536 g – 0.18144 g (0.189 g x 0.96)	Syrian *mithqāl*
0.93 carat	4.36023	4.536 g – 0.17577 g (0.189 g x 0.93)	

One of the substandard solidi represents the Syrian *mithqāl* of 4.35456 g and the weights of the two other ones can be related to this weight standard. Thus, we find a similar situation as in the hoards from Bet She'an and especially Nikertai.

---

[25] For Egypt this situation is well attested by written sources. See: Borek, as footnote 22, p. 47-49
[26] Borek as footnote 22, p. 1, p. 23, pp. 25-31
[27] Borek as footnote 22, pp. 31-38
[28] Borek as footnote 22, pp. 38-49
[29] Borek as footnote 22, pp. 18-19

The *zygostates* in 7th century Syria

The hoards from Bet She'an and Nikertai demonstrate that in Syria after the Arab conquest Byzantine solidi were still used. The hoards contained solidi which were used in the traditional way: i.e. several weight standards were used. Therefore, it is not surprising that the office of the *zygostates* continued under the Umayyads.[30] The reform of 'Abd al Maliks replaced the use of gold coins of several different weight standards by the dinar of just two very similar weight standards (see below). Consequently, *zygostatai* were no longer needed in their traditional function. However, they were still employed to collect taxes.[31] Possible consequences: since the solidi were used according to a large number of different weight standards and the copper coins were struck according to a large number of different weight standards both phenomena may be two sides of the same coin, i.e. it may well be that local weight standards of the solidi were related to local weight standards of the copper coins.

The post-reform Dinar

The dinar which was introduced by 'Abd al-Malik in 77 AH (696/7 CE) was struck according to two different standard weights: The Syrian dinar of 4.2525 g[32] (+/- 0.0405 g) and the Egyptian dinar of 4.2336 g (+/- 0.0432 g).[33] The mean of the two standard weights is 4.24305 g.[34] This may be the reason why in publications the standard weight of the dinar is usually given as 4.25 g. The standard weight of the Syrian dinar and the tolerance to which it was struck is perfectly illustrated by the 136 dinars from the Damascus hoard[35] (histogram 8).

Histogram 8

n x 0.0405 g	Zahl		
106	iiiii iiiii ii	12	
105			110
104	iiiii iiiii iiii	14	

The tolerance which was applied by the mints striking the dinar was about half the tolerance used for striking the solidus. In addition it seems that the standard weight of the dinar was also used as the unit of account. Thus the dinar creates a totally new coinage system. However, this raises the question what happened to the seigniorage? Did it just disappear?

---

[30] Borek as footnote 22, p. 49; and Appendix 4.6, p. 74

[31] Borek as footnote 22, pp. 40-41, p. 45, p. 48

[32] Harald Witthöft, ***Münzfuß, Kleingewichte, pondus Caroli und die Grundlagen des nordeuropäischen Maß- und Gewichtssystems in fränkischer Zeit***, Ostfildern 1984, p. 46

[33] Michael L. Bates, 'Coins and Money in the Arabic papyri' in: ***Documents de l'Islam médiéval - nouvelles perspectives de recherche,*** Actes de la table ronde organisé par le Centre national de la recherche scientifique (Paris 3-5 mars 1988), Institut française d'archéologie orientale du Caire, TAEI 29 – 1991, p. 54, footnote 44. Bates gives 4.23 g. However, 4.2336 g (70 x 0.06048 g, 98 x 0.0432 g) is the standard weight related to 4.35456 g (72 x 0.06048 g) or 4.320 g (100 x 0.0432 g) and therefore fits to the weight system which was used at the time. An alternative would be 4.230 g (94 x 0.0450 g) standard weight to 4.320 g (96 x 0.0450 g). However, the weight of coins suggests a tolerance of 0.0432 g. Further, the grains of 0.06048 g and 0.0432 g) fit to a weight system which is based on the solidus of 4.536 g (75 x 0.06048 g, 105 x 0.0432 g) whereas 0.0450 g does not.

[34] If we disregard an isolated very light dinar the mean of the remaining 40 dinars of the Lajjūn hoard is MW 4.24275 g. Thus this hoard represents the mean of both standard weights. L. A. Mayer, 'A hoard of Umayyad dinars from El Lajjūn', in: ***Numismatics of the Islamic World***, Vol. 23, Frankfurt 2003

[35] Dipl. Phil. Kassem Toueir, ' Ein neuer omayyadischer Goldschatz in Damaskus', in: ***Annales Archéologiques Arabes Syriennes***, Vol XVI (1966) Tome 1, pp. 83-107

The Dinar and its possible relation to the *zakāt*

Maqrīzī reports on the *zakāt*[36]: "The Messenger of God prescribed the *zakāt* on money accordingly: for every five *ūqīyahs* of pure and unadulterated silver he imposed [a *zakāt* of] five dirhams, i.e., the equivalent of one *nawāt*, and for every twenty dinars he imposed half a dinar." Since the *zakāt* of 1/40 is in the magnitude of the seigniorage of Byzantine solidi, it makes sense to examine the possibility that it was designed following this example.

The standard weight of 4.4226 g (specification a4) is 39/40 of the nominal weight of 4.536 g. Since this tolerance is identical to the *zakāt* and since the solidi of Tiberius II. (578-582 CE) circulated at the time of Mohammed (ca. 570-632 CE) it may be that the tolerance of the solidi of Tiberius II were the model for the *zakāt.*

If the Syrian *mithqāl* of 4.35456 g is reduced by 1/40 we get 4.245696 g, which is very close to the mean weight of the Syrian and the Egyptian dinar (4.24305 g). The difference between the two weights is about 1/20 grain and therefore not relevant. Consequently, the difference between the Syrian *mithqāl* and the average weight of the Syrian and Egyptian dinars may be seen as a seigniorage. However, so far nothing indicates that the Syrian *mithqāl* was seen as the nominal weight of the dinar. Further, Byzantine solidi were usually struck to a tolerance which is identical with the seigniorage. In the case of the dinar the tolerance would be less than half the seigniorage. All in all, it is unlikely that the difference between the Syrian *mithqāl* and the average weight of the Syrian and Egyptian dinars was treated as a seigniorage. Consequently, it is very likely that the dinar was struck without a seigniorage. Together with the very small tolerance this suggests, that the intention was to continue the tradition shown by the coin hoards, i.e. to trade gold coins without any seigniorage at weight standards which were kept very precisely.

The Syrian *mithqāl* of 4.35456 g is 1/100 of the *ratl* of 435.456 g (1/75 Babylonian talent)[37] and the *mithqāl* of 4.2525 g is 1/96 of the Baghdadī *ratl* of 408.24 g (1/80 Babylonian talent). Both are weight units that were used in the region since ancient times. Since the difference between the two is about 1/40 it may well be that this relation was the model for the *zakāt.*

Annex

The purpose of this annex is to identify the weight standards according to which Byzantine solidi were struck in the 7th century. In order to achieve a convincing result it was necessary to establish the whole sequence of the relevant weight standards from Justinian I onward. The identification of the weight standards according to which solidi were struck requires a complex approach. It is necessary to consider the weight distribution of the solidi represented in coin hoards, coin weights (preferably those which can be attributed to certain emperors), and written sources of the time.

A second issue was the identification of official weight standards above the standard weights according to which the solidi were struck. These seem to be relevant in consideration of the weight standards represented by published solidi.

---

36 Adel Allouche, ***Mamluk economics: a study and transaction of al-Maqrīzī's Ighāthah***, Salt Lake City 1994, p. 57

37 Dietrich Schnädelbach, 'The weight standard of copper coins as a means for understanding the Syrian tradition of the seventh century', in: Tony Goodwin (ed.) ***Coinage and History in the Seventh Century Near East Vol. 6***, London, 2019, pp. 193-194

Weight standards of the solidus in the time of Justinian

The first weight standard of Justinian I (527-565 CE) is attested by a glass weight which presents the bust of the emperor and around the inscription: DN IVSTINIANVS PP AVC. The given mass is 4.46 g[38] which represents a standard weight of 4.4604 g (specification a1).

	Specification a1		Specification a2	
	N x 0.0378 g	Grammes	N x 0.04725 g	Grammes
Nominal weight	120	4.536	96	4.536
Standard weight	118	4.4604	94	4.4415
Lower limit	116	4.3848	92	4.347
Pass weight	115	4.347	91	4.29975

The second weight standard of Justinian is attested by a weight issued by Zemarchus who was twice eparch of Constantinople the time of Justinian. This is a round bronze weight presenting the bust of Zemarchus above NOB (72 *nomismata*) and around an inscription in Greek: "In the time of Zemarchus, gloriossus, Eparch of [new] Rome, ex-Consul." The given mass is 309.50 g[39] representing the pass weight of 309.564 g (72 x 4.29975 g). See specification a2.

Coin weights presenting the name of Justinian seem to be quite rare. This suggests that the first specification was used only for a short time. The reason for the weight reduction is given by Bijovsky: "In order to finance his military campaigns and pay tribute to the Persians, enormous quantities of *solidi* were struck throughout Justinian's 38-year reign."[40] The weight reduction was probably ordered by John the Cappadocian who was appointed as prefect of the praetorians in 531 CE. He introduced new taxes and was keen to save the money of the state.[41]

Table a1: Solidi stuck by Justinian I at Thessalonica

(g)	no. of solidi
4.47	i
4.46	ii
4.45	i
4.44	i
4.43	i
4.42	II
4.41	-
4.40	ii
4.39	ii
4.38	i
4.37	iiii
4.36	iii
4.35	iii

Histogram a1 40 coins

n x 0.0559872 g	no. of coins	
80	iii	4.478976 g
79	iiiii ii	
78	iiiii iiiii iiii	4.3670016 g
77	iiiii	
76	iii	
75	iii	4.19904 g
74	i	
73	i	
72	-	
71	i	
67	i	
64	i	

[38] Chris Entwistle and Andrew Meek: ***Early Byzantine Glass Weights: Aspects of Function, Chronology and Composition*** https://researchgate.net/publication/306000319...No. 2

[39] Simon Bendall, ***Byzantine Weights***, London 1996, p. 48 no. 126

[40] Gabriela I. Bijovsky, ***Gold Coin and Small Change: Monetary Circulation in Fifth-Seventh Century Byzantine Palestine***, Trieste 2012, p. 211

[41] John Julius Norwich, ***Byzanz. Der Aufstieg des Oströmischen Reiches***, Augsburg 2000, pp. 226-7

(g)	no. of solidi
4.34	i
4.32	ii
4.31	i
4.28	ii
4.27	-
4.26	i
4.22	i
4.21	i
4.20	i

Below one coin of: 4.17 g, 4.08 g, 4.00 g, 3.77 g, 3.58 g
In total 40 coins

The weight distribution of the solidi struck by Justinian I at Thessalonica for Illyricum and Dalmatia is given in table a1. Obviously the nominal weight of these coins is 4.478976 g. Therefore we can expect that the two coin weights referring to this nominal weight, issued by Zemarchus (see below), concern the solidi struck at Thessalonica. Once we examine histogram a1 we see that these solidi were struck according to specification a3.

	Specification a3	
	N x 0.0559872 g	Grammes
Nominal weight	80	4.478976
Standard weight	78	4.3670016
Lower limit	76	4.2550272
Pass weight	75	4.19904

Zemarchus issued two coin weights which are relevant with respect to the nominal weight of 4.478976 g. Both are round bronze weights and are very similar to the one mentioned above. The first one indicates NIH (18 solidi). Its mass is given as 79.50 g[42] which represents 79.501824 g i.e. 18 solidi of 4.416768 g (71 x 0.062208 g). Thus this weight is related to the solidus of 4.478976 g (72 x 0.062208 g). The second weight indicates NΛS (36 solidi) and its mass is given as 155.86 g which represents 155.8683648 g, i.e. 36 solidi of 4.3296768 g (116 x 0.0373246 g) relating to 4.478976 g (120 x 0.0373248 g).

The a.m. coin weights of Zemarchus concern the solidi struck according to specification a3 but – apart from the nominal weight – do not refer to a weight standard thereof. At first glance this is very surprising. However, the weight standard of 4.416768 g (71 x 0.062208 g) offers a possible explanation. At that time the standard weight of the solidi struck at Constantinople was 4.4415 g (94 x 0.04725 g). This is about a half grain above the weight standard of 4.416768 g. Therefore, it looks as if the weight standard of 4.416768 g was used once solidi struck at Thessalonica were presented to the treasury, i.e. this weight standard was used like the standard weight of 4.4415 g would have been used when solidi struck at Constantinople were involved. The second standard of 4.3296768 g is about one third grain below 4.347 g (92 x 0.04725 g), the lower limit of the solidi

[42] Bendall as footnote 39, no. 128

struck at Constantinople. This suggests that this weight was used as a pass weight once solidi from Thessalonica were presented to the treasury. Thus, it seems that solidi which were not struck to the specification of Constantinople had to comply with special requirements once they were used for paying taxes. The solidi struck at Thessalonica demonstrate that solidi were also struck to other weight standards than the ones struck at Constantinople. The respective coin weights issued by Zemarchus provide a very important example since they show that in addition to the coin weights which were related to the standard and pass weight of the specification[43] official coin weights existed that regulated the weights at which these solidi had to be taken by the treasury. If, in addition, one considers that several kinds of light solidi were struck, the large number of weight standards represented by the coin weights recorded by Henri Pottier[44] and other authors is not at all surprising. The individual weight standards which appear in the coin hoard from Bet She'an, Nikertai and other hoards probably represent coin weights of further weight standards.

Weight standards of the solidus in the time of Tiberius II.

A weight standard which is 6.25 % below the nominal weight is specifically mentioned in a papyrus dated to 580 CE.[45] Since the pass weight of 4.2525 g is 6.25 % below the nominal weight of 4.536 g the papyrus probably refers to this weight standard and thus probably confirms the use of specification a4 at the time of Tiberius II. (578-582 CE).

Specification a4

	n x 0.0567 g	weight (g)
Nominal weight	80	4.536
Standard weight	78	4.4226
Lower limit	76	4.3092
Pass weight	75	4.2525

The standard weight of 4.4226 g is well attested by several coin weights. The pass weight is also attested by coin weights. However, these are not as many as could be expected if specification a4 was an important one. Thus specification a4 may represent a local standard. Further, it may be that a major part of the weights representing 4.4226 are pass weights of 91 x 0.046656 g related to the nominal weight of 4.46656 g (96 x 0.0486 g), the aureus of 1/70 gold pound.[46]

Weight standards of the solidus in the time of Maurice

There is a glass weight of 4.43 g presenting the bust of an eparch and around an inscription in Greek reading: "in the time of eparch Ioannes".[47] According to the authors this means either 550 or 582-602 CE. Since in 550 CE solidi were still struck according to the second specification (a2) of Justinian I (527-565) this weight was used in the time of Maurice (582-602). Probably, this weight represents the standard weight of specification a5.

[43] Coin weights representing the SW of 4.3670016 g and the PW of 4.19904 g are well attested.

[44] Henri Pottier, 'Nouvelle approche de la livre byzantine du Ve au VIIe siècle', in: ***Revue belge de numismatique***, no. 150, 2004, pp. 51-133

[45] Borek as footnote 22, p. 43

[46] The aureus of nominal 4.6656 g was prior to 368 CE used together with the heavy solidus of 4.725 g (see below).

[47] Entwistle and Meek, as footnote 38, no. 18

	Specification a5	
	N x 0.0540 g	Grammes
Nominal weight	84	4.536
Standard weight	82	4.428
Lower limit	80	4.320
Pass weight	79	4.266

Weight standard of the solidus in the time of Heraclius

As mentioned above, the hoards from Bet She'an and Jerusalem demonstrate that at the time of Heraclius (610-641 CE) the standard weight was 4.4064 g (68 x 0.0648 g).

Weight standards of the solidi above the standard weight

In the Louvre there is a weight from the time of Justinian I (532/33 CE) the mass of which is given as 322.51 g.[48] Probably this weight represents 322.5096 g i.e. 72 solidi of 4.4793 g (79 x 0.0567 g). This is a solidus weight which is reduced by one grain compared to the nominal weight of the solidus of 4.536 g (80 x 0.0567 g). Justinian's second standard weight of 4.4415 g is 99.16 % of 4.4793 g. Since 368 CE solidi were struck from fine gold (*obryzum*) with a fineness of ca. 99 %.[49] The relation between the second standard weight of Justinian and the weight standard represented by the weight in the Louvre suggests that the latter standard was used to select solidi that contained the standard weight of 4.4415 g in fine gold. In this case a fineness of 99.16 % was assumed. The weight standard of the solidi of Justin I (518-527) until Tiberius II (578-582) published in catalogues is 4.4712 g[50] and consequently above the standard weights according to which they were struck. It seems that the selection of solidi representing the standard weight in fine gold was a general phenomenon. Table a2 compares the standard weights of Justinian until Maurice with the weight standard of 4.4712 g. In all three cases the selection of solidi of 4.4712 g would guarantee that the weight standard in fine gold would be received once the fineness of the gold was about 99 %.

Table a2

Emperor	Standard weight	% of 4.4712 g
Justinian 2nd standard	4.4415 g	99 1/3
Tiberius II.	4.4226 g	98.91
Maurice	4.428g	99.03

48 „...ein justinianisches Münzgewicht aus dem Louvre von 532/33 wird mit 322,51 g angegeben, ..."
Cornelius Steckner, 'Die offene Rekonstruktion mehrdimensionaler Maßsysteme am Beispiel spätjustinianischer Architektur und Amphorenkeramik', in: Dieter Ahrens und Rolf C. A. Rottländer (eds.) ***Ordo et Mensura IV / V***, St. Katharinen 1998, S. 27. Taken from: Ch. Daremberg – E. Saglio, Dictionnaire des antiquitées greques et romaines, s.v. Exagium, Abb. 2850.

49 Robert Lehmann, Karola Hagemann, Artur Lehmann, 'Der Solidushort der Region Hannover', in: Robert Lehmann and Karola Hagemann (eds.) ***Schatzfunde – Fundmünzen, Numismatik zwischen Archäologie, Kriminalistik und Chemie***, Rahden/Westf. 2019, p.272

50 Dietrich Schnädelbach, 'The Roman/Byzantine and the Islamic Weight Systems – Two sides of the same coin', in: Tony Goodwin (ed.) ***Coinage and History in the Seventh Century Near East Vol. 5***, London, 2016, p. 163

The importance of the weight standard of 4.4712 g is shown by the large number of coin weights representing it (table a2).[51] It is very remarkable that many weights represent simple fractions of the pound of 72 solidi: i.e. 12, 6 and 3 solidi. Thus they may be designed to provide exactly these sums in the increased weight standard for specific purposes.[52] Otherwise these weights may have been used to select exactly these sums from circulation. It is remarkable that there are several other solidus weights in the range between 4.49 g and 4.47 g. These may represent weight standards which were used for the same purpose.

Table a3

Unless otherwise indicated the references are those given by Pottier[53]

Reference		grammes	shape	nominal	calculated weight (g)
BM OA 831		53.64	sq	SOL	53.6544 g = 12 x 4.4712 g
HE 381[54]		53.6	sq	12 SOL	53.6544 g = 12 x 4.4712 g
GN 164[55]		26.80	sq	6 N	26.8272 g = 6 x 4.4712 g
	"Incrustations intactes ou bien conservées" weighing 26.8 g				
MZ II-4124		17.88	ro	4 N	17.8848 g = 4 x 4.4712 g
Bend 99		13.41	sq	3 N	13.4136 g = 3 x 4.4712 g
Bend 100	A 36	13.40	sq	3 N	13.4136 g = 3 x 4.4712 g
			weighing 13.4 g		
MZ III-145		13.40	ro	3 N	13.4136 g = 3 x 4.4712 g
KMK 70481	1601	13.40	ro	3 N	13.4136 g = 3 x 4.4712 g
GN 361[50]		4.47	sq	1 N	4.4712 g

Before 368 CE, when the solidus with a fineness of about 99 % was introduced, solidi were struck to a fineness of about 96 %.[56] Solidi struck from gold of 96 % to a nominal weight of 4.536 g represented solidi of 4.35456 g in fine gold. Thus it was assured that solidi struck to weight standards related to 4.536 g would comply with the respective weight standards related to 4.35456 g in fine gold. The introduction of gold of about 99 % fineness ended this simple system.

Once solidi were hoarded people wanted to make sure that the intended sum was absolutely complete. Therefore a slight additional amount was collected. In the case of the Bet She'an and the Nikertai hoard the added amount is about 1 %. The purpose may have been to assure that the intended sum was available in fine gold. Sometimes, once certain weight standards were involved, people wanted to make sure that the intended weight was present in fine gold. Therefore, slightly increased weight standards were used which would make sure to receive the intended weight in fine gold. The need to avoid losses at one time led to the introduction of the office of the *zygostates*. This is not surprising since gold was very valuable at any time.

---

[51] 4.4712 g (115 x 0.03888 g) is a pass weight to the nominal weight of 4.6656 g (120 x 0.03888 g), the aureus of 1/70 gold pound. Thus it may be that the coin weights were once made to serve as pass weights and were later used to deal with solidi according to the increased weight standard.

[52] They may even have been used like the weights issued by Zemarchus for the solid struck at Thessalonica.

[53] Pottier as footnote 44, p. 106

[54] David Hendin: ***Ancient Scale Weights and Pre-Coinage Currency of the Near East***, Nyack 2007

[55] Matteo Campagnolo, Klaus Weber, ***Poids romano-byzantins et byzantins en alliage cuivreux,*** Collections du Musée d'art et d'histoire – Genève, Genève 2015

[56] R. Lehmann, K. Hagemann, A. Lehmann as footnote 49, p. 271

The enigmatic Minting of Standing Caliph Coins in Jund Qinnasrīn

Ingrid Schulze[1]

Among many others, in 2020 I published a gigantic die chain with Standing Caliph coins from the jund Qinnasrīn. Included in this die chain are mint names such as Ḥalab, Anṭākiya, Tanūkh and – astonishingly – Ḥimṣ.[2] In the meantime, I found new die links and was able to expand this and other die chains. In this way, answers to some of the questions asked in 2020 can be found, such as: Are we dealing with main mints, secondary and separate workshops?[3] My main focus on the remaining questions will be on the 'handwritings' of the die cutters, on the iconography.

I start with some curious die links:

bi-qinnasrīn *bi-ḥimṣ* *ma'arrat miṣrīn* undeciphered

Figure 1

A new link with Ḥimṣ has appeared – this time with Qinnasrīn instead of Ḥalab as usual. The depiction of the caliph fits neither the one nor the other mint, which also applies to the linkage of dies known so far. What led to this cross-jund coinage remains mysterious. The second link shows nonsensical legends on the obverse, but the stylised spelling of the mint name is not unusual, while the second reverse shows an undeciphered word on the left and nothing on the right. The overall crude and incompetent presentation speaks for a small separate workshop.

The same applies to the example in Fig. 2: here, however, the special thing is that Sarmīn is linked for the first time, even with two different reverse dies.

In Fig. 3 we also read *sar*, but the expected *mīn* is replaced by a *wāfīn*. The obverse is strange in that the obviously planned *amīr al-mu'minīn* legend is completely unsuccessful and, moreover, NEVER occurs on coins with the mint name Qinnasrīn. In contrast to these inconsistencies, the caliph's

[1] Ingrid Schulze is an independent scholar ingridschulze@wg-s.de

[2] Schulze (2020) p. 161 fig. 23 and p. 163 fig. 24

[3] For the definition cf. the article of W. Schulze 'Where were the Standing Caliph coins with the mint names Tanūkh and Jibrīn struck?' elsewhere in this volume.

depiction seems to be quite competent. One almost has the impression that we are dealing with products from a small workshop with workers of varying competence.

sarmīn *sarmīn* *ma'arrat miṣrīn*

Figure 2

sar / wāfin

bi-qinnasrīn

Figure 3

This short look at four small isolated die links without further die matches does not help us to understand the coinage in Jund Qinnasrīn. Hence the question: what is typical for a mint, what served as a model and was imitated at times in other workshops?

obverse dies exclusively combined with *bi-qinnasrīn*

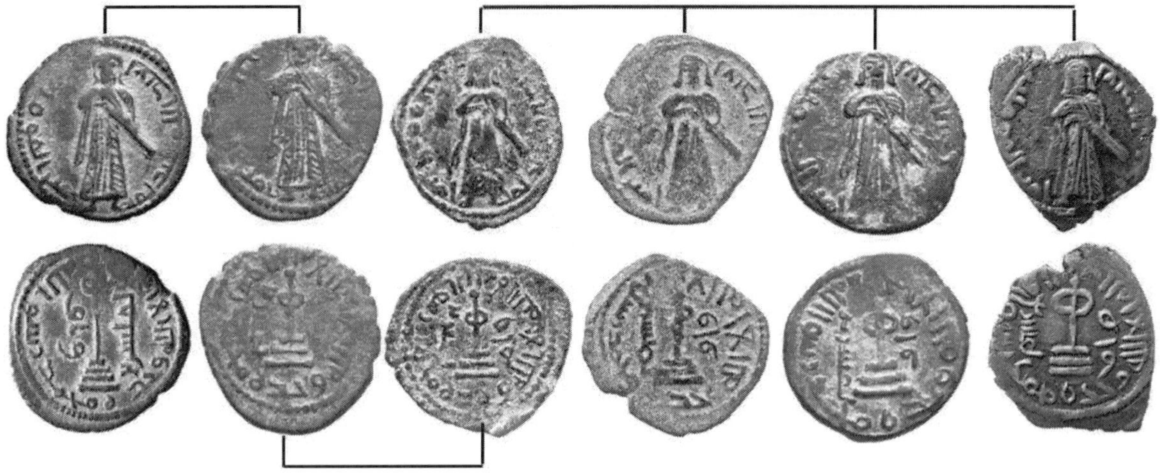

23 2 7 11 4 7

number of specimens recorded so far

Figure 4

One of the most beautiful representations of the caliph is shown on coins with the mint name Qinnasrīn: the figure is carefully worked out and was certainly the model for the second obverse die. The reverses are not quite so well done by the die cutter. They look a little awkward and he obviously had difficulties in placing the word *bi-qinnasrīn*. Presumably there were different die cutters responsible for obverse and reverse dies.

bi-ḥalab rev. legend abbreviated — *bi-qinnasrīn* (retrograde) — *bi-tanūkh* — *bi-tanūkh* — *bi-ḥalab* (retrograde) *wāfin* (retrograde) rev. legend abbreviated

Figure 5

With the obverses in Fig. 5 too, it looks as if the die cutter still had the model in mind, and again he fails with the reverses. Here we are probably dealing with a secondary mint that was oriented towards the Qinnasrīn example and was responsible for several places.

The coins in Fig. 6 show an iconographic contrast and were presumably struck in another secondary mint of Ḥalab. They feature unusual details:

'tippet' and zigzag-streamer / unusual design of the scabbard
blundered legends, partly abbreviated

wāfin retrograde — *ḥalab* ?

Figure 6

Figs 7 and 8 show that the reverses of the coins in Fig. 6 also occur with other obverses, some of which (b and c) are stylistically questionable, while others (a, d, e and f) are still in the conventional style:

Figure 7

Figure 8

Fig. 9 continues with the zigzag-streamers: the production becomes more and more careless, the legends and partly the claimed 'mint names' are hardly readable. At least the first of the *bi-ḥalab* reverses is coupled with an obverse without a zigzag-streamer:

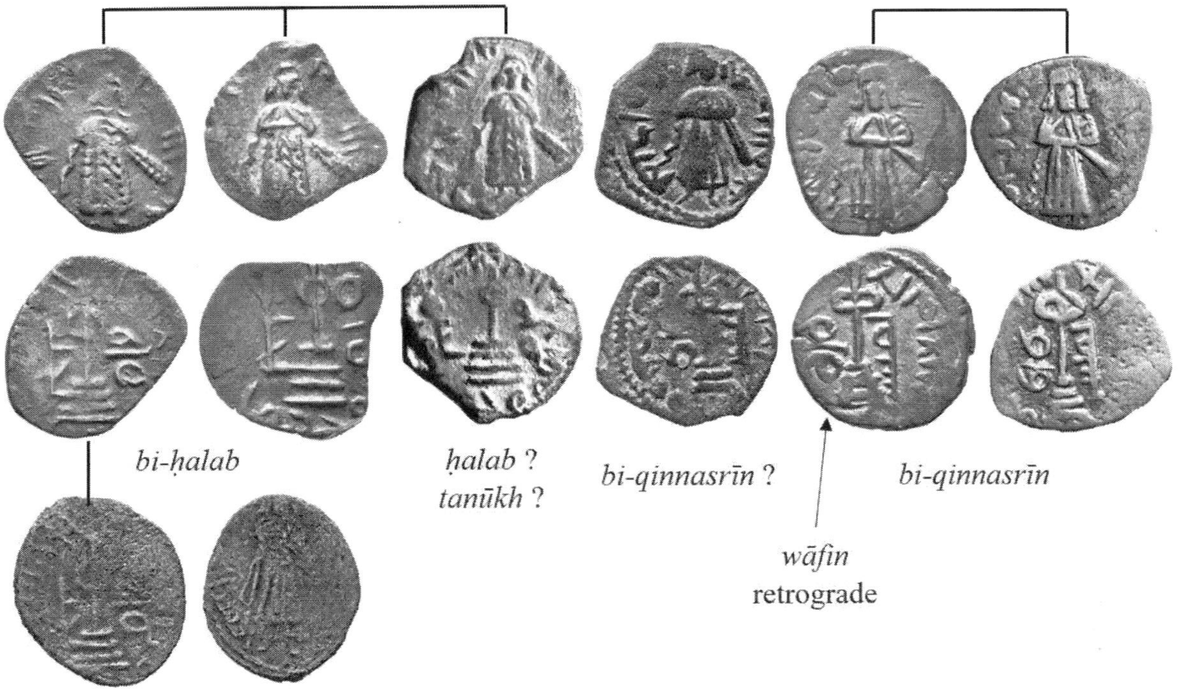

Figure 9

The die cutters of the coins on the preceding figures had a peculiar idea of what they were supposed to do, and they certainly did not work in a main mint.

I used the term 'conventional style' earlier. By this I mean recurring stylistic elements that are familiar to us. I would like to introduce a particularly interesting group:

"chequered sleeves"

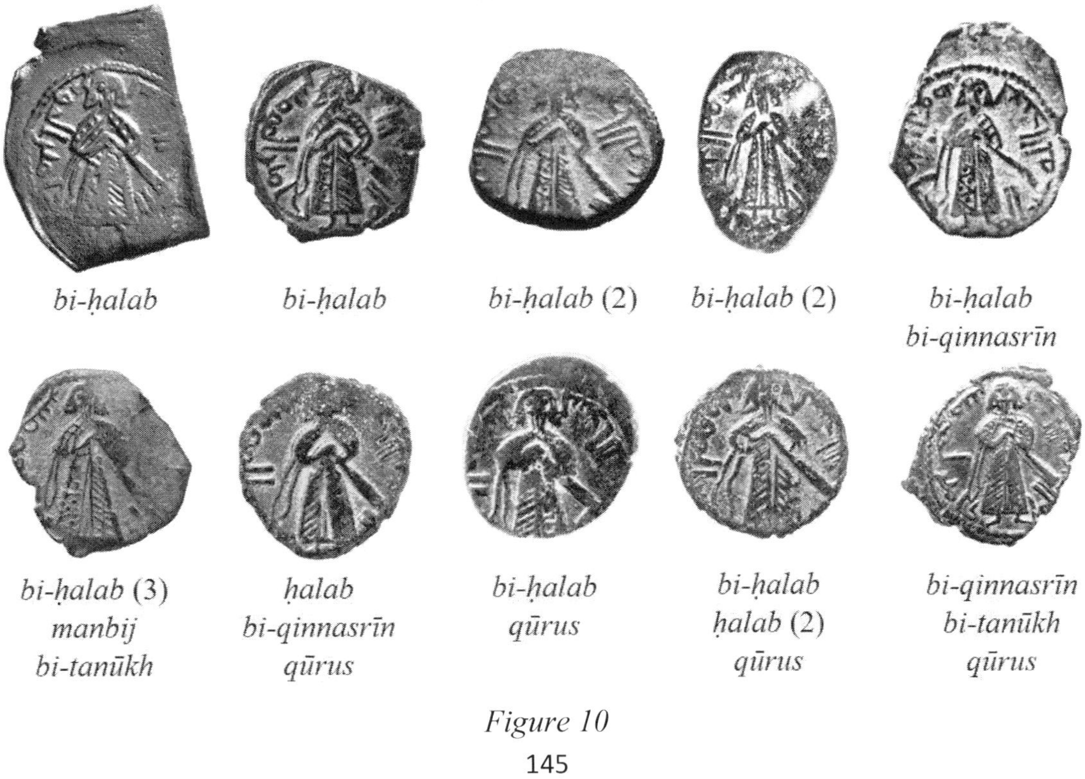

Figure 10

The similarity of the figures is striking, sometimes the dies can only be distinguished by the different positioning of the legend. All five dies in the upper row seem to be made by the same hand. In the lower row changes occur, for example the pattern of the skirt changes. The noted multitude of the ‘mint names’ allows only one interpretation: the pictorial specification comes from a main mint responsible for Ḥalab; this specification was imitated more or less competently in smaller secondary mints and used for several ‘mint names’.

some more “chequered sleeves”

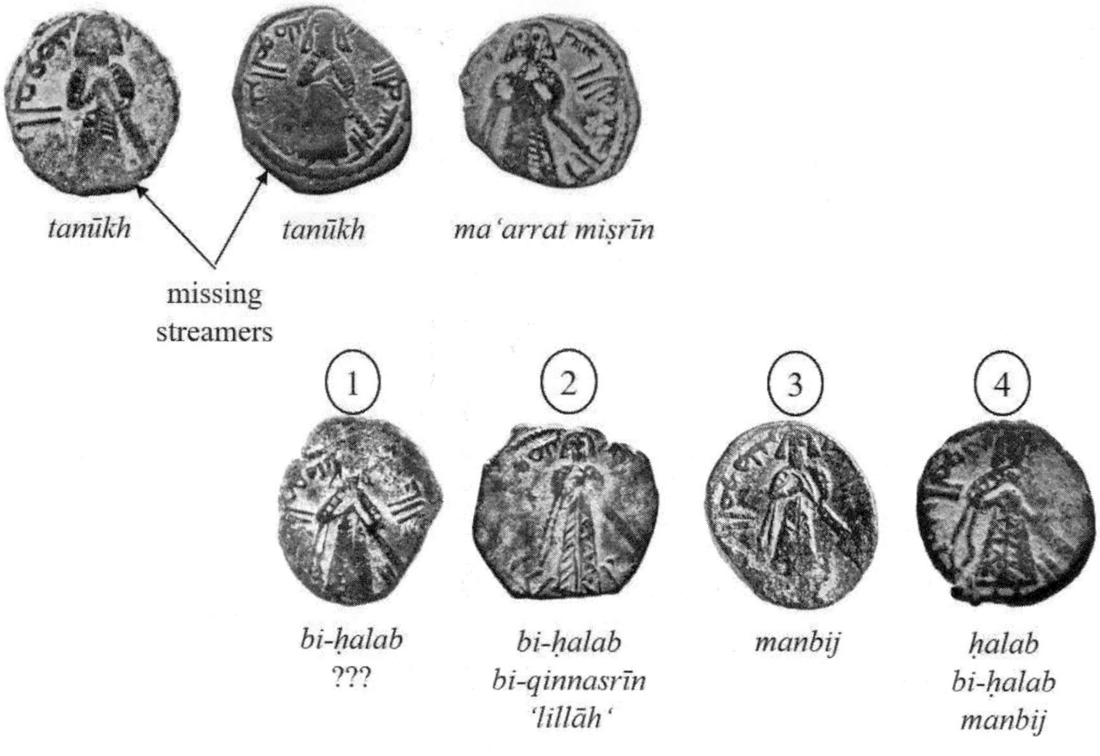

Figure 11

These examples move further and further away from the original. I will now present the last four one after the other:

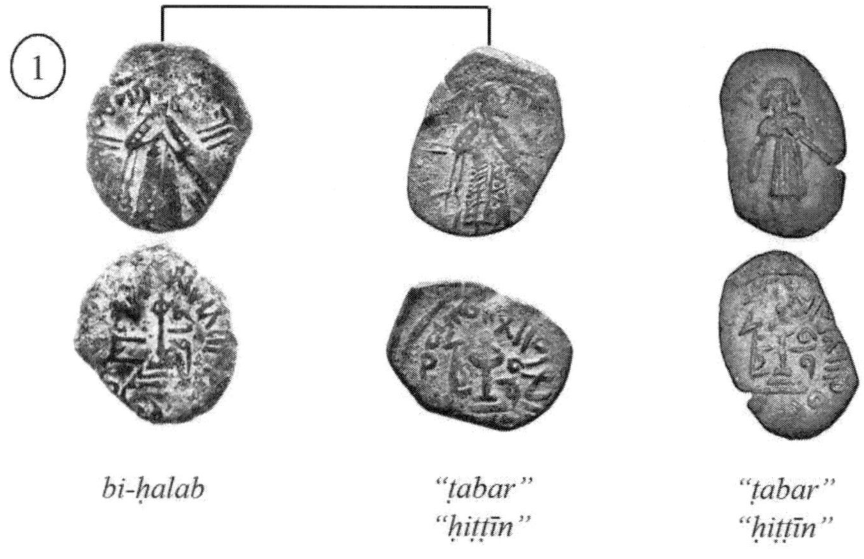

Figure 12

The number 1 from the series was the biggest surprise for me in the compilation of the dies: we see a completely normal *bi-ḥalab* reverse, and on a second coin with the same obverse as 'mint' the word that we have not been able to read or interpret so far: '*ṭabar*'. Tony Goodwin has dealt extensively with this word and the possible meanings,[4] I will not repeat that, especially because Steve Album recently published a '*ḥiṭṭīn*' interpretation.[5] The fact that there are now three dies with this enigmatic name and also a link to Ḥalab confirms Goodwin's assumption that it must be a meaningful name. However, this does not imply that it was a real physical mint. For comparison, on the right the coin with the similar reverse.

Now number 2: the left part of the link has been known for some time,[6] but an addition shows a surprise:

The *lillāh-allāh* Connection

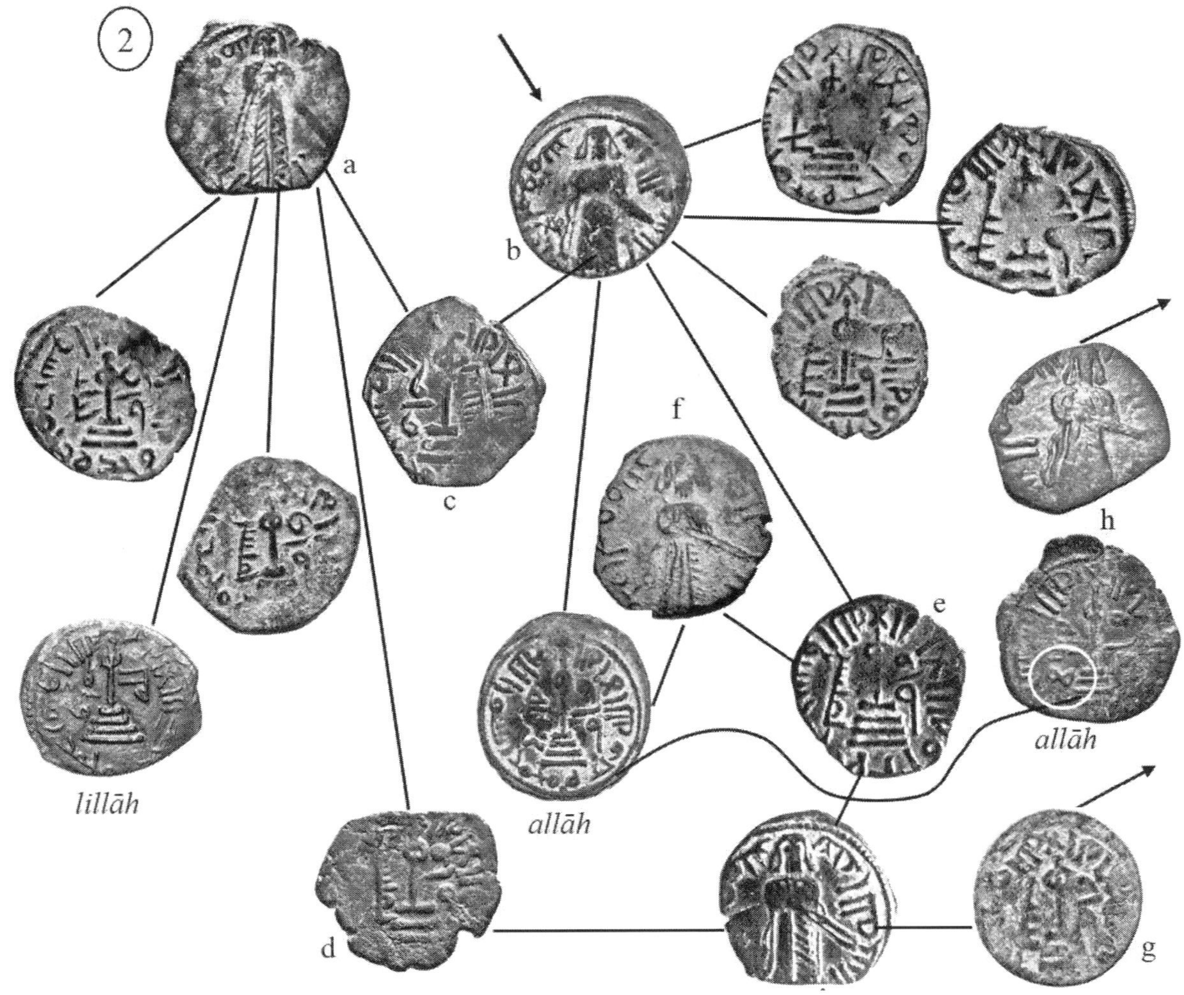

Figure 13

There is another link with a reverse where we read '*allāh*'. And now comes the surprise:
Both obverses (a and b) have a common reverse with *bi-qinnasrīn* (c); thus, both links are connected. But that is not the end of the linkages: two more *bi-qinnasrīn* items (d and e) are added, a new obverse

[4] Goodwin (2017) pp. 152-55; Goodwin (2018) p. 79
[5] Album Auction 43, 05-22, lot 175
[6] Schulze (2015) p. 126 fig. 18; Goodwin (2018) p. 74

link (f), a new reverse (g), and finally another '*allāh*' coin with a new obverse (h) – I will spare you further ramifications (arrows to outside).
However, I would like to point out one more detail: if we look closely at the new '*allāh*' coin (h), we see that there is no correct '*allāh*' at all, but rather a puzzling sign at the beginning (encircled) that does not correspond to any Arabic letter. If you know this coin, you will also see this sign on the first coin. I think we should add a little question mark to the '*allāh*' reading.
So, we have here an interesting network of die connections in which two 'pious' reverses are embedded. Or is the situation not as simple as it looks? Already in my last article I posed the question, precisely for the obverse (b)[7] (arrowed), of whether the coins with the Ḥalab reverse came from a 'main mint' and the die was then further used in a 'secondary mint'.

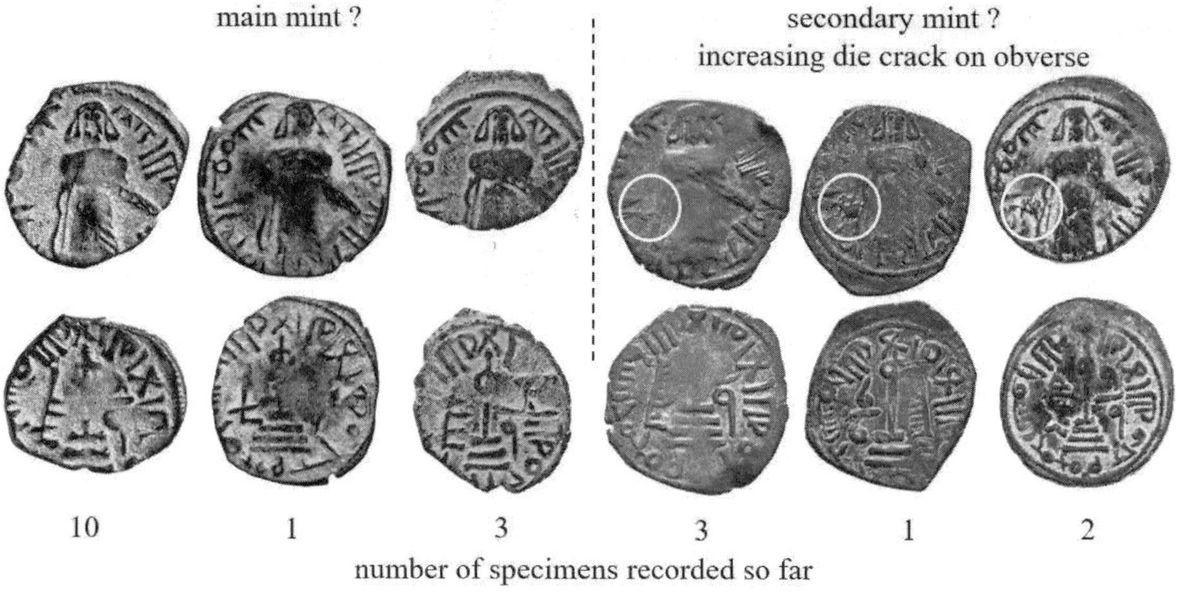

Figure 14

Now with much more material than a few years ago, especially the *allāh* die, which was not known to me at that time, this assumption seems to be confirmed. The die crack on the left of the obverse, which is very clear on some coins, is found exclusively on the specimens showing *bi-qinnasrīn* or *allāh* on the reverse.

As announced above (see Fig. 11), with Fig. 15 we continue with no 3 of the 'chequered sleeves', to an obverse that (so far) is only known with a Manbij reverse. Exactly this reverse is part of a die link that has been known to us for a long time.[8]

[7] Schulze (2020) p. 156 fig. 18
[8] Goodwin (2010) p. 36 fig. 1; Goodwin (2018) p. 43 fig. 4

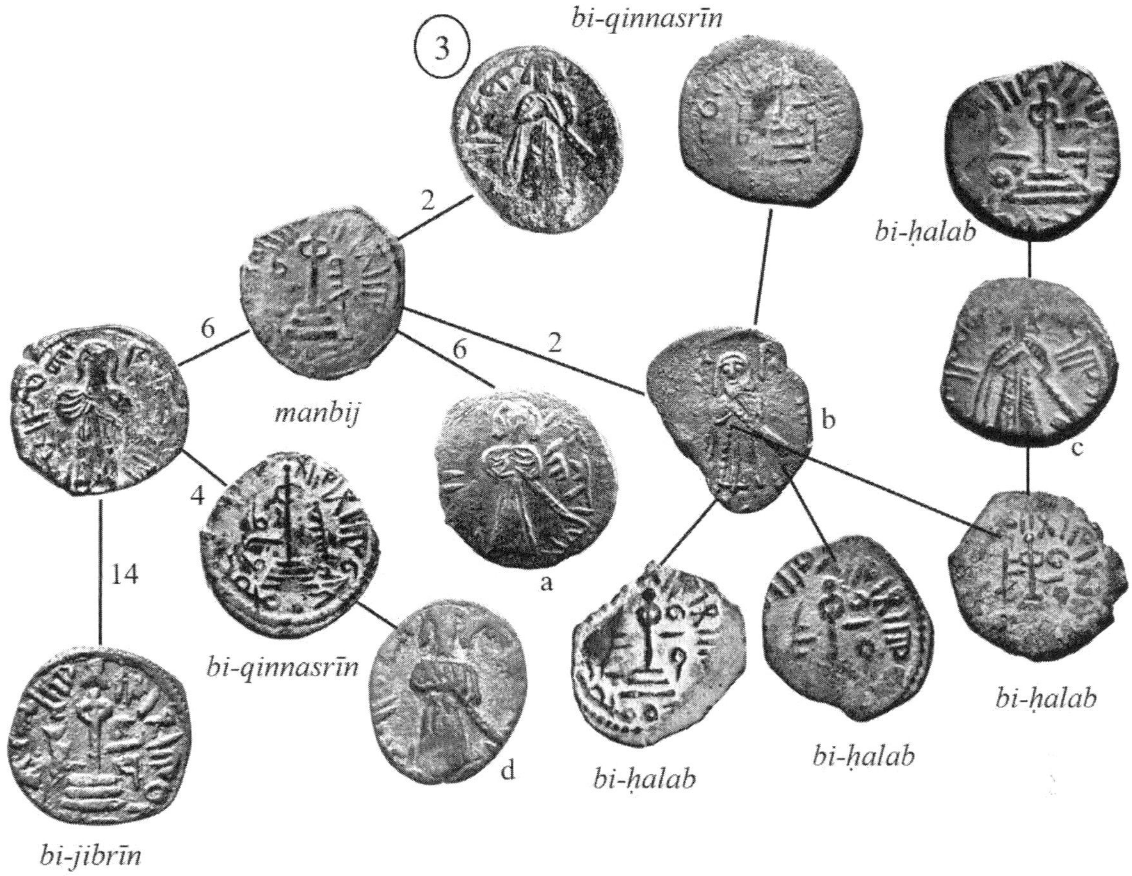

Figure 15

What is interesting here is that most of the coins in this group have the *jibrīn* reverse. Also noteworthy is another obverse (a) paired with the Manbij reverse, of which I found 6 specimens: the die cutter obviously tried to copy the familiar obverse with the prominent shoulders. However, he made a mistake with the legend: he engraved *li-'abd 'abd al-malik*, and when he discovered his mistake, he wrote the missing *allāh* in the field.

Only recently I found another coin (b)with the same Manbij reverse, which was previously known with three different *ḥalab* reverses and a *qinnasrīn* reverse, and curiously, one of the *ḥalab* reverses also exists with a 'chequered sleeves' obverse (c), which in turn has another *ḥalab* reverse. Finally, a new obverse (d) can be added to the *qinnasrīn* reverse of the initial link. Thus, the original link, which until now was about Manbij, gets a new statement: it looks to me as if the entire link comes from a secondary mint of Ḥalab or Qinnasrīn.

We now have four obverses in very different styles with the same Manbij reverse, and at this point I pose the question: what is actually typical for the Manbij coinage?

Fig. 16 shows a selection of Manbij dies of the main type. The iconography is unusual and there is nothing else comparable in jund Qinnasrīn. Remarkable but not unknown is the misspelling on the 2nd and 3rd obverse: the connecting line between *alif* and *mim*.[9]

---

[9] Schulze (2015) p. 127 fig. 20 b

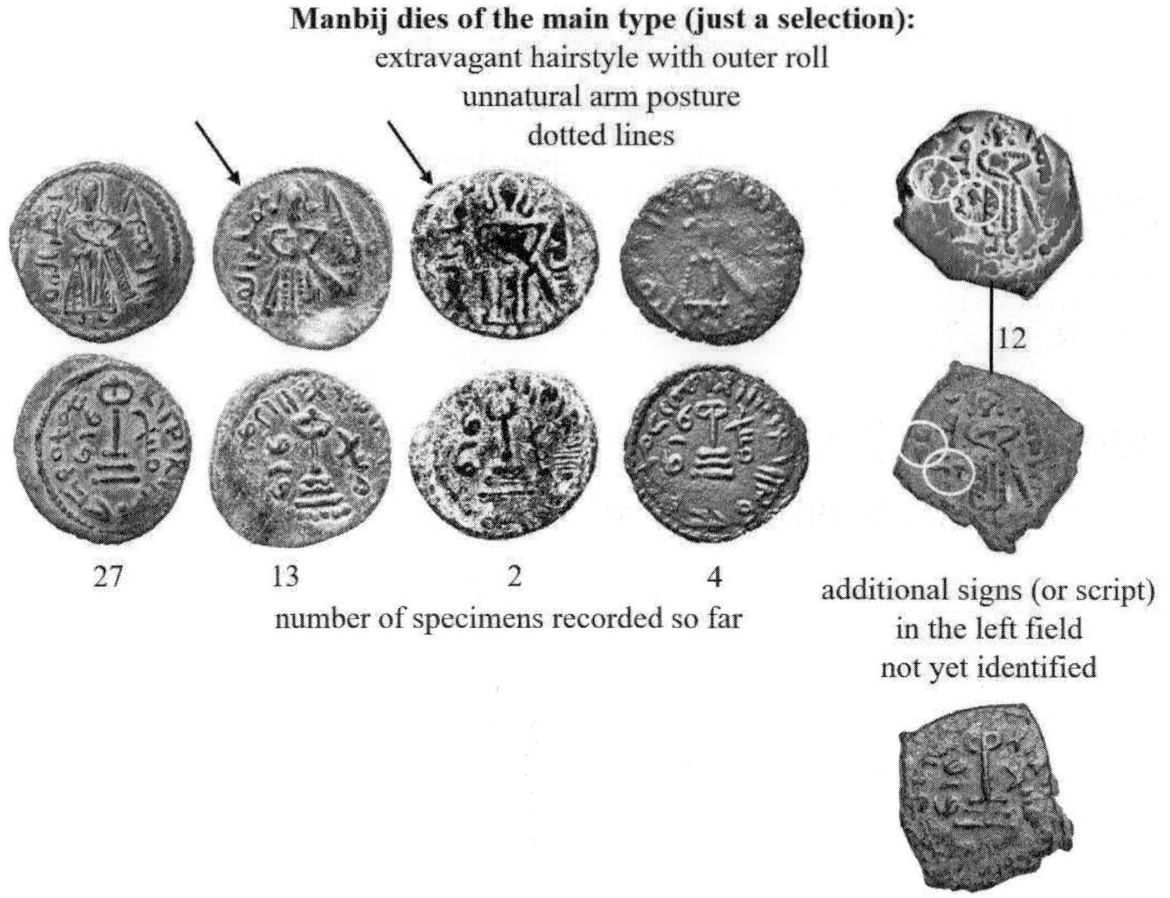

Figure 16

The die chain in Fig. 17 has also been known for some time,[10] but I was able to add another coin (right), and only then noticed a curious detail: the reverses with *manbij* show a cross (left coin) or a star (right coin) instead of the usual *wāfin*. The legends are retrograde.

Fig. 18: It is hardly possible to cut dies more curiously and incorrectly – misspellings, retrograde legends are typical for Manbij! The two coins on the right do not show *manbij* but an illegible word, perhaps *ḥalab*, but judging by style they could well come from the same workshop.

Fig.19 shows some more crude links. Although the 'chequered sleeves' number 4 obverse has a correct legend, the reverses are candidates for a separate workshop with untrained die cutters; the same applies to the second small link, which by style fits neither Manbij nor Jibrīn. Strangely enough, the two *ḥalab* reverses also exist with other obverses showing a star in the right field. Already in 2015 in my article 'Can we believe what is written on the coins?'[11] I pointed out that such additional attributes may have a meaning – an idea that should be treated in another project in the future.

---

[10] Schulze (2015) p. 127 fig. 19
[11] Schulze (2015) pp. 131/2

Crude imitations of the main type

legends partly retrograde and blundered

Figure 17

More crude imitations

Figure 18

Some crude links

Figure 19

The most enigmatic link

Figure 20

Fig. 20 shows a puzzling link which I published, in part, in 2015.[12] It is now possible to expand it and this allows a new interpretation. We see two obverses that are typical for Ma'arrat Miṣrīn. Both have a reverse with the familiar stylised spelling of the mint name (right and left outside) and together they also have the same reverse with a correctly written mint name. It is hard to imagine a more interesting interconnection of the different stylistic features typical of a coinage. So how does this Manbij reverse

[12] Schulze (2015) p. 127 fig. 20 c + d

get in between? As we have just seen, there were some more or less talented die cutters at work in Manbij, why would one ask for two obverse dies in that far away town, which had already been used, as proposed by Goodwin?[13] We can clearly see that the coins with the Manbij reverses do not have worn obverses at all, this means, they have not been discarded and handed in. Did they wander back and forth? I think that is possible, but unlikely. But I am particularly reluctant to imagine that these typical Ma'arrat Miṣrīn obverses circulated in Manbij – they would have been positively exotic there, which to me also applies to the 'chequered sleeves' obverses. Tony Goodwin points out[14] that the Manbij die was probably made by the same engraver who was responsible for the reverse first shown in Fig. 16. I therefore put forward a new theory for discussion: it was the die cutter who travelled, who worked first in Manbij, later in Ma'arrat Miṣrīn, and at his new place of work 'by mistake or habit' cut a false reverse die that never came into use in Manbij, especially since this die in combination with a Manbij-typical obverse is not known so far.

As a small diversion I now present some odd products from a separate workshop with unskilled staff – without further comment.

Crude products of a separate workshop

Figure 21

What follows is a 'stylistic walk'. The initial coins are from Ḥalab, and we are looking for specimens that meet the following criteria:

Main stylistic criteria:
- two separate streamers
- extreme position of the right arm and elbow

Figure 22

[13] Goodwin (2018) p. 42
[14] Goodwin (2018) p. 42

The comparable coins in Fig. 23 show a more or less mutilated *bi-qinnasrīn* on the reverse and the usual *wāfin* is partly replaced by an eight-pointed star. The legends on both obverse and reverse are virtually illegible. Unfortunately, the right coin lacks the streamers, otherwise it fits perfectly into this group, although the mint name looks more like Ḥalab. With one exception, all these coins are (so far) singular, which means, they are not linked.

Figure 23

The exception mentioned is the reverse die of the first coin in Fig. 23, which is also coupled with another obverse (Fig. 24). The iconography of this new obverse die is somewhat different to those in Fig. 23, but with the retrograde legend and two separate streamers it fits in quite well.

Figure 24

Furthermore, I can present in Fig. 25 a duplicate with one coin that can be found in Goodwin's Standing Caliph book under 'uncertain mints';[15] the second small link is already known;[16] and because of the stylistic affiliation to the upper group with extreme position of the right arm and elbow, the 'uncertain mint names' can therefore also be interpreted as a blundered version of *bi-qinnasrīn*:

[15] Goodwin (2018) no 428
[16] Goodwin (2018) p. 78 fig. 34

Figure 25

With the third link in Fig. 26, things get really interesting: twice something like *bi-qinnasrīn* and once *bi-ḥalab*. On the reverses the *wāfin* is back and the star is to be seen on the obverse.
This small link, found under the specification 'two separate streamers and extreme position of the right arm and elbow' brings us right into the middle of the gigantic link that I developed in my last article and partly described as a 'network of incompetence'.[17]

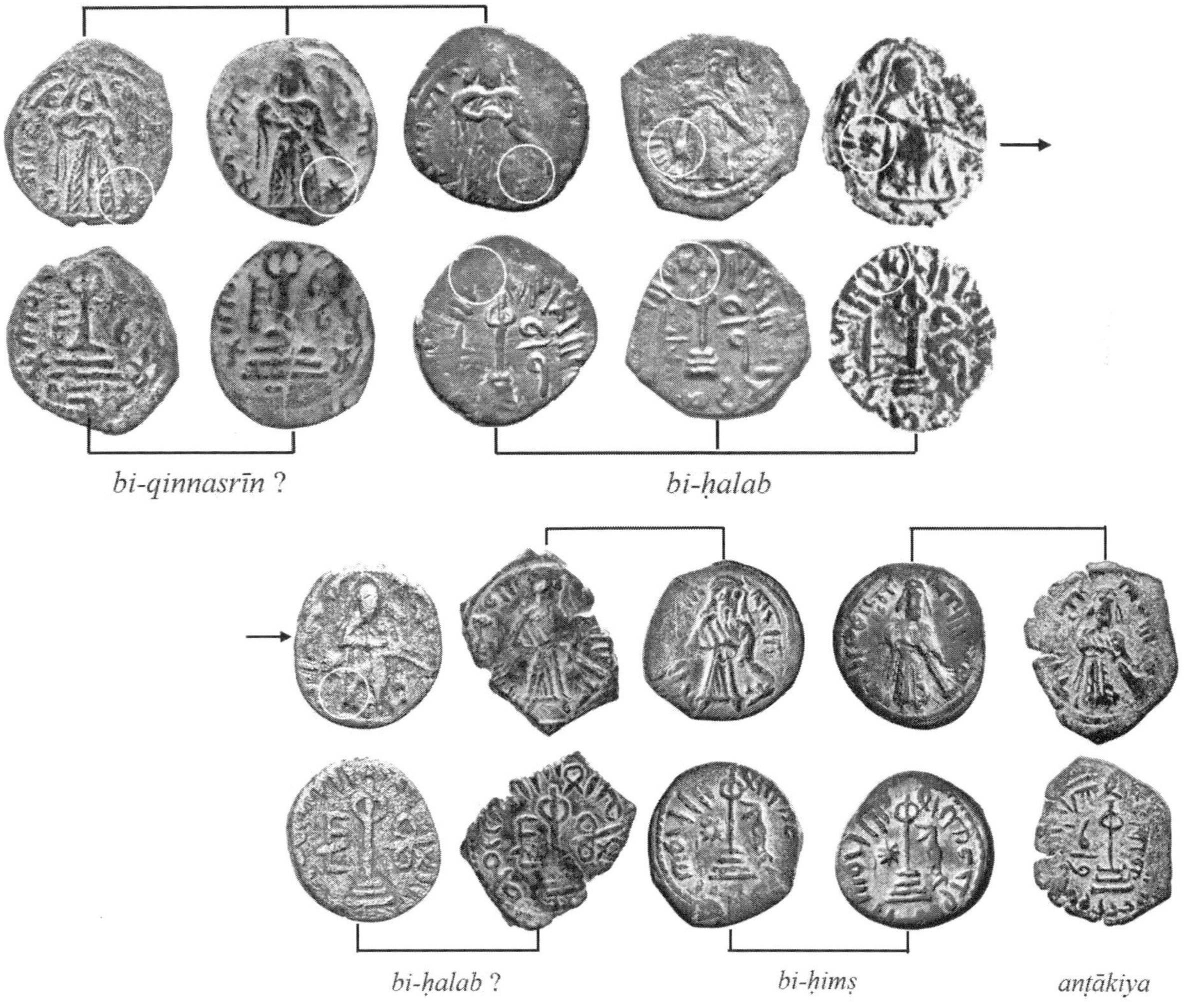

Figure 26

[17] Schulze (2020) p. 157

Fig. 26 is a much-shortened version of the complete die chain as all the linkages can no longer be presented in one diagram. For the full composition I can only refer to figs 20, 23 and 24 of my last article.[18] It was to be expected that more matches would be found, but this one is particularly interesting: firstly, because the new specimens join into the old die chain at the point where a die cutter with a penchant for stars (on both obverse and reverse) was working. Who has imitated whom here? And secondly, because it is the first time that a Qinnasrīn reverse joins the overall link. Obviously, we are dealing with several 'separate mints' between which both personnel and dies were exchanged.

Another small link from the last article[19] (Fig. 27 on the upper right) can also be extended stylistically and will lead us to an astonishing result:

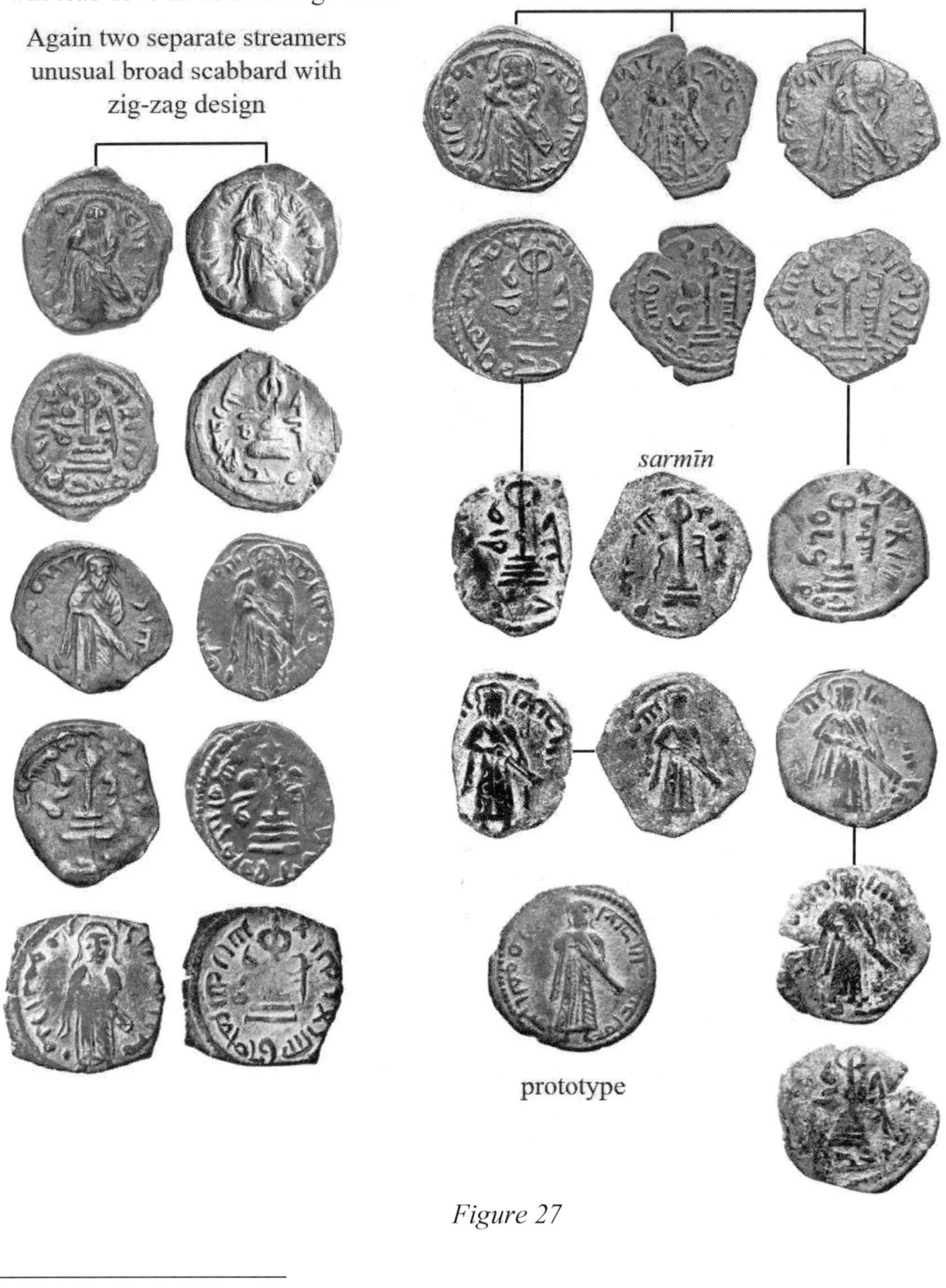

Figure 27

[18] Schulze (2020)
[19] Schulze (2020) p. 156 fig. 19

The greatest stylistic similarity with this crouched, somewhat gnome-like caliph are the specimens on the left that have *ḥalab* on the reverse; the legends are faulty to nonsensical. The coin at the bottom with *bi-ḥalab* is also faulty, but shows a somewhat more pleasing caliph. He could have served as a model. From the initial small link on the right there are some interesting links: to *ḥalab* and to *bi-qinnasrīn*. On the reverse of one of the linked coins we read *sarmīn*! This is a minor sensation in that Sarmīn has not been represented in any chain of dies with different 'mint names' until now, apart from the curious link from a separate workshop on Fig. 2. The prototype for these obverses is quickly found: if one compares the heads with the beard and the slightly wavy hair, it could be that it is the same die cutter who was responsible for the well done Qinnasrīn obverse in Fig. 4. The conclusion might be: the main mint was Qinnasrīn – the further production took place in a secondary mint with untrained die cutters.

Instead of the usual Qinnasrīn reverse with a symbol-on-steps, the series shown in Fig. 28 has a reverse m, a feature otherwise only known on Standing Caliph coins from jund Filasṭīn.

ANS	TG 238	Trade	Trade	Schindel
1998	2018	2016+2020	2022	2016

Figure 28

Sufficient has already been written[20] and speculated[21] about the reverse, instead I focused on the obverse, and discovered that there are some more specimens, unmistakably with the childishly naïve caliph depiction, similarly carelessly struck on irregular flans (Fig. 29). The reverses of these are not pretty, but show a clear *bi-ḥalab*, the symbol-on-steps, and the legend seems to be correct except for the *wāfin* that is retrograde. So, we are again dealing with a workshop that works for both Qinnasrīn and Ḥalab, and at a very low technical level.

Let us have another look at the obverses, which have a special feature: normally the legend is interrupted between 5 and 7h for the hem of the skirt and the feet of the caliph – but here it runs through. I have only found one comparable die and it might well be that it is the same handwriting. The reverses are no surprise: again, we read *bi-ḥalab* and *bi-qinnasrīn* (Fig. 30). Because of the distinctive feature of 'writing under the feet', I think that these coins (Figs 28–30) come from the same workshop.

[20] Goodwin (2018) p. 66 f. and cat. no. 238
[21] Schindel (2016)

bi-ḥalab

Figure 29

bi-ḥalab *bi-qinnasrīn*

Figure 30

Somewhat less distinctive is the writing on another group (Fig. 31 to the left). The slightly tilted posture and the dotted line marking the left side of the skirt are both significant and lead us further to another pair of coins, which we already know from the Manbij-Ḥalab-Qinnasrīn-link (Fig. 15b). Cautiously I place one more coin in this row, because of the slight inclination of the figure, the dotted line, traces of writing under the feet – and the questionable mint name.[22] According to the comparisons made so far, however, there is much to suggest that this so-called '*tabar*' or '*ḥiṭṭīn*' coin comes from the same mint as the other coins.

---

[22] Goodwin (2018) p. 79

bi-ḥalab *bi-ḥalab* *bi-ḥalab* *manbij* *"ṭabar" "ḥiṭṭīn"*

Figure 31

Now I briefly come back to the reverse, where an m replaces the usual symbol-on-steps. This looks highly unusual, but it is not totally unexpected, because occasional examples occur where a normal reverse attribute is replaced by one from a different jund, as in the examples shown below in Fig. 32.

Interchange of typical attributes

m instead of symbol-on-steps

bi-ḥimṣ with *wāfin* instead of star or *ḍarb*

ḥalab with star instead of *wāfin*

Figure 32

Finally, Fig.33 shows again my favourite workshop, the '*epsilon* workshop'. I have already presented the left part of this die link[23] and pointed out that there are some more coins with 'epsilon' and a careful analysis should be done. Of course, I did it, and the result is as follows:

[23] Schulze (2020) p. 159 fig. 21

"*epsilon* workshop"

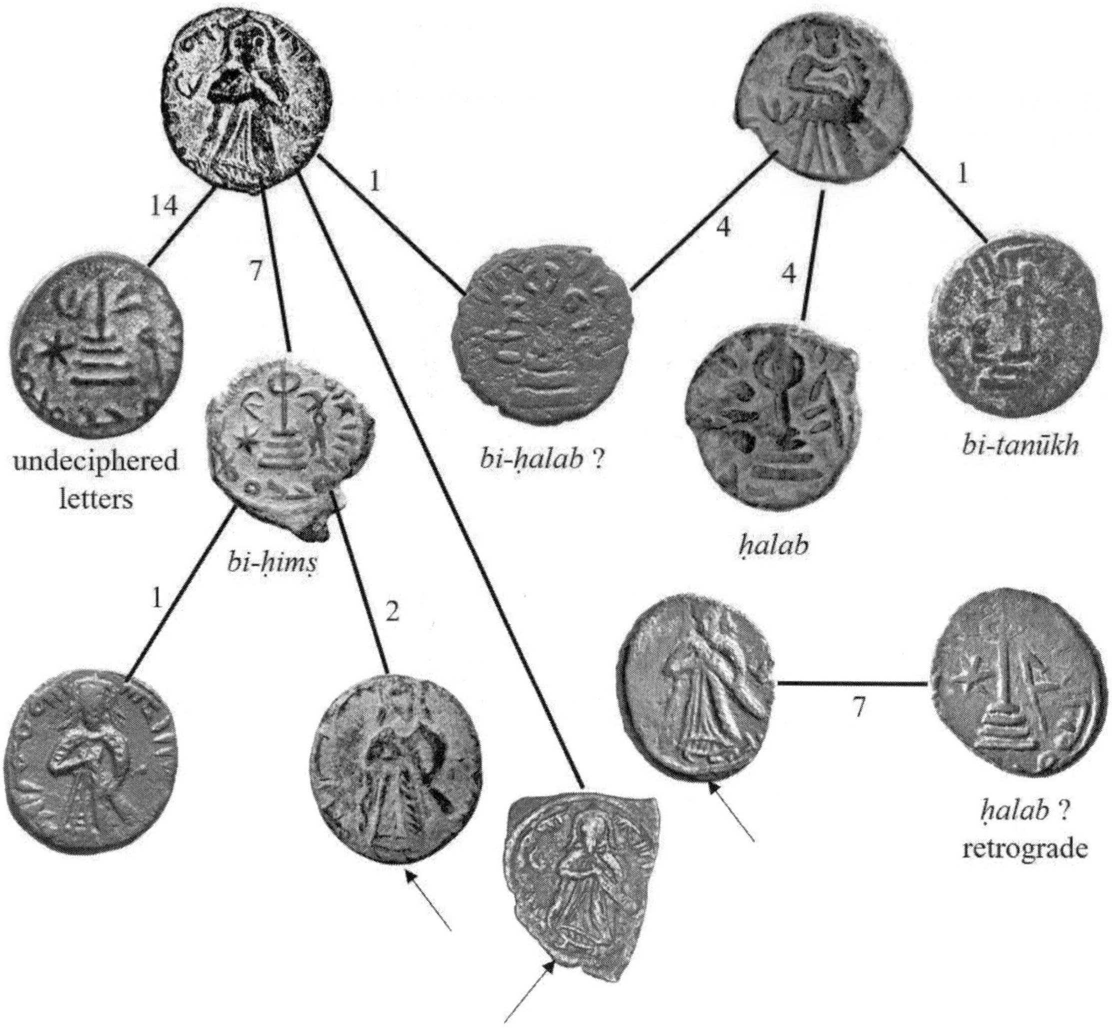

Figure 33

Both 'epsilon' obverses have a common reverse with a somewhat dubious *bi-ḥalab*. There is also a third obverse with a small 'epsilon' in the right field, which could have a retrograde, blundered *ḥalab* on the reverse.[24] A fourth obverse (bottom row, left), which is coupled with the same Ḥimṣ reverse die, fits in well in terms of style. One thing is certain, however: we are dealing with an idiosyncratic die cutter, because this extravagant skirt hem is unique, and particularly curious: feet to the right, feet to the left – here are the dancing caliphs!

I could have extended all the examples, and countless other examples would have been possible – nothing claims to be complete. Nevertheless, I hope I was able to convey with my selection how exciting it is when we follow more the iconography of the obverses instead of stubbornly sorting by 'mint names', because this opens up new points of view. Of course, there have been 'main mints' with their own style – as shown for example for Manbij, and of course there have been main mints for Ḥalab and Qinnasrīn, but alongside them and complementing them, there has been a whole network of smaller workshops working at different levels for several places. At this point I can only

[24] Walker (1956) no. 117; Goodwin (2018) no. 432

repeat my good advice from 2015: 'never believe at first glance in the mint name which is written on an early Umayyad coin'.[25]
Every time I thought 'now I'll finish the work on the paper' new interesting dies appeared on the market. Two of the last discoveries will be presented as conclusion of this article.
The first one is a link between Ḥalab and Ḥimṣ, remarkable because here, for the first time, the obverses seem to come from a main mint:

bi-ḥimṣ *ḥalab*

Figure 34

and in contrast to this finally a last example with a very atypical presentation of the caliph, not unusual for a separate workshop:

Figure 35

[25] Schulze (2015) p. 131

Bibliography

Goodwin, T., 2010, 'Die Links between Standing Caliph Mints in Jund Qinnasrīn' in ***Coinage and History in the Seventh Century Near East* 2** (A. Oddy ed.), London, pp. 35–40.

Goodwin, T., 2017, '"Tabar" – a new Standing Caliph Mint?' in ***Coinage and History in the Seventh Century Near East* 5** (T. Goodwin ed.), London, pp. 152–155.

Goodwin, T., 2018, ***The Standing Caliph Coinage***, London.

Schindel, N., 2016, 'An unusual "Standing Caliph" fals' in ***Journal of the Oriental Numismatic Society* 228**, pp. 15–17.

Schulze, I., 2015, 'Can we believe what is written on the coins? Enigmatic die links and other puzzles' in ***Coinage and History in the Seventh Century Near East* 4** (A. Oddy, I. Schulze and W. Schulze eds), London, pp. 115–136.

Schulze, I., 2020, 'Die Chains and Die Links with the Mint Name Ḥalab' in ***Coinage and History in the Seventh Century Near East* 6** (T. Goodwin ed.), London, pp. 143–164.

Walker, J., 1956, ***A Catalogue of the Arab-Byzantine and Post-Reform Umaiyad Coins*** (A Catalogue of the Muḥammadan Coins in the British Museum Volume II), London.

Where were the Standing Caliph coins with the mint names Tanūkh and Jibrīn struck?

Wolfgang Schulze[1]

With this article I follow in the tracks of Ingrid Schulze's paper 'The enigmatic minting of Standing Caliph coins in Jund Qinnasrīn'[2] and that of Lutz Ilisch, who gave at the Seventh Century Syria Numismatic Round Table at the University Birmingham in November 2002 a paper with the title 'Mints and minting rights for copper coinage in jund Qinnasrīn in the early Islamic period'. In this paper Ilisch touched on the same questions posed in my title.[3]

To date, nine mint names for Standing Caliph coins from jund Qinnasrīn have been clearly identified. These are from North to South: Qūrus, Jibrīn, Manbij, Anṭākiya, Ḥalab, Qinnasrīn, Tanūkh, Ma'arrat Miṣrīn and Sarmīn.

Here you can see eight of them on a map, originally produced for SICA 1 and updated by adding the mint name Anṭākiya[4] and writing Jibrīn's full name 'Jibrīn Qurasṭāyā.

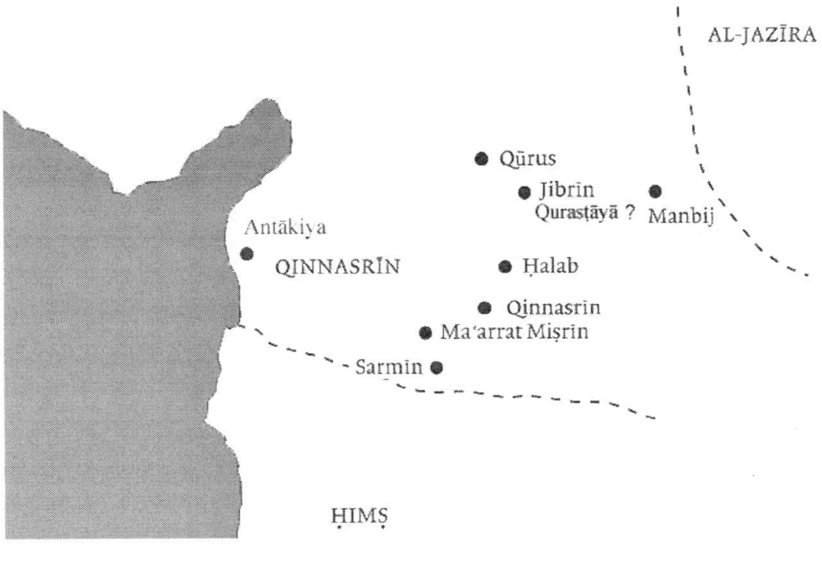

Figure 1: The previously locally assigned mint names

Certainly, one can see that the place for Jibrīn still has a question mark, and for Tanūkh there is no place written on the map because the Tanūkh were a Bedouin tribe and there is no city with this name.

[1] Wolfgang Schulze is an independent scholar schulze@wg-s.de

[2] Elsewhere in this volume.
[3] Unfortunately, Ilisch's paper was never published and exists only as an uncompleted manuscript.
[4] Schulze, W., 2017a.

In addition, for the jund Qinnasrīn a lot of Standing Caliph coins with questionable[5], undeciphered mint names or without any mint name are known.[6]
Based on intensive die studies of the Standing Caliph coins in jund Qinnasrīn, Ingrid Schulze has concluded that the mints just shown were not all physically existing establishments which manufactured coins. What we are reading on the coins are in many cases only 'mint names' produced by a multitude of larger or smaller workshops in the Ḥalab/Qinnasrīn region. This insight of Ingrid Schulze, which has now been confirmed by die studies, coincides with Ilisch's 2002 thesis of 'an administratively illogical but historically reasonable mint network, reflecting the incorporation of a private coin production into a state controlled coin production.'[7] It is interesting to note that this network of smaller mints had easy access to copper, as copper mines were located near Ḥalab at mount Jawshan (now in the western local area of Ḥalab).[8] Finally, the statement that 'in jund Qinnasrīn larger mints, namely Ḥalab and Qinnasrīn, struck coins for and in the name of other places', which I have published several times,[9] is confirmed.

After all this, the question remains where the coins with the mint name Tanūkh were struck.

a

b

Figure 2: Standing Caliph coins with the mint name Tanūkh.
Schulze collection 19.5 x 21.5mm 2.92g(a) and 12h and 20mm, 3.39g 8h (b) [10]

Before starting with explanations where the Tanūkh lived, some words about the jund[11], the administration district, of Qinnasrīn are necessary. After the Arab conquest Qinnasrīn (the classical Chalcis ad Belum) and its districts belonged to Ḥimṣ until Mu'āwiya (governor of Syria since 643 and caliph from 661 to 680) separated Qinnasrīn, Anṭākiya and Manbij and their surroundings as a new jund with Qinnasrīn as the main town of a military district.[12] Qinnasrīn became an army camp, a garrison for mercenaries and tribal warriors, and was starting point for longer war trains to the north. Ḥalab (the classical Beroea) remained less important than Qinnasrīn. In this connection it may be relevant that, after the Arab conquest of Syria, Ḥalab's walls and the citadel were in ruins due to an

---

[5] 'Ḥiṭṭīn', this mint name was first noted in 1996 in Stephen Album's list 123 no. 69; he read it as Ḥiṭṭīn and equated the mint with the location of the famous Crusader battle near the Sea of Galilee. A second specimen appeared in a Morten and Eden auction in 2015 (23.4.15 lot 4) where the mint name was read as 'bi-tabar' for Ṭabarīya. In 2017 (pp. 53-4) and 2018 (p. 79) Goodwin rejected this reading as the first letter was clearly not 'b' and pointed out that the coins must have been minted in jund Qinnasrīn. Subsequently Album (auction 43, May 2022, lot 175) has suggested a different location for Ḥiṭṭīn in Syria located just northwest of al-Raqqa, at the eastern edge of the jund Qinnasrīn. In any case, it is a coinage from the jund Qinnasrīn, possibly struck by a small workshop in the Ḥalab region.
Another question mark is connected with the mint name Sinjār, whose geographical position in jund Ḥimṣ near the border to jund Qinnasrīn is not secured (Cf. Goodwin 2012). However, the Standing Caliph coins with this mint name probably belong to a small workshop in jund Ḥimṣ. This is due to stylistic considerations and the absence of the *wāfin* typical for the Standing Caliph coins in jund Qinnasrīn.
[6] Cf. for example the broader articles of Schulze, I., 2015, 2020 and in this volume.
[7] Ilisch 2002.
[8] Yākūt II, p. 156. Compare also Goldziher 1971, p. 302.
[9] Schulze, W. 2017a, p. 138; 2017b, p. 147 and 2020, p. 168.
[10] All coins presented in this article are shown slightly enlarged.
[11] It is possible that the term jund did not come into use before the reign of the 'Abbasids, but it is used here according to common usage.
[12] Haase 1975, p. 37.

earthquake.[13] It was not until the 8th century that al-Walīd (705-715) or Sulaymān (715-717) had a Friday Mosque built here again.[14] So at the time we are talking about here, Ḥalab was in ruins and, as we shall see, a new Ḥalab arose in the nearby Ḥāḍir Ḥalab.

Regarding Qinnasrīn 'there are reports that Mu'āwiya's son, Yazīd I (caliph 680-683), "destroyed the walls of the city" and "built the capital of the jund in 680". A cursory excavation of Chalcis in 1990 begins to explain this apparent confusion. The classical site had very few Islamic artifacts, suggesting that Islamic Qinnasrīn should be sought elsewhere. Yazīd had dismantled Byzantine defences of the old city and built a new military headquarter and capital (i.e., a miṣr)'.[15]
Where was this 'new' Qinnasrīn situated? The answer to this question results from an archaeological excavation under the leadership of Donald Whitcomb during the years 1998-2002, when the remains of Ḥāḍir Qinnasrīn, situated four kilometres to the east of the classical Qinnasrīn (Chalcis ad Belum) were excavated.

Figure 3: Detail of a map of northern Syria according to the information provided by the Arab geographer Izz al-Dīn ibn Šhaddād (13th century)

Ross Burns describes a Ḥāḍir as 'an area apparently reserved as an encampment for visiting Arab groups.[16] But it is evidently much more. It means a campsite for Arabic semi-nomads. 'Ḥāḍir is rather similar to a town with markets and stone buildings in which the children and elderly people of the half sedentary Bedouins live permanently while from spring to autumn the major part of the population would be migrating with their sheep and cattle'.[17] Qinnasrīn, Ḥalab and other classical cities had such Arab camps already in pre-Islamic times. The Ḥāḍirs also 'are frequently described as transient assembly points for the great commercial caravans and their inhabitants as Bedouin organized caravaneers…The Ḥāḍir was an ethnic suburb inhabited by Arab tribesmen'.[18] During Umayyad rule this Ḥāḍir Qinnasrīn developed from a tribal encampment (ḥirah) to a permanent settlement of late antiquity (ḥāḍir) and to an Islamic town (miṣr) and functioned as the obvious focal point for the new administration.[19]

All of this means that we have to say goodbye to the idea that the classical Qinnasrīn was the Umayyad administrative metropolis. Instead, the new administrative centre in nearby Ḥāḍir Qinnasrīn was created.[20] When I am speaking of Qinnasrīn later in this paper, I am referring to this new foundation.

[13] Haase 1975, p. +17.
[14] Haase 1975, p. +17.
[15] Whitcomb 1998–1999, p. 78.
[16] Burns 2016, p. 76.
[17] Ilisch 2002.
[18] Whitcomb 1998–1999, p. 79.
[19] Walmsley 2007, p. 80.
[20] This corresponds to the somewhat inaccurate description of the new Qinnasrīn by Kennedy 2007, p. 87: 'The Arabs settled outside the walls in what was effectively a new suburb, not in the city itself.'

Who were the Arabs living in Ḥāḍir Qinnasrīn? Al-Balādhurī, the 9th-century Muslim historian, reports: 'The Ḥāḍir Qinnasrīn had been settled by the Tanūkh tribe since they came to Syria and pitched their tents in it. They later built their houses in it.'[21] These sentences are describing 'the movement from pastoral peasantry and ultimately toward tribal urbanities'.[22] This development was in the spirit of new rulers. Al-Balādhuri reports: 'When Mu'āwiyah ruled over Syria and Mesopotamia in the name of 'Uthmān ibn 'Affān he was instructed by him to settle the Arabs in places far from the cities and villages, and allow them to utilize the lands unpossessed by anyone.'[23]

The Christian Tanūkhids fought with the Byzantines against the Muslims. After the battle of Yarmouk, their status as foederati ended. They were described as an autonomous Christian community in Bilād al-Shām. Since around 600 they shared the campsite Ḥāḍir Qinnasrīn with the Ṭaiyi' tribe[24], whose pastures were farther south at the end of the 7th century:

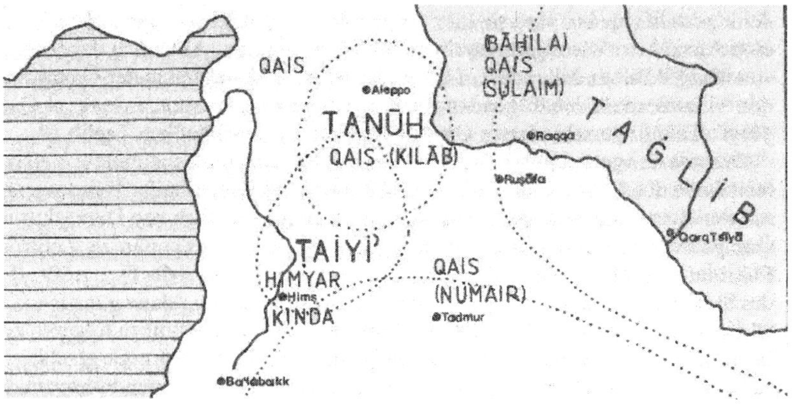

Figure 4: Arab tribes at the time of the second civil war after Rotter 1982[25]

The Ṭaiyi' Bedouins belonged to the Tanūkh confederation.[26]

In summary, it can be said that Qinnasrīn was created as a new city in the area populated by the semi-nomadic Tanūkh and other Arab people.[27] Ḥāḍir Qinnasrīn is not to be confused with al-Ḥāḍir, another Umayyad settlement a few kilometres east of classic Qinnasrīn, which was probably settled by tribes from Iraq.[28]
This 'new' Qinnasrīn became the only capital of a newly established military district; in other junds the old provincial capital was maintained.[29]

It does not seem absurd to assume that the Standing Caliph coins with the mint name Qinnasrīn were minted here. However, the question arises whether the Tanūkh coins also were struck at this place. After all, Qinnasrīn originated as miṣr in the 7th century in an area that was settled by the Tanūkhids long before the Arab conquest. For this reason, it is obvious to look for the mint of the Tanūkh Standing Caliph coins here.
This hypothesis could be confirmed by die-links between coins of Qinnasrīn and Tanūkh (see below).

---

[21] al-Balādhurī 145 (p. 223).
[22] Whitcomb 2006, p. 32.
[23] al-Balādhurī 178 (p. 278).
[24] Haase 1975, p. +16.
[25] Excerpt of Rotter 1982, p. 127.
[26] For this reason, Izz al-Dīn ibn Šhaddād (p. 27) reports Ḥāḍir Qinnasrīn also as Ḥāḍir Ṭaiyi'.
[27] It is interesting to note, that during the excavations very special buildings were discovered that were similar in shape to the tents used by the tribes. Whitcomb 2006, p. 30.
[28] The French excavations in al-Ḥāḍir between 2003 and 2007 only resulted in settlement remains from the Umayyads to the Ayyubids. Cf. Rousset 2012, esp. pp. 11–17.
[29] Haase 1975, p. +38.

However, Ḥāḍir Qinnasrīn was not the only place where the Tanūkh had pitched their tents. Al-Balādhurī reports for the time shortly after the Arab conquest of Syria: 'Close to the city of Aleppo stood a settlement called Ḥāḍir Ḥalab in which different Arab tribes including Tanūkhids lived.'[30] It was a settlement comparable to Ḥāḍir Qinnasrīn. Ḥāḍir Ḥalab was near to Ḥalab[31] – only 'an arrow-shot to the south-west'.[32] Later, in the 13th century, Ḥāḍir Ḥalab became a suburb of Ḥalab.

In his 2002 paper Lutz Ilisch made several proposals for a place where the Tanūkh Standing Caliph coins could have been minted. His favourite site is Ḥāḍir Ḥalab.[33]
What can the coins tell us about this problem? The mint of Ḥalab was certainly very active in jund Qinnasrīn. The Standing Caliph coins of Ḥalab are the most common in jund Qinnasrīn followed by Qinnasrīn itself. So far the following die links have been found for Ḥalab:

- Ḥalab – Qinnasrīn (1)
- Ḥalab – Qinnasrīn (2)
- Ḥalab – Qinnasrīn (3)
- Ḥalab – Qinnasrīn (4)
- Ḥalab – Qinnasrīn (5)
- Ḥalab – Qinnasrīn – lillāh – allāh
- Ḥalab – Qinnasrīn – Qūrus – Tanūkh
- Ḥalab – Qinnasrīn – undeciphered mint name
- Ḥalab – Manbij
- Ḥalab – Manbij – Tanūkh
- Ḥalab – Jibrīn
- Ḥalab – Anṭākiya – Hims
- Ḥalab – Tanūkh – undeciphered mint name – Hims
- Ḥalab – Tanūkh (1)
- Ḥalab – Tanūkh (2)
- Ḥalab – Tanūkh (3)
- Ḥalab – Tanūkh – Anṭākiya

Figure 5: Ḥalab Standing Caliph coins and some of their die links

These are by no means all die links in the Standing Caliph series of jund Qinnasrīn. But this excerpt alone gives a confusing picture. The overall picture is chaotic, and the frequent interlocking between Ḥalab and Qinnasrīn is conspicuous.

Minting of coins in jund Qinnasrīn under Umayyad rule initially was limited to the production of Phase 1 (Pseudo-Byzantine) coins until the introduction of the Standing Caliph coins. In contrast to other junds Phase 2 coins were never minted. This means that a lot of workshops minted crude imitations after Byzantine models. It is known that during Umayyad rule the money circulation was complemented by Roman, Byzantine and other foreign coins, which sometimes had circulated for several hundred years. These old coins – occasionally plain metals pieces, but mostly worn minimi –

[30] Al-Balādhurī 145 (p. 224).
[31] Haase 1975, p. +16.
[32] Le Strange 1890, p. 445 (keyword: Hādir Kalb).
[33] Ilisch 2002 appendix.

formed together with the Phase 1 coins the currency for daily trade[34] [35], which evidently was sufficient for the jund Qinnasrīn up to the introduction of the Standing Caliph coins in the early 690s.
With the first money reform of ‘Abd al-Malik the basic design of the Standing Caliph coppers was prescribed by the administration in Damascus. In contrast to gold and silver coins, providing the population with copper coins was under the responsibility of governors, emirs or bishops.[36] These were responsible for the so-called main mints. Occasionally the right of minting was leased to private entrepreneurs. The output of coins was depending on the demand. Such ‘private mints’ are called secondary workshops.[37] While the secondary workshops still basically adhered to general guidelines, there were also those among them which produced more or less nonsense. We call these separate mints.
I assume that the mints of the jund-capital Qinnasrīn and of the important Ḥāḍir Ḥalab were controlled by the governor. Furthermore, it seems as if both also made coins for and in the name of other places, such as for example Qūrus.[38] It remains unclear whether the mints with the larger output worked continuously.

Since the time of Mu‘āwiya the jund Qinnasrīn was the deployment area for the more or less regular invasions (ghazw) of the Umayyads to the north into Byzantine territory.[39] For these ghazw constantly changing starting camps were needed, to which one could also return. For example, al-Balādhurī mentions that a leader named Salmān b. Rabī had his camp in Qūrus.[40] In such a situation there was a sudden increased demand for small change. The problem could be solved by minting coins with the name of such camps, for example in the case of Qūrus by the Qinnasrīn and Ḥalab mints.

In the meantime, we know that in the region Qinnasrīn/Ḥalab there was a whole series of such temporary workshops. There are different reasons conceivable. On the one hand, as already mentioned, the constantly changing population density could have played a role. On the other hand the Umayyad administration might have given licenses to institutional or private individuals for pecuniary, political or economic reasons. For example, the coins with the mint name of the predominantly Christian Tanūkh may have been struck under responsibility of their bishop. And thirdly, the proximity to the copper mines of mount Jawshan in the neighbourhood of Ḥalab was favourable for the operation of mints.
After all these considerations, the Standing Caliph coins with the mint name Tanūkh and their die links should be examined for their meaningfulness. They can be summarized in this way:

---

[34] Bijovsky 2012, p. 3 and Foss 2015, p. 954. That this phenomenon lasted until the end of the Umayyad rule in 750 can be proved by the coins found in Umayyad houses which were destroyed in Jerash during the earthquake of 749 and never touched until they were excavated by the Danish-German Jerash Northwest Quarter Project in 2012–2016. Cf. Schulze and Schulze 2018 and 2020.
[35] That this phenomenon lasted until the end of the Umayyad rule in 750 can be proved by the coins found in Umayyad houses which were destroyed in Jerash during the earthquake of 749 and never touched until they were excavated by the Danish-German Jerash Northwest Quarter Project in 2012–2016. Cf. Schulze and Schulze 2018 and 2020.
[36] Heidemann 2002, pp. 353–63; Ilisch 2010, p. 129 and 2016, p. 252.
[37] This terminology avoids the previously used and sometimes misleading terms such as ‘semi-official’, ‘irregular’ or ‘pseudo’ mint.
[38] Schulze, W. 2017b, pp. 144–147.
[39] Al-Balādhurī 163 (pp. 251 f.).
[40] Al-Balādhurī 149 (p. 230).

Group A

Tanūkh – Qinnasrīn
Tanūkh – Qinnasrīn – Qūrus

Group B

Tanūkh – Ḥalab – Ḥimṣ – undeciphered mint name
Tanūkh – Ḥalab (1)
Tanūkh – Ḥalab (2)
Tanūkh – Ḥalab (3)
Tanūkh – Ḥalab – Manbij
Tanūkh – Ḥalab – Anṭākiya – Ḥimṣ

Figure 6: Tanūkh Standing Caliph coins and their die links

Graphically, the following picture emerges:

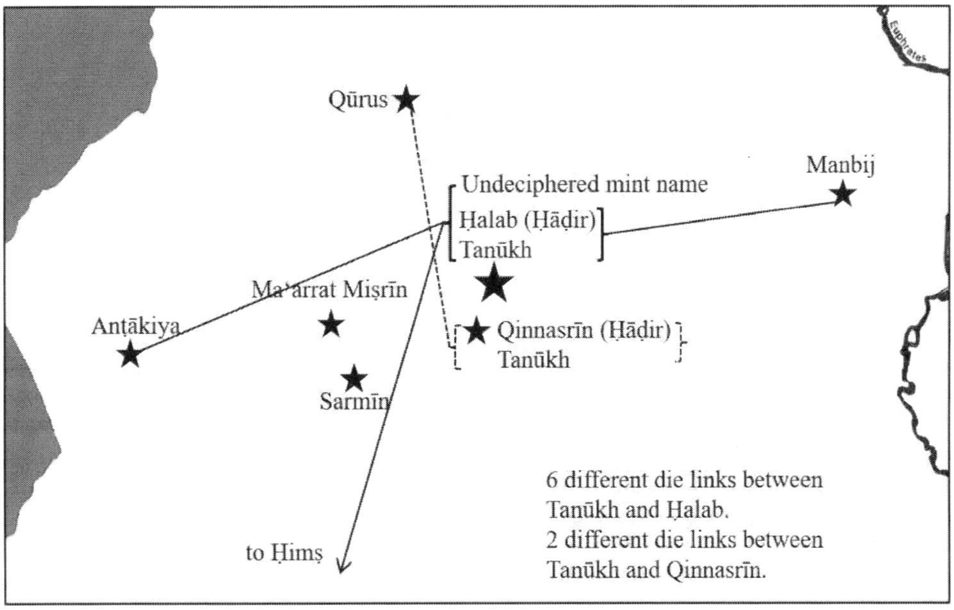

Figure 7: The mint places of Tanūkh and their die links

What can we derive from this compilation?

On the one hand, we found two different groups – the die links from Tanūkh to Qinnasrīn (group A) and to Ḥalab (group B), of which group B is significantly more extensive.

Back to the initial question: Where were the Tanūkh coins struck?
There are no die links between groups A and B. This means that the Tanūkh coins could be struck in different places. Their settlement areas in Ḥāḍir Qinnasrīn and Ḥāḍir Ḥalab are ideal for this. It cannot be ruled out that there were other workshops in which Tanūkh coins were struck or that the minting took place over several periods. But such details are unlikely to be verified.

If one considers that there are also many die links between Ḥalab and Qinnasrīn, we have to conclude that there was a large number of workshops in the Ḥalab/Qinnasrīn area in which coins were minted indiscriminately, probably at different times. Dies were presumably exchanged again and again; new dies were made by inexperienced die cutters who did not know exactly what they were writing. This is the only way to explain that the die links were very different, and there were connections between places that were far apart. When the die cutters had a Ḥimṣ coin in front of them, they wrote that name down, and sometimes they couldn't think of anything better than to use allāh or lillāh as the name of the mint or to invent imaginative names that we can no longer decipher today. Apart from that, the coin legends are often flawed and difficult to read. All of this was irrelevant as long as the basic shape of the Standing Caliph coins ordered by Damascus was preserved.

So, we are dealing with an enormous number of connections of different 'mint' names starting from Ḥalab and Qinnasrīn, which do not give an orderly overall picture. The large number of coins from Ḥalab and Qinnasrīn indicates that the governor's central mints can be found here. Besides different workshops were minting at different times according to the small change need, as was the case before the Standing Caliph coins were introduced.

In short, the coin system in jund Qinnasrīn was chaotic. Ingrid Schulze's studies prove that in addition to the central mints of Ḥalab and Qinnasrīn, there was a larger number of workshops where Standing Caliph coins were produced naming other real mints or with nonsensical 'mint names'. This also applies to the coins with the mint name Tanūkh that were most likely minted in Ḥāḍir Qinnasrīn and/or Ḥāḍir Ḥalab.

Now I would like to continue with the question where the coins with the mint name Jibrīn were struck.

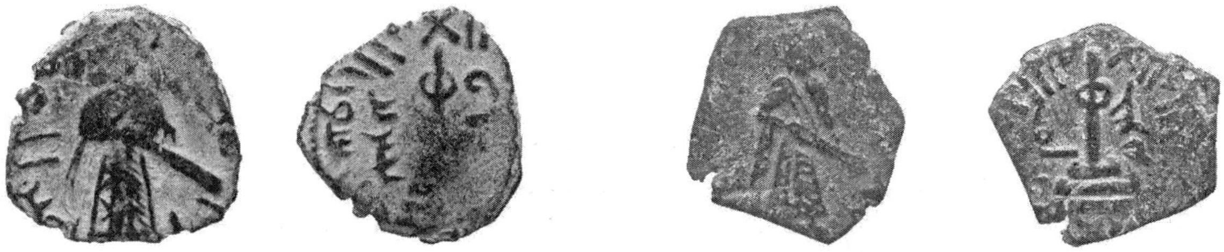

a b

Figure 8: Standing Caliph coin with the mint name Jibrīn.
Schulze collection 17mm 2.53g 7h (a) and 17 x 19mm 2.71g 9h (b)

In search of the Jibrīn mint I could see that Jibrīn is a common local name in greater Syria.

Because of the 'northern' style of the coins with the mint name Jibrīn and the corresponding find occurrence[41] we can exclude Bayt Jibrīn in Palestine. Apart from this all Standing Caliph coins with the *wāfin* to the right or left of the symbol on steps were exclusively minted in jund Qinnasrīn. For the same reason, Sāqiyat Jibrīn in the north of Bayt Jibrīn and a Jibrīn between Dimashq and Ba'labakk, mentioned by Le Strange,[42] cannot be considered.

Not on modern road maps, but on Google maps a Jibrīn can be found some kilometres north-east of Ḥamā. This place is to be seen on Dussaud's map VIII of 1927:

[41] Ilisch 2002.

[42] Le Strange 1890, p. 464.

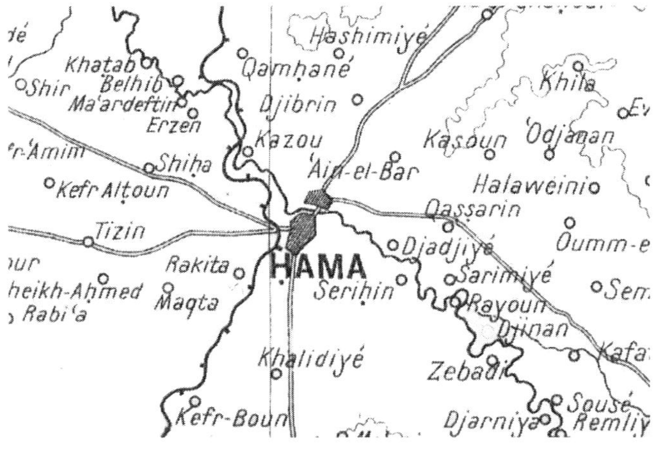

Figure 9: Excerpt of Dussaud, Topographie Historique de la Syrie Antique et Médiévale, 1927, map VIII

Because this Jibrīn near Ḥamāh is never mentioned in the historic literature and seems to have no importance it can be excluded from our search. If anything, Umayyad coins would have been minted in and for the then important city of Ḥamāh. We also know that the coinage in Ḥamāh first started under the Ayyūbids.[43] Finally, Ḥamāh was not situated in jund Qinnasrīn and would not have minted Standing Caliph coins with *wāfin*.

The next candidate is Jibrīn or Jibrīn Qurasṭāyā, situated about 40 kilometres north of Ḥalab. As already shown above (Fig. 1) this is the place where the Jibrīn mint was previously suspected. The reason for this was a passage from al-Balādhurī's historical work. Al-Balādhurī reports for the time of the Arab conquest of Syria that Abu 'Ubaida on the way from Ḥalab to Qūrus already accepted the submission of the population of Qūrus here in Jibrīn near 'Azāz.[44] This Jibrīn certainly was no city, but a small village and was never mentioned by historians or geographers later[45]. It was of no administrative or economic importance[46] and this is one of the reasons that previously a mint was only suspected here very carefully and with a question mark.

In contrast to the Jibrīn Qurasṭāyā just discussed we know of another Jibrīn, already mentioned by the geographer Yākūt al-Rūmī in the 13th century[47] and by the geographer Izz al-Dīn ibn Šhaddād (also from the 13th century):

Figure 10: Excerpt of a map after the geographer Izz al-Dīn ibn Šhaddād

---

[43] Korn 1998.

[44] al-Balādhurī 149 (p. 230). Referring to al-Balādhurī also reported by Izz al Dīn ibn Šhaddād p. 278 f.

[45] Already by the 10th century the geographer al-Muqaddasī makes no mention Jibrīn Qurasṭāyā.

[46] Ilisch 2002.

[47] Yākūt II, p. 101.

and finally, by Dussaud:

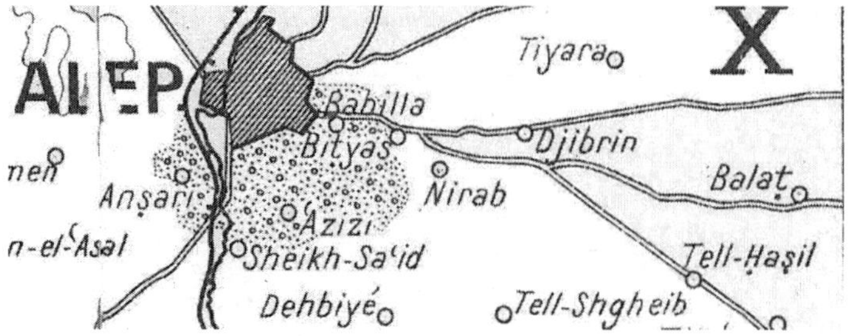

Figure 11: Excerpt of Dussaud 1927, map X

This Jibrīn is situated about 8 kilometres east of Ḥalab and can still be found on modern maps of Syria. It was on the old trade route between Edessa and Ḥalab. It is possible that during the seventh century it was another Ḥāḍir near to Ḥalab where Bedouins lived in their tents. I found an interesting picture of 1903 in the www showing Jibrīn near Ḥalab:

Figure 12: Postcard of 1903 showing conical huts in Jibrīn near Ḥalab

The conical huts, which resemble tents, are striking. It has already been discussed above that the nomads or semi-nomads set up their tents in the Ḥāḍirs and later built permanent houses in the style of their tents. Should a Ḥāḍir tradition have been preserved here until the 20th century? We do not know and will not be able to evaluate it in the near future due to the warlike destructions in Syria.

After all, it does not seem impossible that this Jibrīn was a Ḥāḍir in the nearby Ḥalab area, where coins could have been minted as in other places. Anyway, for the reasons given this Jibrīn seems to me more likely as a mint place than the previously accepted Jibrīn Qurasṭāyā – only mentioned once by al-Balādhurī.

Now I will precede with the coins themselves and their die links checking whether this theory can be reconciled with them. Because of the rarity of the Jibrīn Standing Caliph coins I can only present three die links. One of them, the die link between Jibrīn and Ḥalab looks like this:

Ḥalab Jibrīn Jibrīn Jibrīn

Figure 13: Die link Jibrīn – Ḥalab

Furthermore, there are die links between

Jibrīn – Qinnasrīn – Manbij[48]
and
Jibrīn – Manbij[49]

Graphically, the following picture emerges:

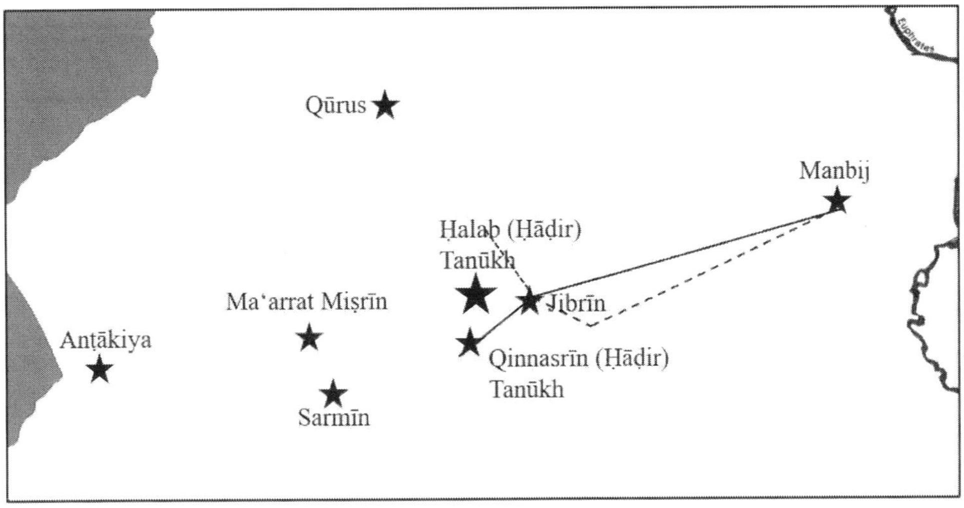

Figure 14: Jibrīn and its die links

Just like the die links of Tanūkh, we have connections to Ḥalab and Qinnasrīn. So, there is much to suggest that the rare Jibrīn Standing Caliph coins were minted in a small workshop also creating Ḥalab and Qinnasrīn coins. Furthermore, it is not unlikely that the linked Manbij coin was also created here, because the aforementioned location of Jibrīn on the trade route to Edessa also leads via Manbij.

---

[48] This die link was first published in Goodwin 2010, p. 36, but now three additional obverses of the Manbij reverse are known.
[49] The other die links were found by Ingrid Schulze.

Apart from this, Ingrid Schulze has noted that the linked Manbij coin does not stylistically match the coins minted in Manbij.

After all this, I propose to accept Jibrīn as one of the workshops that worked in the Ḥāḍir Ḥalab/ Ḥāḍir Qinnasrīn area.

Summary

The mint names that appear on the Standing Caliph coins in jund Qinnasrīn are not to be trusted. The coins on which we read Ḥalab or Qinnasrīn were not minted in the classical places Aleppo (Beroea) or Qinnasrīn (Chalcis ad Belum), but in Ḥāḍir Ḥalab or Ḥāḍir Qinnasrīn. Here we also find a convincing answer to the question of the minting place for the coins with the inscription Tanūkh. The coins with the mint name Jibrīn were most likely minted east of Ḥalab in the village of the same name, whose mint belonged to the network of small private workshops that operated in the Ḥalab/Qinnasrīn area next to the larger mints in Ḥāḍir Ḥalab and Ḥāḍir Qinnasrīn. The mints of Ḥāḍir Ḥalab and Ḥāḍir Qinnasrīn were presumably under state control, while the small private workshops supplemented from time to time the need for money. From numerous die links and the use of fancy names or the omission of mint names it is clear that this network of mints also produced coins with the names of other places like Qūrus, Manbij, Anṭākiya , Ma‘arrat Miṣrīn or Sarmīn. For example, in Qūrus or Anṭākiya there was no physical mint.

Bibliography

al-Balādhurī	Abu-l‘Abbās Aḥmad ibn Jābir al-Balādhurī, ***Kitāb Futūh al-Buldān***, translated by P. K. Hitti, (Piscataway, NJ, 2002).
al-Muqaddasī	Shams al-Dīn Abū ‘Abd Allāh Muhammad bin Ahmad bin Abī Bakr al-Bannā’ al-Shāmī al-Muqaddasī, ***Aḥsan al-Taqāsīm fī Ma‘rifat al-Aqālīm***, translated as ‘The Best Divisions for Knowledge of the Regions’ by B. Collins (Reading 2001).
Bijovsky 2012	Bijovsky, G., ***Gold Coin and Small Change: Monetary Circulation in Fifth – Seventh Century Byzantine Palestine*** (Trieste 2012).
Burns 2016	Burns, R., *Aleppo – A History*, (London 2016).
Dussaud 1927	Dussaud, R., ***Topographie Historique de la Syrie Antique et Médiévale*** (Paris 1927). https://books.openedition.org/ifpo/3692?lang=de
Foss 2015	Foss, C., ‘Coinage and circulation in Byzantine Palestine’, ***Journal of Roman Archaeology* 28**, pp. 954–56.
Goldziher 1971	Goldziher, I., **Muslim Studies Vol. 2**, (New York 1971). Translation of ‘Mohammedanische Studien Zweiter Theil’, Halle 1890.
Goodwin 2010	Goodwin, T., ‘Die Links between Standing Caliph Mints in Jund Qinnasrīn’, ***Coinage and History in the Seventh Century Near East* 2** (A. Oddy ed.). Proceedings of the 12th Seventh Century Syrian Numismatic Round Table held at Gonville and Caius College, Cambridge on 4th and 5th April 2009 (London 2010), pp. 35-40.

Goodwin 2012 — Goodwin, T., 'Sinjār – A new Standing Caliph mint in Syria?', ***Journal of the Oriental Numismatic Society* 211**, p. 18 f.

Goodwin 2017 — Goodwin, T.,' "Tabar" – a new Standing Caliph mint?', ***Coinage and History in the Seventh Century Near East* 5** (T. Goodwin ed.), Proceedings of the 15th Seventh Century Syrian Numismatic Round Table held at Corpus Christi College, Oxford on 17th and 18th September 2016 (London 2017), pp. 152–155.

Haase 1975 — Haase, C.-P., ***Untersuchungen zur Landschaftsgeschichte Nordsyriens in der Umayyadenzeit,*** PH.D. thesis oft he University Hamburg 1972 (Kiel 1975).

Heidemann 2002 — Heidemann, S., ***Die Renaissance der Städte in Nordsyrien und Nordmesopotamien. Städtische Entwicklung und wirtschaftliche Bedingungen in ar-Raqqa und Ḥarrān von der Zeit der beduinischen Vorherrschaft bis zu den Seldschuken*** (Leiden 2002).

Ilisch 2002 — Ilisch, L., ***Mints and minting right for copper coinage in Jund Qinnasrīn in the early Islamic period,*** Unpublished paper given at the 7th Century Syrian Numismatic Round Table held at the University of Birmingham on 23rd and 24th November 2002.

Ilisch 2010 — Ilisch, L., 'Coinage and Economy of Syria-Palestine in the Seventh and Eights Centuries CE', ***Money, Power and Politics in Early Islamic Syria – A review of current debates*** (J. Haldon ed.) (Farnham 2010), pp. 125–146.

Ilisch 2016 — Ilisch, L., 'Einordnung und Datierung der Münze aus dem großen Hof', *Qasr al-Mschatta. Ein frühislamischer Palast in Jordanien und Berlin Vol. 1*, ***Berliner Beiträge zur Bauforschung und Denkmalpflege* 16** (Johannes Cramer *et al* eds) (Petersberg 2016), pp. 249–261.

Izz al-Dīn ibn Šhaddād — Izz al-Dīn ibn Šhaddād, ***Al-a'laq al-Ḫatīra fī ḏikr umārā' al-Šām ẉa'l-Ğazīra***, translated into French by A.- M. Eddé as 'Description de la Syrie du Nord' (Damascus 1984).

Kennedy 2007 — Kennedy, H., ***The Great Arab Conquests*** (Philadelphia 2007).

Korn 1998 — Korn, L., ***Sylloge Nummorum Arabicorum Tübingen, Ḥamā IVc Bilād aš-Šām* III**, (Tübingen–Berlin 1998).

Le Strange 1890 — Le Strange, G., ***Palestine under the Moslems***. Reprinted from the original edition 1890 (Beirut 1965).

Rotter 1982 — Rotter, G., ***Die Umayyaden und der zweite Bürgerkrieg*** (Wiesbaden 1982).

Rousset 2012 — Rousset, M.-O., ***Al-Hadir, Étude archéologique d'un hameau de Qinnasrin*** (Lyon 2012).

Schulze and Schulze 2018 — Schulze I. and Schulze W., 'Working with Coins in Jerash: Problems, Solutions, and Preliminary Results', ***The Archaeology and History of Jerash – 110 Years of Excavations*** (A. Lichtenberger and R. Raja eds), Jerash Papers 1 (Turnhout 2018), pp. 195–205.

Schulze and Schulze 2020 — Schulze I. and Schulze W., 'The Coins of the Jerash Northwest Quarter Project and the Umayyad Money circulation in Jund al-Urdunn', ***Metal Finds and Coins, Final Publications from the Danish-German Jerash Nordwest Quarter Project*** **II** (A. Lichtenberger and R. Raja eds), Jerash Papers 7 (Turnhout 2020), pp. 125–171.

Schulze I. 2015 — Schulze I., 'Can we believe what is written on the coins? Enigmatic die links and other puzzles', ***Coinage and History in the Seventh Century Near East*** **4** (A. Oddy, I. Schulze and W. Schulze eds). Proceedings of the 15th Seven Century Syrian Numismatic Round Table held at The Hive, Worcester, on 28th and 29th September 2013 (London 2015), pp. 115–135.

Schulze, I. 2020 — Schulze, I., 'Die Chains and Die Links with the Mint Name Ḥalab', ***Coinage and History in the Seventh Century Near East*** **6** *(T. Goodwin ed.)*. Proceedings of the 16th Seventh Century Numismatic Round Table held at The Hive, Worcester on 6th and 7th April 2019 (London 2020), pp. 143–164.

Schulze, W. 2017a — Schulze, W., 'Anṭākiya – A new Standing Caliph mint and die links in the jund Qinnasrīn', ***Coinage and History in the Seventh Century Near East*** **5** (T. Goodwin ed.). Proceedings of the 15th Seven Century Syrian Numismatic Round Table held at Corpus Christi College, Oxford on 17th and 18th September 2016 (London 2017), pp. 129–140.

Schulze, W. 2017b — Schulze, W., 'The Standing Caliph coins with the mint name Qurūs', ***Coinage and History in the Seventh Century Near East*** **5** (T. Goodwin ed.). Proceedings of the 15th Seven Century Syrian Numismatic Round Table held at Corpus Christi College, Oxford on 17th and 18th September 2016 (London 2017), pp. 141–157.

Schulze, W. 2020 — Schulze, W., 'The Standing Caliph Coins with the Mint Name Qūrus – A new Die and a New Die Link', ***Coinage and History in the Seventh Century Near East*** **6** (T. Goodwin ed.). Proceedings of the 16th Seventh Century Numismatic Round Table held at The Hive, Worcester on 6th and 7th April 2019 (London 2020), pp. 165–168.

Walmsley 2007 — Walmsley, A., ***Early Islamic Syria. An archaeological assessment*** (London 2007).

Whitcomb 1998–1999 — Whitcomb, D. S., ***The Hadir Qinnasrin Project, Annual report 1998–1999*** https://oi.uchicago.edu/research/projects/hadir-qinnasrin-project

Whitcomb 2006 — Whitcomb, D. S., 'Archaeological Evidence of Sedentarization: Bilad al-Sham in the Early Islamic Period', in: Stefan R. Hauser (ed.): *Die Sichtbarkeit von Nomaden und saisonaler Besiedlung in der Archäologie. Multidisziplinäre Annäherungen an ein methodisches Problem.* ***Orientwissenschaftliche Hefte*** **21**; Mitteilungen des SFB 'Differenz und Integration' 9 (Halle 2006), pp. 27–43. http://www.nomadsed.de/uploads/tx_pdfviewer/owh9_whitcomb.pdf

Yākūt — Yākūt al-Rūmī, ***Kitāb Muʿǧam al-buldān***, ed. F. Wüstefeld (Leipzig 1870).

The Standing Caliph coins with the mint name Qūrus
– Third approach –

Wolfgang Schulze[1]

Twice already, I have published on the Qūrus Standing Caliph coins in articles in the Proceedings of the Seventh Century Syrian Numismatic Round Table in 2017 and 2020.[2] In the article of 2017, I already forebodingly remarked that 'the numismatic research of the 7th century Syria is a work in progress' and that we can await new knowledge about the coins with the mint name Qūrus. Accordingly, I was able to introduce a new die and a new die link in the 2020 article.

In the 2017 article I presented two different groups of Qūrus coins, the first with the obverse dies O1 - O3 and a second with O4. The second group is not connected with the first one and will be discussed later in this paper. There are new findings for both groups, which will now be presented. Some repetitions cannot be avoided, but they will be limited to what is necessary. For the remaining details I may refer to my 2017 and 2020 articles.

First group

So far we have known for the first group four obverse dies O1-O3a and two reverse dies R1 and R2.

O1/R1 O2/R2 O3/R1 O3a/R2

Figure 1

[1] Wolfgang Schulze is an independent scholar schulze@wg-s.de

[2] 'The Standing Caliph coins with the mint name Qūrus', ***Coinage and History in the Seventh Century Near East*** **5** (T. Goodwin ed.). Proceedings of the 15th Seven Century Syrian Numismatic Round Table held at Corpus Christi College, Oxford on 17th and 18th September 2016 (London 2017), pp. 141–157 and 'The Standing Caliph Coins with the Mint Name Qūrus – A new Die and a New Die Link', ***Coinage and History in the Seventh Century Near East*** **6** (T. Goodwin ed.). Proceedings of the 16th Seventh Century Numismatic Round Table held at The Hive, Worcester on 6th and 7th April 2019 (London 2020), pp. 165–168.

In my earlier articles I have demonstrated that all these coins are linked to each other and in addition to Standing Caliph coins with the mint names Qinnasrīn and Ḥalab:

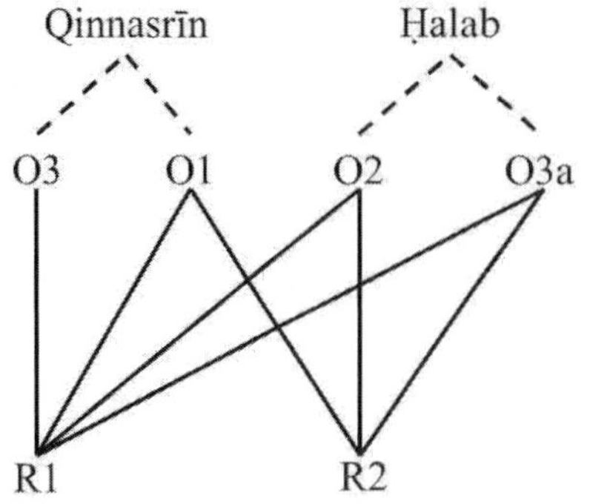

Figure 2

In September 2020 I was able to purchase a Qūrus coin that shows a new obverse die:

Figure 3

This is a very poorly preserved example, but when compared to O1-O3a, the difference is nevertheless clear. The new die can therefore be designated as O3b.

Figure 4

It can be clearly seen that the previously known obverse dies O1-O3a depict the caliph's skirt with diagonal lines on his right side. In contrast, the skirt on the new obverse die O3b shows at this place a zigzag line with dots in the gussets. It is more difficult to see that the stripes falling down from the caliph's right elbow on O3b have a slightly different shape than on O1-O3a. The reverse die of the new coin is R1 and thus fits into the known scheme according to which all the dies of this first group are linked to each other.

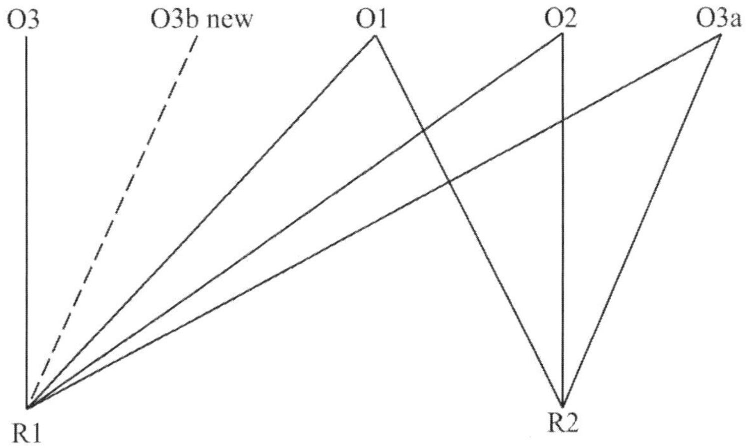

Figure 5

There is more to report about the first group: So far it is known that O1 and O3 are linked to Qinnasrīn and O2 and and O3a are linked to Ḥalab. Now Ingrid Schulze found out that the link between O3 and Qinnasrin can be expanded to Tanūkh.

Qūrus O3/R1 Qinnasrīn Tanūkh

Figure 6

Graphically, this looks like this:

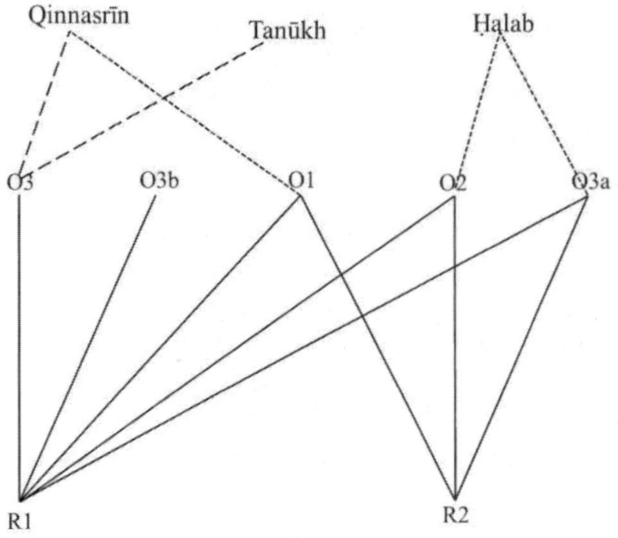

Figure 7

To summarise the first group, we now know of five different obverses and two different reverses. All of these are linked to each other. In addition, there are further links to Ḥalab, Qinnasrīn and Tanūkh. All this confirms once again my observation in the 2017 and 2020 articles that the coins with the mint name Qūrus were not minted in a mint physically present in Qūrus, but in a smaller or larger workshop in the Ḥāḍir Qinnasrīn/Ḥāḍir Ḥalab area.

Second group

In 2017, I presented another group of coins with the mint name Qūrus that was considered the standard reference for Qūrus coins from the 19th century until well into the 21st century. We know of two such coins in the Jena and in the Tübingen collection, which were published by de Saulcy and Walker as line drawings.

De Saulcy 1839 | Walker 1956 | Jena | Tübingen

Figure 8

Instead of the usual *Qūrus* possibly one can read *bi-Qūrus* (of Qūrus) or *li-Qūrus* (for Qūrus). Considering the crude striking these coins could not regarded as minted in a governmental mint. This was further evidenced by the fact that **stylistic** links to other coins with senseless inscriptions were known.

Jena Tübingen Schulze coll. Trade 2021

Figure 9

In the meantime, however, Ingrid Schulze has found two **direct** links to this group.

Jena	Tübingen	Trade 2020	Priv. coll.
O4/R3	O4/R3	O4/senseless rev.	O4/Ḥalab rev.

Figure 10

This die link shows once again that the 'classic' Qūrus coins are linked to a coin that bear undeciphered and meaningless inscriptions, and to another one showing the mint name Ḥalab.

After all this – especially on the basis of the new direct links – we can assume that the second group of coins with the mint name Qūrus, like the first one, does not belong to a firmly established mint in the place of the same name. Instead, it can now be assumed with great certainty that this group was produced in a small – possibly private – workshop in the greater area around Ḥāḍir Qinnasrīn and Ḥāḍir Ḥalab. A connection between the first and the second group due to die links is (so far) not discernible.
In my first article of 2017 on the Qūrus coins, I was able to publish a catalogue with 25 of these rare pieces. In the meantime, 18 new Qūrus coins have become known. To ensure completeness, I have included them in a new catalogue, which also will contain some other minor updates.

Catalogue[3]

No.	Location	Published/Remarks	Wt. in g	Dia. in mm	Die axis	Die nos
1	ANS New York, inventory number 2005.28.2		3.302	15.4	12	O1/R1
2		CNG electronic auction 298 (March 2013) lot 432	3.85	-	6	O1/R1
3		Trade (January 2014)	-	-	-	O1/R1
4	Goodwin collection	Goodwin (2018) no. 339 (6h) = Goodwin (2005) p. 44 (3h)	2.63	-	3	O1/R1
5	Schulze collection	Morton and Eden auction 82 (October 2016) lot 118 = auction 85 (April 2017) lot 169	3.18	17-19	12.30	O1/R1
6*		Album auction 31 (May 2018) lot 206	2.98			O1/R1
7*		Album auction 31 (May 2018) lot 208	3.02			O1/R1
8*	Schulze collection	Leu web auction 6 (December 2018) lot 1472	3.32	16	6	O1/R1
9*	Schulze collection		4.14	15.5x23	1	O1/R1
10*		Trade (February 2014)	3.60	17-19	3	O1/R1
11*		Trade (December 2017)	2.72			O1/R1
12	ANS New York, inventory number 1998.25.74		3.305	17	-	O1/R2
13	FINT (Tübingen), inventory number LA4A6		3.77	16.5	11	O1/R2
14		Trade (February 2014)				O1/R2
15	Foundation collection		3.27	17.5	-	O1/R2
16		Album auction 25 (May 2016) lot 124	2.79	-	-	O1/R2
17*		Savoca 2nd black auction (February 2020) lot 230 = Leu web auction 16 (May 2021) lot 4296	3.25	15	11	O1/R2
18	Priv. coll. Lebanon		-	-	-	O2/R1
19	Goodwin collection	Goodwin (2018) no. 340	3.74		12	O2/R1
20	FINT (Tübingen), inventory number AN3C5		3.10	17	1	O2/R2

[3] The catalogue entry 'Goodwin (2018)' refers to the publication by Tony Goodwin, The Standing Caliph Coinage (London 2018). For the rest of the literature, I refer to the bibliography in my 2017 essay.
The newly included coins are marked with an asterisk after the catalogue number.

21		SICA no. 673 (ex Shamma collection)	3.64	-	6	O2/R2
22		Kölner Münzkabinett auction 32 (May 1982) lot 576	-	-	-	O2/R2
23	Private collection GB		2.95	16	12	O2/R2
24	Goodwin collection	Goodwin (2018) no. 341	3.24	15	4	O2/R2
25		SICA no. 672 (ex Shamma collection)	3.28	-	12	O2/R2
26		Morton and Eden auction 72 (December 2014) lot 482	3.31	-	-	O2/R2
27		Album auction 25 (May 2016) lot 123	3.57	-	-	O2/R2
28*	Schulze collection	Leu web auction 8 (June 2019) lot 1993	3.68	17-18	6	O2/R2
29*	Schulze collection	Leu web auction 15 (February 2021) ex lot 3400	3.13	18	1	O2/R2
30	Schulze collection	Kölner Münzkabinett auction 32 (May 1982) lot 575	3.72	17-22	2	O3/R1
31	Foundation collection		2.94	20	8	O3/R1
32	Foundation collection		3.03	23	12	O3/R1
33*	Schulze collection	Trade (February 2019)	2.88	20	8	O3/R1
34*		Savoca auction 87 (October 2020) lot 2135 – incorrectly classified as Sinjār	3.16	20	-	O3/R1
35*		Album auction 30 (January 2018) lot 181	3.00			O3a/R1
36*		Baldwin's of St. James's Auction 4 (May 2017) lot 104	3.46			O3a/R1
37*	Schulze collection	Morton & Eden auction 89 (October 2017) lot 139	4.26	17	3	O3a/R2
38*	Schulze collection	Trade (September 2020)	2.65	17-18	12	O3b/R1
39	Orientalisches Münzkabinett Jena, inventory number 303-FO9	De Saulcy (1839) Pl. II, no. 11; Walker (1956) p. 40, J2 (both line drawing)	4.97	20	-	O4/R3
40	FINT (Tübingen) inventory number 2014-1-8		3.24	22	9	O4/R3
41*	Private collection		3.83		2	O4/Halab rev.
42*	Schulze collection		3.11	20.5	6	O4/senseless rev.
43*		Leu web auction 11 (February 2020) lot 2322	3.37	21	4	O4/senseless rev.

The Legends of the Most Common Variety of the Two Imperial Bust Type of Arab-Latin Gold Coinage from North Africa

David Woods[1]

The striking of Arab-Latin gold coinage in North Africa seems to have begun shortly after the Arab re-capture of Carthage from the Byzantines in AH 79/ AD 698-99 and continued until the introduction of purely Arabic epigraphic gold coinage in AH 100/ AD 718-19. The gold coinage struck during this period can be divided into three successive types. In his recent authoritative study of this coinage, Jonson referred to these as the Two Imperial Bust type (Fig. 1), the Latin Epigraphic type, and the Arabic/Latin Bilingual type.[2] Coins of the Two Imperial Bust type bore no date, while those of the other two types did, revealing that coins of the Latin Epigraphic type began to be struck in AH 84/ AD 703-4, and those of the Arabic/Latin Bilingual type in AH 97/ AD 715-16. The coins of the Two Imperial Bust type are so called because they retain the two imperial busts of their Byzantine model on the obverse, those of the emperor Heraclius and his eldest son Heraclius Constantine as depicted on Byzantine solidi of the period AD 613-31. They also retain a mutilated form of the large cross upon steps from the reverse of these solidi on their reverse. Hence the gold coins of the Two Imperial Bust type very strongly resemble their original Byzantine model. The main change lies in their replacement of the Latin legends of the obverse and reverse of their model with completely new Latin legends bearing no resemblance whatsoever to the traditional Byzantine legends.

Fig. 1: Arab-Latin solidus (c. 15mm, 4.26g), Two Imperial Bust type. Jonson, OD5/RD7. Ex Nomos AG, Auction 2 (18 May 2010), lot 230. © Nomos AG.

The obverse legend of the Byzantine solidi of the period AD 613-31 simply stated the names of Heraclius and his eldest son Heraclius Constantine, while the reverse legend referred to the victory of the emperors, with an additional mintmark in the exergue. However, the legends of the Arab-Latin

---

[1] David Woods is the Head of the Department of Classics at University College, Cork, Ireland: d.woods@ucc.ie.

[2] See T. Jonson, ***A Numismatic History of the Early Islamic Precious Metal Coinage of North Africa and the Iberian Peninsula***, pp. 32-40. This is a doctoral dissertation successfully submitted at the University of Oxford in 2014 which Jonson has kindly made available online (https://independent.academia.edu/JonsonTrent). More recently, see A. Fenina, 'L'arabisation du monayyage d'Ifrīqiya: étapes et signification', in J.L. Fournet, J.M. Mouton, and J. Paviot (eds.), ***Civilisations en Transition, II: Sociétés multilingues à travers l'Histoire du Proche-Orient*** (Byblos, 2016), pp. 115-168; A.A. Armada, 'Del sólido al dinar. En torno a las primeras emisiones áureas del Magreb (76/695- 696 – 100/718-719). Nuevas perspectivas', ***Revista Numismática Hécate*** 4 (2017), pp. 88-113.

solidi of the Two Imperial Bust type seem to have been purely religious in nature. They did not name the caliph or any of his local officials, they did not celebrate victory or any other real or desired achievement, and they did not say where these coins had been struck. Jonson records 55 examples of this type which he classifies according to the 7 different obverse legends which they bear.[3] However, 23 of the 55 examples – 8 solidi, 2 semisses, and 13 tremisses – belong to the same variety with obverse legend beginning NONEST. While this obverse legend has not been fully explained, there is general agreement as to most of its content and its wider significance. In contrast, the reverse legend presents far more problems and remains poorly understood at best. It is the purpose of this note to offer new readings and translations of both.

The Obverse Legend

Jonson identified 8 different obverse dies used to strike the NONEST variety of the Twin Imperial Bust type, but only one (his OD1) preserves what seems to be the full form of the obverse legend.[4] When the letter forms are standardized for ease of comprehension, this reads:

NONESTDSNISIPSESOLCSETNONABETV

All the other obverse dies preserve abbreviated forms of this legend with only slight variations between them. Fortunately, the first half of this legend is easy to read, and there is general agreement that it should be expanded as follows:

NON EST D(*eu*)S NIS(*i*) IPSE SOL(*us*).
'There is no God except himself alone'.

As has been long recognized, this is a translation into Latin of the first part of the *shahāda*, the Islamic statement of faith.[5] However, the second part of the legend is much more difficult to read. One problem faced by those attempting to read it lies in deciding between the variations in the legends preserved by the different dies. For example, the second half begins with the sequence CS in the case of OD1, but all the other dies preserving this element record it as CIS instead. A second problem lies in identifying the final two letters of the legend. They are preserved by OD1 alone, and seem to read TV, but this is by no means certain.

Walker was not aware of the longest form of the legend and expanded the second half of the form known to him as C(*u*)I S(*ocius*) N(*on est*), literally 'to whom there is no ally', that is, 'He has no ally'.[6] He interpreted the letters CI as an abbreviation of the dative singular of the relative pronoun, where this was used as a possessive dative with the verb 'to be' (*est*). However, the longest form of the legend proves that the verb *est* is not actually present in the legend, so this reading cannot be allowed to stand.

---

[3] Jonson, ***A Numismatic History*** (see n. 2), pp. 91-2.
[4] Jonson, ***A Numismatic History*** (see n. 2), pp. 92-3. The coin struck with OD1 is CNG, Triton VI (14 January 2003), lot 1189.
[5] See e.g. J. Walker, ***A Catalogue of the Muhammadan Coins in the British Museum, II: A Catalogue of the Arab-Byzantine and Post-Reform Umaiyad Coins*** (London, 1956), p. xcix.
[6] Walker, ***A Catalogue of the Arab-Byzantine*** (see n. 5), p. 54, no. 143. In this he followed H. Lavoix, ***Catalogue des monnaies musulmanes de la Bibliothèque nationale*** (Paris, 1887), p. 39, in his reading of the same legend on the copper coinage instead. This reading continues to be repeated. See e.g. M.L. Bates, 'Roman and early Muslim coinage in North Africa', ***Yarmouk Numismatics*** 8 (1996), pp. 9-17, at 15; G. Bernardi, ***Arabic Gold Coins Corpus I*** (Trieste, 2010), p. 101; Fenina, 'L'arabisation du monayyage d'Ifrīqiya' (see n. 2), p. 127; Armada, 'Del sólido al dinar' (see n. 2), p. 96.

It is clear that the sequence ABETV at the end of the legend on OD1 preserves the main verb of second half of the legend, but this is obviously incomplete as no form of the verb ends –TV. This seems to abbreviate the ending of the 3rd-person singular form of the verb in the passive, – *tur*. Hence the verb should probably be expanded to read (*h*)*abetu*(*r*) 'he/she/it is had/ held'. Jonson recognises that the legend contains a form of the verb *habeo* 'to have/hold', but reads it as (*h*)*abet* 'he/she/it has'. He refuses to accept a passive form of the verb here because he has already decided that the sequence CS (OD1) or CIS (all other obverse dies) should be expanded to read (*so*)C(*io*)S or (*so*)CI(*o*)S 'allies', a noun in the accusative plural as the object of an active verb.[7] One could correct this expansion to read (*so*)CI(*u*)S, a noun in the nominative singular, instead, and his apparent objection to the passive verb would disappear. However, the more important difficulty is that the expansion of the sequence CS or CIS in this manner is untenable. It is highly unlikely that anyone would have abbreviated a word by omitting the first syllable in this manner because this would have rendered the abbreviated word unrecognisable. Jonson seeks to defend the idea that an engraver might have abbreviated a word in this way by pointing to the fact that the name of Heraclius was spelled without the initial H on the solidi of Byzantine Carthage. Yet this represents a very different phenomenon, the dropping of the initial H in spoken Latin, a development that had begun as early as the 1st century BC even, but had gathered pace over the centuries.[8] It was not a deliberate form of abbreviation. He also draws attention to the fact that Carthaginian solidi of Constantine IV sometimes omitted the initial C from his name, but this was no more than a blunder, one of many such in the legends of these coins. Finally, one should note that ET serves as an adverb rather than a conjunction in this case. The result of his analysis is that Jonson reads the second half of the legend as follows:

(*so*)CI(*o*)S ET NON (*h*)ABET.
'He does not have allies also'.

In contrast, if one respects the fact that OD1 clearly reveals that the verb is passive and expands the initial C (OD1) or CI (all other obverse dies) as C(*ui*) or C(*u*)I, as Walker suggested, where this is the dative of agent as normally used with passive verbs rather than a possessive dative, one can read this legend as follows instead:

C(*u*)I S(*ocius*) ET NON (*h*)ABETV(*r*).
'By whom an ally is not also had'.

Jonson does briefly consider the possibility that the S in this legend could abbreviate *socius* 'ally', but argues that 'it is unlikely that the engraver would have chosen to use single letters to abbreviate a word, especially in the middle of the legend'.[9] Against this, one can argue not only that *socius* was an extremely common Latin term, but that it was also exactly the sort of term that one would have expected to find in this context, in a phrase completing the *shahāda*, something denoting a companion of some type. Hence there should have been no difficulty understanding what the S alone meant here. This means that the obverse legend reads in full as follows:

NON EST D(*eu*)S NIS(*i*) IPSE SOL(*us*) C(*u*)I S(*ocius*) ET NON (*h*)ABETV(*r*).
'There is no God except himself alone, by whom an ally is not also had'.

---

7 Jonson, ***A Numismatic History*** (see n. 2), p. 96.
8 See J. Herman, ***Vulgar Latin***, trans. R. Wright (University Park, PA, 2000), p. 38.
9 Jonson, ***A Numismatic History*** (see n. 2), p. 95.

The Reverse Legend

Fig. 2: Arab-Latin solidus (16mm, 4.35g), Two Imperial Bust type.
Ex Heritage Auctions, NYINC Signature Sale 3063 (16 Jan. 2018), lot 32117. © Heritage Auctions.

Jonson identified 15 reverse dies (RD) where 13 of these seemed to depict slight variations of the same legend.[10] To these, one should add the reverse die of a solidus recently offered for sale (I will refer to it as RD16 for the sake of convenience) (Fig. 2). The main variations in the legends may then be analysed as follows (where spaces do not represent spaces in the legends, but have been inserted to assist comparison and dotted lines represent missing or illegible letters):

RD16	D · E	D N	CI PI	AS	MN	ET	OMN N AN	
RD1	DE	D N	CI PI	AS	OA	E	....	NO AVC : SC
RD14	DE		....			ET	OMN A	MAN SCI
RD5	DE	D N	CI PI	AS	MA	ET	ONM A	
RD7	DE	D NO	CI	AS	MA	ET	OMN A N	
RD10	DE	D NM	CI	AS	MA	EP	OMN A IN	
RD15	DE	D NV		BS	M	ET	OMN N IN	MANO

Walker attempted a partial reading of the legend of RD7 as follows:

DE(*us*) D(*ominus*) NO(*ster*) CIAS MA(*gnus*) ET(*ernus*) OMN(*i*)A N(*oscens*)[11]
'Our Lord God, wise (?), great, eternal, all-knowing'.

The most problematic element of this reading is the interpretation of the sequence CIAS as a bungled form of the adjective *sapiens* 'wise'. He reached this conclusion on the basis that CIAS seemed to be an abbreviated form of the sequence NEIPAS, as he misread the sequence NCIPIAS (as in RD1, RD5, RD16 above), which he misinterpreted as a retrograde form of SAPIENS.[12] Jonson does not even attempt a reading of the first part of the legend before the conjunction ET, and speculates rather half-heartedly that the latter part could be expanded to read 'either ET OMN(*i*)A IN MA(*nu*) [*eius*], 'and everything is in [his] hands' or even ET OMN(*i*)A IN MA(*nu*) [*eius*] SCI, 'and know that everything is in [his] hands', but offers no support for either reading of the text.[13]

---

[10] Jonson, ***A Numismatic History*** (see n. 2), p. 97.

[11] Walker, ***A Catalogue of the Arab-Byzantine*** (see n. 5), p. 54, no. 143. Again, this is often repeated. See Bates, 'Roman and early Muslim coinage' (see n. 6), p. 15; Fenina, 'L'arabisation du monayyage d'Ifrīqiya' (see n. 2), p. 127; Armada, 'Del sólido al dinar' (see n. 2), p. 96.

[12] For a similar conclusion based on the same misreading of this legend on copper coinage, see Lavoix, ***Catalogue des monnaies musulmanes*** (see n. 6), p. 39.

[13] Jonson, ***A Numismatic History*** (see n. 2), p. 99, although he should translate 'hand' rather than 'hands'.

As one reconsiders this problem, one first searches for a main verb. Since the sequence CIPIAS (RD1, RD5, RD16) resembles the 2nd- person singular of the present subjunctive of the verb *capio* 'I take, receive', properly spelled CAPIAS rather than CIPIAS, one may tentatively treat it as such.[14] One is encouraged to do so by the facts both that this is the form of the verb used for expressing a prayer, the optative subjunctive, or subjunctive of desire, and that this legend seems to begin by addressing the Lord God as if in prayer. Furthermore, the identification of CIPIAS as a form of the verb *capio* 'I take, receive' is entirely consistent with the reading of the apparent final sequence IN MANO (clearest in RD15), or similar, to be a slightly corrupt rendering of *in manu*, meaning either 'in [your] hand' or 'in [your] host'.[15] Finally, if this is a verb in the 2nd-person singular, and God is being addressed directly, then the terms used of him are in the vocative case. This means that DE may abbreviate *domine* 'lord' rather than *deus* 'God', and I will tentatively assume that it does. Fortunately, it does not substantially affect the translation whether one prefers to expand the first letters of the legend as D(*omin*)E D(*eus*) N(*oster*) or DE(*us*) D(*omine*) N(*oster*). Hence the first part of the legend seems to read:

D(*omin*)E D(*eus*) N(*oster*) CIPIAS
'Lord Our God, may you take ...'

The next question is whom or what it is hoped that God will take. The presence of the conjunction ET between two groups of letters suggest that these groups identify the objects of the verb CIPIAS. Hence MA (RD5, RD7, RD10) or MN (RD16) seems to identify one object and OMN A (RD7, RD10, RD14) or OMN N (RD15, RD16) seems to identify a second object. Interestingly, the variants in these two cases reveal the occurrence of the same error in each instance, the confusion of A and N, where the preponderance of the evidence suggests that one should probably prefer to read A rather than N. The sequence OMN suggests some form of the adjective *omnis* 'all, whole'. This leaves the letter A alone to abbreviate the name of this second object, where this was probably thought sufficient because the name of the object was so obvious from the general social or political context. One obvious possibility is the name of Africa, so the wish is that God will take the whole of Africa in his hand or host. This is supported by the fact that the name of Africa occurs in the reverse legend of the next type of gold coin, the Latin Epigraphic type, and is in fact the only place that these coins mention.[16] Then, if one interprets the term abbreviated by A as a geographical term, one should probably interpret the MA or MN in the same manner. In that case, the obvious suggestion is that one should prefer the reading MA in abbreviation of the name of Mauretania. Hence one strong possibility is that the legend asks God to take Mauretania and all of Africa in his hands, where these terms are used to describe broad regions rather than particular provinces with the former Byzantine exarchate of Africa.

One must next explain the apparent final element of the legend that only survives on two reverse dies, the sequence SC (RD1) or SCI (RD14). While Jonson translates SCI at one point as if it was the singular imperative of the verb *scio* 'I know', in other contexts SC or SCI would normally suggest an abbreviation of some form of the adjective *sanctus* 'holy'. In this case, the sequence SCI should abbreviate S(*an*)C(*t*)I which could be either the masculine nominative plural, masculine genitive singular, or neuter genitive singular of this adjective. Given the meaning of *sanctus*, one immediately

[14] The apparent stem CIP- could suggest that one is dealing with a compound of *capio* such as *accipio* 'I take, accept' or *recipio* 'I regain, take back', but the legend does not preserve any clear evidence for the presence of the necessary prefix.

[15] A certain ambiguity arises here because the same noun *manus* can mean either 'hand' or an 'armed force, band, troop'.

[16] The reverse legend of all three denominations was normally some abbreviation of the following, or some slight variant thereof: *In nomine domini misericordis solidus feritus in Africa* 'In the name of the Lord, the Merciful, [this] solidus was struck in Africa'. See Jonson, ***A Numismatic History*** (see n. 2), pp. 122-29, 133-37.

suspects that this is in fact the first word of the legend, agreeing with D(*omine*)E that follows next, rather than the last word, in which case the form SCI cannot be correct, because it would not be in agreement with D(*omin*)E, and should probably be corrected to read SCE instead, in abbreviation of the vocative S(*an*)C(*t*)E. This identification of SC or SCI as the first rather than the last word in the legend is supported by the occurrence of a device consisting of two pellets, one on top of the other, immediately before the SC in the case of RD1. This can now be recognised as a marker indicating the point where the legend began and ended.[17] This means that the sequence AVC which occurs immediately before this marker on RD1, and for which there appears to be no evidence otherwise, is in fact the last word of this legend. It appears to abbreviate the adjective *augustus* 'revered, sacred'. While this term was awarded by the Roman senate as a cognomen to the first emperor and became a standard imperial title subsequently, it is not used in that sense here. Here it can only be an adjective agreeing with the preceding noun MANO, properly *manu*. Hence in its fullest form the inscription should probably be expanded to read as follows:

S(*an*)C(*t*)I D(*omin*)E D(*eus*) N(*oster*) CIPIAS MA(*uretaniam*) ET OMN(*em*) A(*fricam*) IN MANO AVG(*usta*)

In correct classical spelling, this would read:

S(*an*)C(*t*)E D(*omin*)E D(*eus*) N(*oster*) CAPIAS MA(*uretaniam*) ET OMN(*em*) A(*fricam*) IN MANV AVG(*usta*)

One can then translate this as either 'Holy Lord Our God, may you take Mauretania and the whole of Africa in (your) sacred hand' or 'Holy Lord Our God, may you receive Mauretania and the whole of Africa in (your) sacred host'. In either case, it appears to be a prayer for God to take control of Mauretania and the whole of Africa. Bearing in mind that it was the Arab conquerors who struck these coins, this was in effect a prayer to God that he would support the completion of their conquest of north-western Africa.

Conclusion

None of the surviving examples of the NONEST variety of the Twin Imperial Bust type preserves a complete and unambiguous legend on either obverse or reverse. However, it is arguable that Jonson's OD1 displays relatively little abbreviation and, most importantly, contains no error of any kind. While all of the reverse dies display some error, his RD1 (from the same coin) seems to preserve the fullest version of the legend with minimal error, although several letters are either illegible are off-flan. The content of the obverse legend is, not at all surprisingly, a version of the *shahāda*. In contrast, the content of the reverse legend reveals it to be an original composition created for the local circumstances, a prayer for the completion of the conquest of Mauretania and Africa.

[17] This interpretation is supported by the use of a similar pair of pellets to mark the beginning of the Latin legend on the Cii variety of the so-called York gold shilling struck in Anglo-Saxon England during the mid-7th century. Three pellets one above the other seem to serve the same function on the Ciii variety of the same type. In general, see T. Abramson, 'England's earliest coinage with particular reference to the York group of gold shillings', ***British Numismatic Journal*** 89 (2019), pp. 1-18. On the reading of their inscriptions, see D. Woods, 'Reading the inscriptions on the York group of Anglo-Saxon gold shillings', ***British Numismatic Journal*** 90 (2020), pp. 67-76.

Umayyad Caliphal Seals

Nitzan Amitai-Preiss[1]

Both historical sources and archaeological objects tell us about the past of a place.

The writing of Islamic history started already during the third quarter of the seventh century by Syrian writers who wrote about the Islamic conquests. But those books have been lost, and they are only mentioned in treatises written in the ninth and tenth centuries.[2] Other historical sources writing about the Umayyad period are even from the Mamlūk period. Such are, for instance, two sources that wrote about ʿAbd al- Malik's monetary reform that took place in 696-697 CE: Rashīd al-Dīn's *Jāmiʿ al-tawārīkh* (composed c. 1310) and al-Damīrī's *Ḥayāt al-ḥayawān al- kubrā* (composed c. 1371-2).[3]

Historical sources writing about Umayyad Palestine are non-existent except for one Samaritan source dating from 1355 C.E., written in Arabic. This source only seldom writes about communities other than the Samaritans. The period this source covers is from the early Islamic period until the days of Muḥammad ibn Tughj the Ikhshīd (c. 935 C.E.).

When we turn to administration, some knowledge of it is found in compilations of the third Islamic century.[4] Due to this lack of knowledge about the history and administration of Palestine, the information we can gather from archaeology becomes even more important. A major archaeological source is the various kinds of administrative objects originating from Umayyad Palestine which have been found in the last 120 years. Some are small portable objects such as coins, seals, weights and stamped glass vessels, while others are monumental inscriptions.

The current article will discuss lead seals. Three groups of seals have the same technical solution to the problem of how to connect a seal to a cloth sack or to a wooden box, that being a rivet that connects to or into the surface to which the seal was attached. The groups are a set of caliphal seals, a group of governors' seals,[5] among them a set from the days of Saʿid b. ʿAbd al-Malik the governor of Filasṭīn,[6] and a group of seals bearing a religious phrase on the obverse.[7]

The current article is about the caliphal seals, that is, seals bearing the name of a caliph. Among the 280 lead Umayyad seals I know of, which I have studied and researched, there are 21 caliphal seals, dating from the reigns of most of the caliphs from ʿAbd al-Malik (65-86 AH/685-705 CE), the fifth

[1] Dr Nitzan Amitai-Preiss is a lecturer of Islamic Archaeology at the Hebrew University of Jerusalem, (Israel). She is also a numismatist. e-mail: amitaipr@mscc.huji.ac.il

[2] Elad A. 'The Beginning of Historical Writing by the Arabs: The Earliest Syrian Writers on the Arab Conquest', *Jerusalem Studies in Arabic and Islam*, 28, 2003, pp.65–152.

[3] Milstein R. 'A New Source for the Monetary Reform of ʿAbd al- Malik', *Israel Numismatic Journal*, 16, 2008, pp.174–175.

[4] Donner F.M. 1998. *Narratives of Islamic Origins the Beginning of Historical Writing*, Princeton, 166-171, esp. 167.

[5] Amitai-Preiss N. 2007, 'The Administration of Jund Filastin and Jund Al- Urdunn during the Umayyad and Early ʿAbbasid Periods According to Seals and Other Small Finds', Ph.D. diss., Ben Gurion University, Beer Sheba, Israel, pp.125–230, Nos.22–31.

[6] Amitai-Preiss N. 2022. 'Seals and Measures from the Days of Saʿīd ibn ʿAbd al-Malik', in Hanstein S., Vardanyan A. and Ilisch P. (eds), *Studia Numismatica et Islamica in Honorem Lutz Ilisch,* Berlin, pp. 97–102.

[7] Amitai-Preiss N. 2007, see Note 5 above, pp.131–134, Nos.32, 35, 38–41.

Umayyad caliph, to Marwān b. Muḥammad (127-132 AH/744-750 CE), the last Umayyad caliph.[8] Some caliphs (ʿAbd al-Malik, al-Walīd, Marwān b. Muḥammad) have more than one seal known with their name, sometimes identical and sometimes with various different legends.

Each one of these seals bears the following components: a short religious phrase (the *basmallah*), a caliphal title, the name of a caliph. One seal from Hishām's reign and two from that of Marwān b. Muḥammad bear a date (the seals of Marwān b. Muḥammad each have a different date), four seals (one of ʿAbd al-Malik's seals and three of Marwān b. Muḥammad – see below) bear an official's name and three seals bear part of a sūrah from the Qurʾan. One such seal is one of the seals from the days of ʿAbd al-Malik that bears an expression found twice in the Qur`an: 17: 35 and 26: 182,[9] and two other seals are the two seals of Marwān b. Muḥammad that bear a date.[10] Those two seals carry the same part of another surah: 26: 181. All three seals mentioned now bear part of a Qurʾanic verse that warned merchants to not forge the volume or weight of their goods during their trading with customers.[11]

The provenance of all except one of the seals of this group, which I call caliphal seals, is not known.

The Seal of ʿAbd al-Malik

Discussion: ʿAbd al-Malik (r. 685–705 CE), the fifth caliph of the Umayyad dynasty, is the first Umayyad caliph whose seals and weights we have. He initiated an administrative reform in 77/696/7. The first line in ʿAbd al-Malik's two previously known seals is the title *ʿabd Allāh* "the servant of God" (Nos. 1 and 2 in the catalogue below). This is also the case on this caliph's glass stamps.[12] (D'Ottone Rambach 2017:188–190. In that publication, Nos. 1, 2, 5, 9 and 11 bear only *ʿabd Allāh*, and Nos. 1, 3, 4, 6 and 7 have *li-ʿabd Allāh*). This is the first time an object from the time of ʿAbd al-Malik bearing a verse from the Qurʾan has been found. The last two lines of this seal read: *zinū bil-qisṭās al-mustaqīm*, a phrase that is found twice in the Qurʾan – in 17: 35 and 26: 182. The full legend of this seal is No.3:

The servant of God /ʿAbd al-Malik the / commander of the faithful. Weigh (pl.)/ with scales / of justice

The Arabic word *qisṭās* comes from the Greek, from the Attic measure of liquid and dry volume, ξέστης (xestēs), which is equivalent to 545.5 ml (the Roman sextarius), both dry and liquid.[13] Qisṭās is one of the foreign words that entered the Qurʾan.[14]

One Qur`anic verse (11 [Hūd]: 85) connects both measures and weights and keeping the land safe from the corruption of the merchants during trading processes:

---

[8] I want to thank Father Stephan Maxfield for the fruitful discussion we conducted about my lecture at the 2022 Round Table.

[9] Amitai-Preiss N. and Berman A. 'Three Official Objects from the Early Islamic Period', *Israel Numismatic Research*, 17 (2022), p. 242, seal No.1.

[10] Amitai-Preiss N. 'An Umayyad Lead Seal with the Name of Marwān b. Muhammad', *Al-Qantara* 18/1 (1997), pp.233–42; and Amitai-Preiss N. 2007, see Note 5 above, pp.122–123, No.17.

[11] This latter mentioned verse, Q 26: 181, *awfūa al-kayla wa-la takūnūa min al-muhsirīn*, is also found on another kind of lead seal from Palestine, with a rivet on its back, but there it is found on its own, without a caliph's name or date, just a *basmalla* at the opening of the legend, prior to the Qurʾanic verse. See Amitai-Preiss 2007, note 5 above, p.131, Nos.32–34 (No. 32 is Khalili PBS 526, No.33 is from another die with the same legend held in a private collection in Israel. A third seal, No.34, is a from Christie's catalog, 2001:Islamic Art and Manuscripts, Tuesday 16 October 2001, London, p.134, No.15. No picture is provided, so it is not clear whether it is from the same die as either the above mentioned No.32 or No.33).

[12] D'Ottone Rambach A. Arabic Glasses (coin weights, jetons and vessel stamps) from Umayyad Syria, in T. Goodwin (ed.), *Coinage and History in the Seventh Century Near East,* 5, *Proceedings of the 15th Seventh Century Syrian Numismatic Round Table held at Corpus Christi College, Oxford on 17th and 18th September 2016*, 2017:188–190.

[13] Qisṭās, https://en.wikipedia.org/wiki/Ancient_Greek_units_of_measurement#Volume (retrieved July 27, 2022)

[14] Jeffery, A. 2007. *The Foreign Vocabulary of the Qur'an*, Leiden, pp.238–239.

وَيَٰقَوۡمِ أَوۡفُواْ ٱلۡمِكۡيَالَ وَٱلۡمِيزَانَ بِٱلۡقِسۡطِۖ وَلَا تَبۡخَسُواْ ٱلنَّاسَ أَشۡيَآءَهُمۡ وَلَا تَعۡثَوۡاْ فِي ٱلۡأَرۡضِ مُفۡسِدِينَ

My people! Give full measure and weigh with justice, do not diminish the goods of others, and do not go about creating corruption in the land.

The Terms for the Seals

One sealing (No. 5 and No. 6) has two non-identical seals with the name of al-Walīd (r. 705-715 CE) connected to each other by a rivet. The term for such a sealing is found engraved within its inscription on one of the two seals. It is called a *mikyalah*.[15] Also seal **No.19** below, from the days of Marwān b. Muḥammad, bears the seal name *mikyalah*.

Mikyalah seems to be the term for a seal with the name of a caliph, *kayl* could be the term for a seal of a governor belonging to the Umayyad family. The full legend of this seal of Saʿid b. ʿAbd al-Malik is: *amara bi-ṣanʿat al-kayl* (or *muddī*) *alladhi nuqisha li-rabbihi Saʿid b. ʿAbd al-Malik bi-sanat sabʿ wa-* [*ʿishrīn wa-miʾa*]. The verb *naqasha*, found here used in the passive voice, is the term used by mediaeval authors for seals used by caliphs.[16] Here it is on a seal of a son of a caliph who was a governor.

ṣanʿah refers to the making or manufacturing of a seal (Seals Nos. 6 from the reign of al-Walīd and No.19 from the reign of Marwān b. Muḥammad in the catalogue below).

We do not have a *mikyalah* for all the caliphs whose seals have survived, and no other term for the object is specified on the other 18 lead seals with a name of a caliph that we know about.

Other lead objects that look like a seal with a rivet at their back side are called *muddī*, a volume measure. One is called *muddī Filasṭīn*, from Yazīd's reign and specifically the year 101 A.H./719-720 CE.[17]

Another *muddī* is known from the days of Saʿīd b. ʿAbd al-Malik, who was governor of Filasṭīn. I believe the *muddī* is from the period after he was contested and dismissed from office by two rebels who were brothers, Saʿīd and Diabʿān, sons of a former governor of Filasṭīn who thought they deserved to be governors in place of a son of ʿAbd al-Malik, the caliph who died in 705 CE. Sa`id and Diab`an who saw themselves as descendants of a ruling family by tradition, took advantage of the weak ruler in the capital Damascus, to expel Saʿīd b. ʿAbd al-Malik.

Names of Officials

On each of the four seals: 3, 18, 19 and 20 a name of an official appears (these names will appear below). By checking in *al-Shāmilah* site of scanned Arabic books, no conclusive identification of these four minor officials could be established. As for two of the three names that appear each on a seal from the days of Marwān b. Muḥammad (Nos.18-19), they appear on a seal from 127A.H, No.18 and on a seal of 128 A.H., No.19, it may mean that we have here an opportunity to read by the seals' legends and dates, a moment of change of two officials' service in such a position of

[15] Amitai-Preiss N. 'Umayyad Vocabulary on Administrative Objects from Palestine', in Callegher B. and D'Ottone (eds), *3rd Assemani Symposium on Islamic Couns, Trieste, EUT 2012*, (Numismatica antica a medievale, studi, 2), pp.281–282.

[16] Porter V. 2011. *Arabic and Persian Seals and Amulets in the British Museum*. London, p.3.

[17] Amitai-Preiss N. 'Early Islamic Volume Measurements', in Goodwin T. (ed.), *Coinage and History in the Seventh Century Near East 5, Proceedings of the 15th Seventh Century Syrian Numismatic Round Table Held at Corpus Christi College, Oxford on 17th and 18th September 2016*, 2017, pp.197–198.

issuing the seals, one of which No.19 is called *mikyalah*. At the current knowledge and research, we have no idea how long was this position occupied by each one of these officials.

On seal No.3, from the days of ʿAbd al-Malik, the name Muḥammad b. ʿAbd al-Rahman is engraved. He is not a known person.

On three seals of Marwān b. Muḥammad (Nos.18-20 below in the catalogue):

On No.18: ʿUthmān b. al-Walīd – year 127 AH/ 744-745 CE.

On No.19: Yazīd b. Sulaymān – year 128 AH/745-746 CE.

On No.20: the governor ʿAbd al-Salām.

The Nature and Function of the Caliphal Seals

The nature of the inscription and the design of the seals with a rivet at their back indicates that they must have been used to seal a bag of something. The inscription implies that the caliph, and the clerks of his administration who were below him in the hierarchy, were prepared to vouch for the correct weight of what was in the bag.

It is most unlikely that the contents of the bag were perishable. Therefore I think it may be that the substance was valuable – as it needed to be weighed. I suggest it was raw copper, silver, or gold.
The seals would mostly be found where the goods went and were opened, rather than where they were first sealed. This follows the pattern of a seal of another type, that was unearthed at Yatir in the Negev, in the south of Israel, that bears the term 'the market of Iliya' (i.e., the market of Jerusalem).[18]

Conclusions

It is expected that new types of caliphal seals found in the future will shed additional light on the Umayyad administration, such as names of more minor officials under the caliphs or new names of governors of Filasṭīn and al-Urdunn throughout the Umayyad period, or the terms for the seals themselves. This will add more tesserae to the mosaic of Umayyad administration that is revealed to us, adding to the minimal knowledge we find in the ʿAbbasid sources or some Mamluk sources that write about the Umayyad history and administration.

[18] Amitai-Preiss N. 'Evidence for Commercial Connections', *Israel Numismatic Journal,* 19, 2016, p. 111, No. 6.

Catalogue

All except for No.8 (which has its inscription on both sides of the bulla) the seals are inscribed on one side only, Side B -their back has a nail.

1. A Seal of ʿAbd al-Malik

عبد الله / عبد الملك/ ا مير المؤ/ منين

Transliteration

ʿabd allāh/ ʿAbd al-Malik/ amīr al-mu/ ʾminīn

Translation

The slave of God/ʿAbd al-Malik/ The caliph (lit. commander of the faithful)

Nasser D. Khalili collection of Islamic art PBS 546. 20.79 g, 25-35 mm

2. A Seal of ʿAbd al-Malik

عبد الله/ عبد الملك / امر به/ محمد بن/ عبد ال/ رحمن

Transliteration

ʿabd allāh l ʿAbd al-Malik/ amara bihi/ Muḥammad b./ ʿAbd al-/ Raḥman

Translation

The slave of God /ʿAbd al-Malik/ordered it/ Muḥammad b. / ʿAbd al- /Raḥman

Khalili collection PBS 534. 22.96 g, 25-33 mm

3. A Seal of ʿAbd al-Malik

امير المؤمنين/ زنوا/ القسطاس/ المستقيم/ عبد الله /عبد الملك

Transliteration

ʿabd allāh / ʿAbd al-Malik/ amīr al-muʾminīn/ zinū/ al-qisṭās/ al-mustaqīm

Translation

The slave of God / ʿAbd al-Malik/ The caliph/ Weigh (pl.)/ with scales/ of justice

Private collection, Israel. 20.835 g, 30 mm

4. A Seal of al-Walīd

[بسـ]ـم الله / [ا] مر عبد الله / [ا] لوليد ا مير / [الـ]ـمؤمـ[نين] / الوفا [لله]

Transliteration

Bism Allāh / amara ʿabd allāh / al-Walīd amir / al-muʾminīn / al-wafā lillāh

Translation

In the name of Allah / Ordered the slave of Allah, al-Walid the caliph / Honesty [belongs] to Allah

Khalili collection PBS 558. 9.5 g, 20x25 mm

5. A seal of al-Walīd (comprised of two seals connected by a nail to each other)

A

B

Seal A

[بسم الله] /...../ عبد الله الو ليد ا مير المؤ/ منين اصلحه الله و اف

Transliteration

Bism Allāh /... / ʿabd allāh / al-Wa / līd amir / al-muʾ / minīn / aṣlaḥahu allāh wāf ...

Translation

In the name of Allah / … / the slave of Allah / al-Walid the caliph / Allah be good to him, Honesty(?) [belongs to Allah? or: Full weight/volume].

Seal B

[بسم الله] / امر بصنعة /هذ ه مكيلة /عبد الله الو / ليد ا مير المؤ منين اصلحه / الله و اف

Transliteration

Bism Allāh /amara bi-sanʿat / hādhihi mikyalah / ʿabd allāh al-Wa / līd amir al-muʾ / minīn aṣlaḥahu / allāh wāf ...

Translation

In the name of Allah / ordered the making / of this *mikyalah* / the slave of Allah al-Wa / lid the caliph / Allah be good to him, Honesty(?) [belongs to Allah? or: Full weight/volume].

Khalili collection PBS 570. Seal A: 22x26 mm; seal B: 24x27 mm.

The two sides are connected by a nail and are inseparable.

6. A seal of al-Walīd

/ ...عبد الله / [ا] لوليد / مير الـ / مـ[ؤمنين]

Transliteration

... / ʿabd allāh / al-Walīd amir al- /muʾminīn

Translation

... / the slave of Allah al-Walid the caliph

Khalili collection PBS 551. 15.27 g, 22mm. A nail on side B.

7. A seal of al-Walīd

...عبد الله الـ / [وليـ]د ؟ ا مير / المؤمنين

Transliteration

... / ʿabd allāh al- / Walīd amir / al-muʾminīn

Translation

... / the slave of Allah al-Walid the caliph

Private collection, no. 24. 20-30mm.

8. Bulla of Sulaymān b. ʿAbd al-Malik as caliph (96-99 AH/715-717 CE)

Side A:

[ب]سم الله / عبد الله / [سليـ]من امـ /

Side B (a direct continuation of side A):

ير / المـ[ؤ] منين

Transliteration

Bism allāh ʿabd allāh Sulaymān amir al-muʾminīn

Translation

In the name of Allah, the servant of Allah, Sulaymān the caliph

Christie's 2001, p. 134, no. 5. 10 mm.

9. A seal of Yazīd b. ʿAbd al-Malik (101-105 AH/720-724 CE)

عبد الله / يزيد امير /المؤمنين

Transliteration

ʿabd allāh / Yazīd amir / al-muʾminīn

Translation

The servant of Allah, Yazīd the caliph

Khalili collection PBS 561. 22.06 g, 23-33 mm. A nail on side B.

10. A seal from 110 AH/728-729 CE (the reign of Hishām b. ʿAbd al-Malik)

.... [بسم الله ?] / سنة عشرة

Transliteration

..... [*basamalh*?]/ *sanah ʿashara*

Translation

...... [in the name of Allah?] /year 10 = since this is an Umayyad seal, judging by its script the only possibility is that it is [1]10

Christie's 2001, p. 134, no. 6. 14 mm.

11. A seal of Hishām b. ʿAbd al-Malik (105-125 AH/724-743 CE)

بسم الله/ عبد الله /[هـ]شام امير /المؤمنين

Transliteration

Bism allāh / ʿabd allāh / Hishām amir/ al-muʾminīn

Translation

In the name of Allah, the servant of Allah, Hishām the caliph

Christie's 2003, on page accompanying the catalogue, no. 10.

31-33 mm. A nail on side B.

12. A seal of Hishām b. ʿAbd al-Malik, identical wording to no. 12 above, except for a missing first line. As Christie's catalogue does not include a division into lines, nor a photograph, it is impossible to determine if the same die was used for both these seals.

Khalili collection PB 540. 15.87 g, 30 mm.

13. A seal of Hishām b. ʿAbd al-Malik, identical wording to no. 12 above, except for a missing first line. The first line seems to be *ʿabd allāh*; the space above it is too narrow to contain a previous line.

British Museum R47033.

14. A seal of Hishām b. ʿAbd al-Malik (105-125 AH/724-743 CE)

]// المؤ[منين// م امير // هشا عبد الله

Transliteration

ʿabd allāh Hishā/m amir/ al-mu[*ʾminīn*]

Translation

The servant of Allah, Hishām the caliph
22-28 mm

Amitai-Preiss N. and Farhi Y. 2010. 'A Small Assemblage of Lead Sealings, Weight and Coins from the Early Islamic Period', Israel Numismatic Journal 17:233, No.1.

15. A seal of Hishām b. ʿAbd al-Malik (105-125 AH/724-743 CE)

عبد الله // هشام امير // المؤمنين // .... م / و

Transliteration

ʿabd allāh / Hishām amir/ al-muʾminīn / ... mīm or *waw*

Translation

The servant of Allah, Hishām the caliph … M / W

Casanova, "Arab seals," pl. 2. 50 mm.

16. A seal from of 120 AH/737-738 CE (during the reign of Hishām b. ʿAbd al-Malik, but whose name does not appear explicitly)

بسم الله / عبد الله / [ا] مير ? / ا مير / المؤمنين / unclear Arabic letters/ في صدر سنة / عشرين ومئة

Transliteration

Bism Allāh / ʿabd allāh / [a]mīr ?/ amir/ al-muʾminīn / unclear Arabic letters / fi ṣadr sanat / ʿishrīn wa-miʾah

Translation

In the name of God, the servant of Allah, [A]mir? the caliph [made?] at the beginning of the year 120

Khalili collection, PBS 591.

17. A seal of Marwān b. Muḥammad (127 AH/744-745 CE)

[بسم الله] / [الر]حمن الرحيم / [ا]وفوا الكيل ولا / [تـ]كونوا من / [المـ]خسر[ين] / [اقيـ]م في خلافة / [عبد] الله مرون ام[ير] / [الـ]مؤمنين اصلحه / الله واطال بقائه / [على يـ]دي عثمن بن الوليد / [سنة سـ]بع وعشرين ومئة

Transliteration

[Bism allāh] / [al-ra]ḥmān al-raḥīm/ awfūa al-kayla wa-lā /takūnū min / [al-mu]khsir[īn] / [uqī]ma fī khilāfat / [ʿabd] allāh Marwān am[ir] / [al-]muʾminīn aṣlaḥahu /allāh wa-aṭāla biqāʾahu / [ʿalā ya]day ʿUthmān b. al-Walīd / [sanat sa]bʿ wa-ʿishrīn wa-miʾah

Translation

In the name of Allah, the Merciful, the Compassionate. Give full measure and to not be of those who cheat. Made during the caliphate of the servant of Allah, Marwān the caliph, Allah be good to him and extend his life, by the hands of ʿUthmān b. al-Walīd in the year 127.

Christie's 2001, pp. 134-135, no. 12.

99.23 g, 49-66 mm.

18. A seal of Marwān b. Muḥammad (128 AH/745-746 CE)

بسم الله / الرحمن الرحيم / اوفوا الكيل ولا / تكونوا من المخسر[ين] / اقيم قي خلاقة عبد / لله مرون ا مير الـ / المؤمنين اصلحه الله / واطال بقائه على / دى يزيد بن سليمن سنة ؟ / ثمان وعشرين [ومئة]

Transliteration

Bism allāh / al-raḥmān al-raḥīm/ awfūa al-kayla wa-lā /takūnū min / al-mukhsir[īn] / uqīma fī khilāfat ʿabd / allāh Marwān amir al- / al-muʾminīn aṣlaḥahu allāh / wa-aṭāla biqāʾahu ʿalā / yaday Yazīd b. Sulaymān sanat? thamān wa-ʿishrīn [wa-miʾah]

Translation

In the name of Allah, the Merciful, the Compassionate. Give full measure and to not be of those who cheat. Made during the caliphate of the servant of Allah, Marwān the caliph, Allah be good to him and extend his life, by the hands of Yazīd b. Sulaymān in the year 128.

Amitai-Preiss, 'An Umayyad Lead Seal with the Name of Marwān b. Muhammad', *Al-Qantara* 18/1 (1997), 233-42

140 g, 60-65 mm

19. A seal of Marwān b. Muḥammad

بسم الله / ا مر بصنعة / هذ ه مكيلة / مرون ا مير المؤ / منين على يدى الأمير / عبد السلام

Transliteration

Bism Allāh /amara bi-sanʿat / hādhihi mikyalah / Marwān amir al-muʾ / minīn ʿalā yaday al-amīr / ʿAbd al-Salām

Translation

In the name of Allah. Ordered the making of this *mikyalah* the slave of Allah Marwān the caliph, at the hands of the governor ʿAbd al-Salām.

Khalili collection PBS 559. 18.86 g, 20-29 mm. A nail on side B.

20. A seal of Marwān b. Muḥammad

[بسم الله] / [اقـ]يم في خلاف[ـة] عبد / [الله] مرون [ا مير] / [المؤ] منين اصلحه / [الله]

Transliteration

[Bism allāh] / [uqī]ma fī khilāf[at] / ʿabd [allāh] Marwān [amir] / [al-muʾ]minīn aṣlaḥahu /[allāh]

Translation

In the name of Allah, made during the caliphate of the servant of Allah, Marwān the caliph, Allah be good to him.

Christie's 2001, p. 134, no. 1. 22-32 mm. Side B: either smooth or with a nail, only side A is shown in the catalogue so it cannot be known for certain. Judging by the previous examples, there is a nail.

21. A seal with unclear formula (uncertain whether this belongs to the group of seals bearing the name of a caliph or the group of seals bearing the name of a governor who is a caliph's son)

بسم الله ... / / unidentified letters / unidentified letters / unidentified letters / unidentified letters / unidentified letters

Translation: the basmallah followed by five lines of unidentified letters

Burūda site. 53-58 mm.

The Significance of the Monetary Reforms of ʿAbd Al-Malik

Marcus Phillips[1]

De tous les appareils enregistreurs, capables de révéler à l'historien les mouvements profonde de l'économie, les phénomènes monétaires sont sans doute le plus sensibles. Mais ne leur reconnaître que cette valeur de symptôme serait manquer à leur rendre pleine justice, ils ont été et ont, à leur tour, des causes: quelque chose comme un sismographe qui non content de signaler les tremblements de terre, parfois les provoquerait.

Marc Bloch 1933

Abbasides, during reigns of, Saracens opulent.

Adam Smith 1776[2]

Introduction

Every year the Royal and the British Numismatic Societies hold a joint meeting where they discuss a subject of mutual interest and in 2021 to celebrate the 50th anniversary of the decimalisation of the UK currency they chose the subject of coin reforms. The plan was to look at different currency reforms throughout history from ancient times to modern; reforms that succeeded, reforms that failed, and to see if are there any common factors? Because of the pandemic the meeting was postponed to 2022 and then cancelled at the last minute.

This paper, to some extent, covers the same ground as the one I was intending to give at the RNS / BNS meeting but is quite different in scope. At the RNS / BNS meeting I would have been talking to an audience that was interested in comparing different coin reforms but knew very little about the reforms of ʿAbd al-Malik (65–86/685–705). Here, I am assuming that the reader has a working knowledge of the reforms and the events that led up to them.[3] Instead I am looking at the wider picture that has emerged in debates among historians about the historical identity of the early Islamic state and how the reforms have been interpreted in the context of this debate.

What struck me, looking at the papers in the original programme, and I mean no disrespect to their authors, is that there was nothing in the history of re-coinages and currency reforms that compares in ambition, scope and speed with that of ʿAbd al-Malik. What made it unique was that the reform was an integral part of a historical process that extended far beyond a change in coinage, and the fiscal system and culture in which it functioned. This is a vast subject, and this short paper can only deal with some of the issues involved, in particular those where numismatics has a significant role to play in the interpretation of the momentous changes which took place.

---

[1] Independent scholar, formerly co-editor of *The Numismatic Chronicle*. senmerv@hotmail.com
I was unable to give this paper at the Round Table meeting owing to being ill with Covid. As ever I am grateful to Susan Tyler-Smith for her help and advice especially with regard to the Sasanians.
[2] The first quotation is the opening sentence of 'Le problème de l'or au Moyen Age'. The second, is the first entry in the first edition of the *Wealth of Nations*. This index was not compiled by Smith himself.
[3] There is a good, up to date, survey of the whole process in Goodwin, *Standing Caliph Coinage*, pp. 12–24.

Coinage Reforms

The aim of a recoinage is to solve a problem(s) with the existing coinage. It succeeds to the extent that it solves the problem(s) and the length of time the solution lasts.
The most commonly encountered problems are:

1. Changes in the political situation.
2. The coinage has become over- or under-valued: too much of it or too little.
3. There is a gap in the denominational structure: too many high value coins and no small change, or vice versa.
3. Significant sections of the population find the designs unacceptable.
4. Technological developments such as the invention of the screw press.
5. Changes in the supply of precious metals, for example the discovery of new mines.

Some of these 'problems' reflect profound historical changes, others are merely technical developments. The two obvious factors in ʿAbd al-Malik's reform are a change in the political situation and the need to find a design that was generally acceptable to people using the coins. 'Changes in the political situation' may simply mean the replacement of one ruler by another but it can, as in this case, mean a good deal more. The reform was triggered by ʿAbd al-Malik's victories over both the Byzantine Empire and his Arab opponents: the Zubayrids and the Kharajites. This in turn obliged him to create a unified coinage for the territories where he had just established his rule. The need for a new coinage in the freshly conquered territories may have been apparent since the Arab conquest half a century earlier but ʿAbd al-Malik was the first Arab ruler to be able to attempt to issue a coinage that would circulate in both Syria and Persia with their different coinage traditions.

That ʿAbd al-Malik[4] decided, after some hesitant experiments, to adopt a wholly aniconic coinage is usually attributed to Muslims' attitude to images, especially those of living people, as unacceptable on coins. I will argue that this is not the whole explanation and in any case the question remains why he chose the legends he did. If 'success' is to be defined by sheer longevity then ʿAbd al-Malik's basic design, which lasted for centuries, must be regarded as perhaps the most successful in the history of numismatics.

ʿAbd al-Malik's political programme

I have already emphasised that ʿAbd al-Malik's coin reform was part of a comprehensive political programme. The reform of the coinage and the drastic nature of the changes involved need to be studied in this context. ʿAbd al-Malik aimed to establish not only his own, and his dynasty's, rule but also the future of the Arab state. This involved administrative reforms such as making Arabic the language of government and enhancing the status of Jerusalem by constructing the Dome of the Rock. More broadly, in Robert Hoyland's phrase, he sought to make Islam the ideology of Arab rule. He had just emerged from a war which he had been fighting on two fronts and during which his prospects of success, indeed his very survival, must at times have seemed doubtful.[5] Thus, ultimately, the success of the reform of the coinage was bound up not merely with the fortunes of ʿAbd al-Malik's dynasty but the whole future of the Arab state. To what extent ʿAbd al-Malik was

---

[4] We have no idea of the extent of ʿAbd al-Malik's personal involvement in the reforms. He certainly could not have carried them out in Iran without his brutal but effective representative al-Ḥajjāj b. Yūsuf and al-Ḥajjāj certainly played a role in shaping policy. There are references to a Jewish mastermind behind the reform, Sumair al-Yahudi, but there are doubts as to his existence, Tye, 'Sumair', p. 2. To keep saying 'ʿAbd al-Malik or his advisers' would clutter the text but it may be assumed.

[5] The war is usually referred to as the second *fitna* (civil war) but ʿAbd al-Malik was also fighting a foreign power: the Byzantine Empire. For convenience I have retained the word *fitna* to describe the whole conflict.

consciously aware of it is uncertain, but the success of the reforms depended ultimately on the degree to which Arab rule brought prosperity to the newly unified territories because this would make it more acceptable to the public at large.

The Arab 'Revolution'. Two recent interpretations

Traditionally the reform dinars and dirhams have been regarded as being as 'revolutionary' as the Arab conquest. Recently, some historians have begun to emphasise the evolutionary aspects of the phenomenon. For example, it is argued that the cultural developments that led to the adoption of a purely aniconic coinage had already been anticipated. In economic terms, and in total contrast to the West the Arabs maintained the classical fiscal system based on a land tax. Another school of thought has argued that the economic changes which occurred, which dramatically reversed a long period of economic decline and created an early form of capitalism, could be described as revolutionary. Both schools of thought are approaching the subject from different angles, but they have one point in common: the importance of coinage and in particular its availability. Yet despite its obvious importance the numismatic evidence has either been ignored or mis-interpreted by the scholars involved.

The nature of historical change, and the concept of 'Late Antiquity'

The Arab conquest was part of a period of historical change which is characterised as the transition from 'Ancient to Medieval'. However one defines these terms, indeed whether one even regards them as useful, there is no denying that the rule of two great empires, Rome and Persia, was replaced over large swaths of territory by people who had little history of coin use. The administration in the West broke down in the early fifth century but it was nearly four centuries before a new currency system based on a single denomination, the silver penny, emerged.

In Michael Hendy's famous formulation, the changes in the West can be characterised as a 'move from public to private'. That is, minting ceased to be a primarily fiscal tool for the extraction of tax by a centralised state and became a mechanism for the collection of rent by landowners and the circulation of private cash. This reflected the shift in the basis of power from control of a paid army and bureaucracy to the ownership of land.[6] The result was a drastic reduction on the amount of coinage issued and used, and the emergence, under the early Carolingians, of a currency consisting of a single denomination: the silver penny (with occasional halfpennies). A single denomination worth, say, £20, in modern money cried out for 'reform' but although the value of different pennies came to vary enormously, the system lasted for over four hundred years.

Compared to the West the transformation in the East was characterised by its extraordinary speed. Not only that, but the coinages of two Empires were involved. In both conquered areas, Syria and Iran, a transitional coinage emerged but lasted only some 50 years.[7] We are less well informed about the fiscal system in the Sasanian Empire but there seems little doubt that the coinage primarily served a tax raising role. What followed under the Arabs is discussed below.

I would argue that historical change – social, political, and economic – for it to be sustainable, has to be a gradual process rather than one resulting from a sudden cataclysmic revolutionary event. In the case of the Arab conquest one is confronted with a historiography that suggests that the changes reflected in the coinage and elsewhere were, indeed, just that: the result of a single catastrophic event. To later Muslims the key event was the revelation of Muḥammad but to a person living in seventh century Iran or Syria it was the Arab conquest. The extraordinary rapidity of this conquest

---

[6] Hendy, 'From public to private'. For additional references see Phillips, 'Coinage and the early Arab state', pp. 54–5.

[7] The transitional coinage persisted in more remote regions, notably Sistan and Ṭabaristān, for much longer.

reinforces the notion of a sudden cataclysmic change in which an invasion of 'warlike Bedouin hordes' wiped out the 'classical' states of Iran and Byzantine Syria.[8]

As already pointed out the reform of ʿAbd al-Malik was not a reaction to the initial conquest, but to his victories in the second *fitna* and the war with Byzantium. The reform, therefore, was at least in part a reflection of strains that had developed within Islamic society after the conquest, but recently some historians have emphasised that it also reflects historical trends that pre-dated the Arab conquest.

The term 'Late Antiquity' has, of course, a long history but usually referred to the last two centuries of the Roman Empire as a time of gradual decline in traditional values and the rise of Christianity. It has acquired the meaning of a specific historical epoch thanks largely to the work of Peter Brown. His *World of Late Antiquity* (1971) argued that the distinction between 'Ancient' and 'Medieval' implying a sudden break from one to the other was a false concept. Furthermore, the later Roman Empire was not simply a decadent form of the classical version but enjoyed a new vibrant culture. There was, however, a significant change in people's attitude to the Empire itself. The concept of Roman citizenship ceased to exist. People defined themselves by their religious affiliations. Thus:

> The arrival of the Arabs merely cut the last threads that had bound the provincials of the Near East to the Roman empire. In the Arab empire nobody was a 'citizen' in the classical sense. This was the final victory of the idea of the religious community over the classical idea of the state.

Brown says little about coinage but he does emphasise that the key point of ʿAbd al-Malik's reformed coinage was not its lack of imagery but that it was struck in the name of God, not a secular ruler. He makes another point relating to the change in coin design on the solidi of Justin II (565–78):

Figure 1. Solidus of Justin II (565–78) with 'Aphrodite' reverse. 4.48 g. CNG Electronic Auction 458 (18 December 2019) lot 578

> … when the Emperor placed the classical winged genius [sic!] of Constantinople on his coins in 570 the provincials were shocked. They thought he had become a pagan. What they wanted was the simple charged emblem of the cross.[9] (Fig. 1)

Brown includes the reform of the coinage 'the first fully Arabic' coins, as just one item in the list of changes which occurred in the late Seventh Century as 'The Eastern Mediterranean began to take on its Islamic face'. His fundamental point is that none of this was totally new but more the culmination of long standing social and cultural trends.

---

[8] Cf. Walker, *BMC Arab-Byzantine*, p. xvi.

[9] Brown, *World of Late Antiquity*, pp. 187 and 181. This derives from John of Ephesus (*c*.507–*c*.588) who states that the figure of Constantinople was taken to be Aphrodite. It had already been cited by Arnold Jones, 'Numismatics and history', p. 15, who took it as proof that the subtle messages numismatists derive from coin types were beyond the understanding of the 'masses' who used the coins. Neither Brown nor Jones question whether John's account should be taken at face value. John's actual text, at least in the only currently available translation, merely says that Justin 'introduced a female figure'.

Islamic 'Late Antiquity'

Brown regarded 'Late Antiquity', as far as Islam and the Arabs were concerned, as ending with the fall of the Umayyads. Quite recently the concept of an 'Islamic Late Antiquity' has been adopted by Islamic historians. In Hugh Kennedy's words:

> The concept of 'Islamic late antiquity'...has now achieved a general currency among historians as a hermeneutic device for interpreting and explaining the first three centuries of Islam rule in the Middle East, roughly from the time of the prophet until the middle of the tenth century. Sizgorich uses the term to describe a pattern of inter-communal relations and the role played by religious violence in maintaining the boundaries between different sects and groups – a pattern that he saw extending from late Antiquity (as described in the accepted Peter Brown model) into the early Islamic period with more communities and actors entering the fray. As such, his work played an important part in undermining those sharp but unhelpful barriers that still separate the world of late antiquity from the world of early Islam, both inside the academy and outside.[10]

In contrast to Brown therefore, Islamicists, or at least those who follow Sizgorich, see 'Late Antiquity' as extending to the collapse of the ʿAbbāsid dynasty in 334/946. In practice Kennedy sees this as merely the culmination of a process dating back to the civil wars that followed the death of Harun al-Rashid (193/809) and can be more clearly observed in the temporary sequestration of the caliphs in Samarra between 861and 870 and the revolt of the Zanj (869–83). By the early decades of the tenth century the government was running increasingly short of cash and resorting to tax farming and the sale of state assets. The result has striking parallels with Hendy's 'public to private' model:

> The privatisation of taxation resembled the process of change and decay that characterised the end of imperial administration in much of fifth century Gaul and sixth century northern Italy. It represented in a very real sense the end of Islamic late antiquity and the disappearance of that most important legacy of the ancient world: the system of public taxation.[11]

Kennedy does not mention Hendy but his article would appear to be a first attempt to answer Hendy's 'challenge' that somehow the divergent models of coinage which, in his opinion, developed in Byzantium and the West needed to be complemented by a similar study of developments in the contemporary Arab world.[12] Kennedy is an acknowledged authority on Islamic state finance and this article is a welcome attempt by an Arabist to compare developments in east and west.

The continuation of the ancient fiscal system under Islam: the land tax

Kennedy's essential point is that for its first two centuries Islamic rule can indeed be described as 'Late Antiquity' because it marked the continuation of a tax system based on agricultural land. This was a direct contrast with events in Northern Italy, Gaul and Spain where the invading populations

[10] H. Kennedy, 'The Middle East in Islamic late antiquity'; Sizgorich, *Violence and Belief in Late Antiquity*. This does not discuss the coinage.
[11] Kennedy, 'Islamic late antiquity', p. 401.
[12] Quoted Phillips, 'Coinage and the early Arab state', pp. 68–9. I have to mention that page 68 of my article contains an unfortunate typo: 'not' should be inserted between 'do' and 'particularly' three lines up from the bottom! In other words I meant to say 'I do not recommend' not, as printed, 'I do recommend'.

were settled on the land. From the beginning the Arab leaders were keen to settle their soldiers, particularly the Bedouin and their dependents, in the newly created garrison towns, Kufa and Basra, as well as more established settlements.[13] They were paid a pension, *ʿatā*', (literally 'gift'), which necessitated large amounts of coin.

> According to narrative sources the number of military settlers in Basra around 670…was some 80,000 with around 120,000 in their families, while in Kufa at the same time there were some 60,000 with 80,000 dependents. Even if all the fighting men had been paid only the lowest rate of '*ʿatā*', 200 dirhams per year, this would still have meant that an enormous amount of coined money was in circulation. …Like the late Roman and Sasanian empires, but unlike contemporary western Europe and even contemporary Byzantium, coined money was in regular use for all types of transactions at all levels of society except possibly the very poorest in remote rural areas.

In earlier writing Kennedy has quoted some of the more fantastic figures such as the claim by al-Balādhurī (*c.*205–79/*c.*820–92 that the total annual revenue collected amounted to 60,000,000 dirhams, as though they were genuine. But even if we dismiss such claims as exaggerated, it still remains that a large amount of coin was available.[14] Although referred to as 'dirhams' they can only have been Sasanian drachms plus the, somewhat lighter, Arab-Sasanian issues.

The fiscal system was, Kennedy argues, a continuation of that of the Sasanians. The key was the area known as the *Sawad* which stretched from Ctesiphon to the head of the Persian Gulf. According to later accounts this provided four times as much revenue as Egypt and five times as much as Syria and Palestine together. It was conquered early on by Bedouin tribesmen but the Sasanian fiscal system and its functionaries were preserved intact.[15] The '*ʿatā*' system could not have worked without them and their records.

The vast revenues of the *Sawad* were of no use to ʿAbd al-Malik in the second *fitna* since it was largely occupied by his enemies. There is considerable doubt about how much he was able to extract from Egypt and there was a consensus that what was collected in Iraq or Egypt should remain there. ʿAbd al-Malik had been obliged to rely on what he could collect from Syria plus his own estates.[16] Naturally this was a situation he sought to reverse after his victories. A standing army under the control of the caliphs and paid for by taxation was the obvious solution. Even after the inevitable Iraqi tribal revolts had been overcome this still did not mean that all the revenue of the *Sawad* went to Syria. ʿAbd al-Malik and al-Ḥajjāj b. Yūsuf (*c.*40–95/*c.*661–714) solved the problem by moving large numbers of Syrian troops to Iraq where they could maintain order and have direct access to the taxation revenue of the locality. A centralised coinage went from being desirable to being a necessity, even though it took a long while for the territorial divisions of gold in the West and silver in the East to be overcome.[17] The new arrangements meant an increase in the demand for coined silver. The new mint of Wāsiṭ, half way between Basra and Kufa, coined silver on an industrial scale. This raises the question where did this silver come from? Was it simply obtained by melting down existing stocks or did the Arabs have access to sources of precious metal which had hitherto been unavailable?

---

[13] Kennedy, 'Islamic late antiquity', pp. 392–4.
[14] Kennedy, 'Armies of the caliphs', pp. 19–21, 71–4.
[15] For details see Morony, *Iraq after the Muslim Conquest*, pp. 99–125.
[16] Phillips, 'Coinage and the early Arab state', p. 67. See also Kennedy, 'Islamic late antiquity', p. 367.
[17] The standard account is still Heidemann, 'Merger of two currency zones'.

In his survey of the role of tax in other areas conquered by the Arabs Kennedy has to admit that he has virtually no evidence for post conquest Syria beyond the papyri from Nessana. These indicate that:

> ... the transfer of resources from the local inhabitants to the Arabic tribes was at this stage much simpler and on a much smaller scale than in contemporary Iraq. *The documents give little evidence for the use of coin* and none of any central administrative apparatus. But it would be rash to extrapolate from this to the rest of Syria. Nessana was always a small town on the margins of the desert The taxation system in a developed agricultural area near the center of power – the Ghuta of Damascus for example – might have been much more developed. (My italics)[18]

Another problem for Kennedy's thesis is that Syria was not conquered by the Bedouin but by members of the prophet's tribe – the Quraysh and other tribes from the Hijaz, in other words the early Muslim elite plus Arabs who lived there before the conquest. It was this elite that is said to have started the great economic revival envisaged by some scholars. The availabilty of coinage in Syria is discussed below.

As for the reform itself, Kennedy places it squarely in the context of ʿAbd al-Malik's fiscal and administrative reforms, in particular the adoption of Arabic as the language of administration. Unfortunately his comments on the coinage contain a number of errors:

> Until ... around 700 the Muslim authorities had used coins based on Byzantine and Sasanian models: the gold dinar of the Byzantines and the silver dirhem of the Sasanians. Both sort of coins were embellished with human images but were sometimes overstruck with short Arabic inscriptions. The new coins, though based on the weights and materials of the previous ones, were entirely epigraphic, giving religious inscriptions, names of rulers and the date and place of minting. For the purposes of this discussion, the important thing was the imposition of a form of monetary standardisation, albeit based on the gold standard of the west and the silver standard of the east.[19]

In Iraq the coins used were a mixture of old Sasanian ones and new Arab imitations, but the former predominated. In Syria and Egypt the only coinage of any significance was in copper. Precious metal coins were few and of an experimental nature. Of the reform coins in precious metal only the silver gave the place of minting, and dinars and dirhams remained anonymous until the time of the ʿAbbāsids. The first name to appear in 145H (762/3) was that of the caliph's son not the caliph himself.[20] There was certainly a degree of monetary standardisation but the circulation areas of the two metals remained separated for a long time.

More to the point perhaps, Kennedy misses what seems to be an important point which is relevant to his argument. Until the reform, in monetary terms Syria and Egypt remained part of the Byzantine empire. The gold coins they used were the products of Constantinople and this was a matter of indifference to the Arabs. It was only after the reform that they became independent of the solidus. As far as weight is concerned the new dinar was slightly lighter than the solidus but the silver dirham was approximately seven tenths of the old Sasanian drachm. Why this weight was chosen has never been satisfactorily explained.[21]

---

[18] Kennedy, 'Islamic late antiquity', p. 396.

[19] Kennedy, 'Islamic late antiquity', p. 399.

[20] Comprehensive discussion in Bates, 'Who was named on Abbasid coins'.

[21] This is in spite of an extensive literature dating back to the first Arabic annalists who discussed it at length.

New metal? The myth of Sasanian gold

The idea, first, that the Arabs had access to important, new, sources of precious metal and second, that this was of decisive importance in determining both the success, indeed the very nature, of Arab rule was, as far as I know, first argued by Maurice Lombard.[22] His pioneering article of 1947 is still, despite its date, heavily relied on by authors such as Jairus Banaji in their interpretation of the economic foundations of early Islam. Lombard was principally concerned with the Mediterranean, and he also took a long-term view of Muslim economic expansion which he saw as based on gold. He was naturally interested in how this started and concluded that even in its earliest stages the Arab conquest had a significant effect on bullion supply. In complete contrast to Brown and Kennedy's concept of Late Antiquity he saw the conquest as essentially negating, not enhancing, pre-existing trends.

Lombard describes the world of Late Antiquity as one of steady Roman decline caused by an increasing shortage of gold. This was because the Byzantines continued to export gold in spite of losing their mineral sources in Dacia and Ethiopia. Between the fifth and seventh centuries the amount of coinage in circulation 'shrank by 20%'. This weakened Roman commerce and led, among other disasters, to the loss of their domination of the maritime route to India.[23]

The main recipient of the gold, according to Lombard, was Sasanian Persia. Solidi flooded out of the Byzantine empire to buy Persian luxury goods. In addition, the political weakness of the Byzantine state meant that throughout the sixth century the emperors were obliged to pay the *Shahanshah* successive tributes of '20 to 30,000 gold pieces' as well.

What happened to all this gold? The Sasanians followed Persian tradition in maintaining an essentially monometallic silver currency, a tradition Lombard thought derived ultimately from their access to silver mines. Instead:

> Les monnaies byzantines ne courent pas dans l'Empire, sâssânide, pas plus que les monnaies romaines ne couraient dans le Royaume parthe: elles y sont fondues et transformées en lingots, en bijoux, en mobilier précieux de toute sorte, qui vont s'enfouir dans les palais et les harems des souverains et des grands seigneurs perses. L'or qui franchissait la frontière de l'Euphrate était donc perdu pour la vie des échanges. Rôle de « pays mangeur d'or »: tout le métal monétaire arraché au circuit méditerranéen s'immobilise dans les trésors de l'Iran et de la Mésopotamie. C'est là que les conquérants musulmans le trouveront.[24]

There are a number of problems with this model. To begin with it was illegal for private citizens in Byzantium to export precious metal.[25] This ban was quite possibly broken at times but the unauthorised transport of gold and silver beyond the imperial frontiers must have a been a hazardous and expensive affair. The state of course ignored its own rules and paid large sums to foreign friends, and enemies, in the form of subsidies, ransoms, bribes, presents and so on. As far as payments to the Sasanians were concerned, they only became serious in 532 when Khusro I (531–79) took advantage of Justinian I's Mediterranean preoccupations and had to be bought off with mixed results. Payments tended to be spasmodic, if quite frequent, after that but would have ceased

[22] Lombard, 'Les bases monétaires d'une suprématie économique'. Maurice Lombard (1904–65) was highly regarded by contemporaries but he published relatively little in his lifetime. Ferdinand Braudel wrote that he '... aura été le plus doué, le plus brillant historien de notre génération, le seul qui fut incontestablement de la classe d'un Marc Bloch'. Goff and Braudel, 'Maurice Lombard', p. 713.
[23] Lombard, 'Les bases monétaires', pp. 145–7.
[24] Lombard, 'Les bases monétaires', pp. 146–7.
[25] Hendy, *Studies*, pp. 257–60.

after 591 when Khusro II (590–628) was forced to rely on Maurice (582–602) to restore him to the throne. More generally they do not compare in size with the payments made to Western peoples: Franks, Lombards and Avars.[26] Furthermore, although the state may have discouraged the export of precious metals, it encouraged their import and Lombard's view of the Byzantine-Persian trade as being entirely one-way is not necessarily correct. Lombard himself described Egypt as a magnet for precious metals from the West but that it then acted as a 'sponge' in soaking up gold and not putting it to productive use.

There is clear evidence, on the other hand, of 'de-thesaurisation' of Sasanian silver. According to al-Ṭabarī (224–310/839-923), when Khusro II was deposed his enemies accused him of, among other crimes, of raising extortionate taxes and being a miser.[27] When the Arabs captured Ctesiphon in about 637 they found, in addition to all manner of precious metal artefacts, a huge quantity of silver coins (dirhams). In his, now outdated, study, of the coin reforms of ʿAbd al-Malik, Philip Grierson calculated this as nine thousand million dirhams.[28] He emphasised that this was 'no doubt exaggerated' but figures like this have a habit of becoming established in the historical literature. Grierson, dependent on Hermann Zotenberg's abbreviated translation of al-Ṭabarī, worked it out from a statement that 12,000 dirhams were given to the 60,000 soldiers who took part in the capture of Ctesiphon which amounted to four fifths of the total, the remaining fifth being allocated to the caliph, ʿUmar b. al-Khaṭṭāb (13–23/634–44). The full text states that the 12,000 dirhams were given to every horseman and adds 'no infantry having participated at the conquest'. An earlier passage mentions that 60,000 were present at the conquest which may or may not be the same people.[29] How realistic are these figures? 60,000 cavalry is an astonishing number. According to Fred Donner not only were the Arab armies considerably smaller but cavalry was in very limited supply and the 'brunt of the fighting seems to have fallen upon the infantrymen'. The figure of '12,000 men' appears in the sources to describe the size of the Arab armies at the battles of al-Qadisiyya and Jalula and Donner thinks this exaggerated.[30] It may even be a *topos*.

There is, however, clear numismatic evidence that at some stage after the Arab conquest a number of hoards with a terminal date of 601/2 which had been stockpiled, presumably in the royal treasury, were released into circulation.[31] The date of their release is obscure and they could have come from other treasuries beside Ctesiphon, but they must have been found some time before the reforms of ʿAbd al-Malik. The hoards are so numerous that it can probably be assumed that they did make a significant contribution to the amount of silver in circulation in the lands of the old Sasanian empire. But one should beware of taking too much notice of precise figures quoted by the Arabic annalists.

If the Arabs had found much gold it would most likely have stayed in the region in which it was discovered and certainly not have all been sent to Syria or the Hejaz. There is no trace of an upsurge of gold ornaments in Iran at the time of the conquest and certainly none of it was coined. Sasanian gold must have been looted but on present evidence the quantities were not that significant.

---

[26] Useful list in Hendy, *Studies*, pp. 260–3. Hendy argues that, despite their size there is no sign that these payments caused any strain to the Byzantine economy until, possibly, the reign of Maurice since his attempts to reduce military pay caused a revolt which cost him his throne.
[27] Bosworth, *History of al-Tabari*, 5, *Sāsānids*, p. 383. The text specifically refers to the land tax.
[28] Grierson, 'Monetary reforms of ʿAbd al-Malik', pp. 259–60. This is just one example of Grierson's uncritical use of the Arabic historians.
[29] Juynboll, *History of al-Tabari*, 13, *Conquest of Iraq*, p. 29.
[30] Donner, *Early Islamic Conquests*, pp. 221–30. Kennedy, 'Armies', pp. 10–11 emphasises the key role of infantry in the battles in the early stages of the Arab conquests.
[31] Tyler-Smith, *Coinage reforms of Khusrau II*, chapter 4.

Other new sources of gold

Lombard saw the period leading up to 700 as one of exploitation of booty which was superseded by administrative reform. He had already suggested that Syria and Egypt absorbed gold without spending it. It was mostly stored in churches. Prior to the reforms the Arabs had relied on the church authorities for much of the administration of the country. This changed with the reforms of ʿAbd al-Malik whereby the Arabs began to create their own administrative machinery and began to tax the churches. As a result masses of gold was released onto the market though it was inevitably a drawn out process.

Lombard was taking a long-term view, but it was largely confined to the Mediterranean. He was interested in the whole process of how gold (not silver) became the basis of Arab prosperity and consequently Arab rule. He has some interesting detail on how the caliphs came to an arrangement with the *matâlib* (literally treasure hunters but in this context tomb robbers) whereby they could keep their loot provided they gave the government a fifth share of the profits.[32] The sources for this date from the ninth century but it is not clear when it started. For Lombard this was just one more example of the 'liberation' of hoarded gold which was the equivalent of the discovery of new gold mines. This came somewhat later as the Arabs came into contact with the gold miners of the Western Sudan:

> La remise en circulation ainsi échelonnée de grosses quantités d'or thésaurisées dans le Proche et le Moyen-Orient est un des faits capitaux de l'histoire économique du haut moyen âge. A une époque où le volume d'or neuf extrait des mines n'est pas encore très considérable, elle équivaut à la découverte de nouveaux gisements métalliques. Mais, dans le domaine de l'exploitation minière aussi, la conquête musulmane devait marquer une étape décisive.

Lombard's view of the reforms of ʿAbd al-Malik was limited by the lack of available data. He quite rightly saw the monetary reforms as an integral aspect of a wide-ranging political settlement. He showed little interest in the ideological aspect of the new coins. He did not have any information on the finds of post-conquest Byzantine gold and copper coins in Syria, so assumed that the Arabs made do with existing coin stocks which of course gradually diminished; hence his emphasis on supply and dethesaurisation of hoarded metal. Whereas for Brown the supplanting of the (Syrian) Umayyads by the (Iraqi) ʿAbbāsids was crucial in moving the centre of gravity of Arab civilisation from west to east, Lombard ignored it.

Lombard's successors and the first capitalists

Andrew Ehrenkreutz essentially agreed with Lombard's conclusions but criticised him for not asking why the Arabs needed so many coins.[33] Releasing large amounts of cash on a stagnant economy would have caused an inflation, of which there is no record. The increase in coin availability therefore must have been a response to increased demand which must in turn have reflected an expanding economy. This expansion was largely due to a mass migration of unskilled labour from the Hejaz, some of whom enjoyed the benefits of the *ʿatā* system. Those who did not at least had the benefit of seeing their taxes, which were no worse than they had been under the old empires, being retained and re-invested in the local economy instead of being sent off to foreign capitals. He followed Lombard in emphasising the deterioration of coin stocks in both east and west being under the impression that the circulation of silver in the old Sasanian empire was increasingly

---

[32] Lombard, 'Les bases monétaires', p. 149. Apparently, the kings of Spain came to a similar relationship with the tomb robbers of South America.

[33] This paragraph summarises three articles: 'Money', 'Pirenne Thesis' and 'Silent Force'. They repeat a good deal but 'Pirenne Thesis' is the most useful.

debased. Trying to make do with the two coinage systems left over from the Byzantine and Sasanian empires was retarding economic growth and administrative reform. While it may have had an ideological component the prime purpose of the reform was economic.[34]

What now seems extraordinary is that neither author mentions the second *fitna*. They speak as though the whole Arab community enjoyed the blessings of peace and a unified fiscal system. This was a reflection on the essentially harmonious nature of the conquest after the prevailing elites had been removed. If this had not been the case, then the economic progress they postulated could not have taken place.

More recently Jairus Banaji has modified his two predecessors' arguments and argued that Arab economic expansion began immediately after the conquest. According to him Byzantine solidi and Sasanian silver 'continued to circulate in vast quantities'.[35] He anticipates Kennedy by insisting that this was because the Arabs continued to use the same fiscal system as their predecessors, based on the land tax. Indeed the economy was even more 'monetised' than before, partly because of the release of hoarded gold but also because the Arabs completed the process of paying taxes in cash instead of kind. Thus he followed Lombard in his insistence on the vast amounts of gold released from the Sasanian treasury but ignored his suggestion that the release of hoarded gold in Syria and Egypt only became significant in the eighth century, largely as a consequence of ʿAbd al-Malik's reforms. At the same time he tends to discount Lombard's point about later supplies of new gold from the Sudan.

It was not just a matter of bullion supply. The Arab ruling class, especially the caliphs, were far more business friendly than their imperial predecessors. Indeed, their outlook could be described as 'proto-capitalist'. This is not a new notion. Authors such as Eliyahu Ashtor and Patricia Crone had already emphasised the 'pre-modern capitalist' identity of medieval Islamic society. They saw this as only really blossoming in the days of the ʿAbbāsid caliphate. Banaji sees the process as developing quickly in the 640s, emphasising the acquisitiveness and entrepreneurial skill of the Arabs, of whom ʿUthmān (23–35/644–56) and Muʿāwiya (41–60/661–80) are singled out.[36] But this commercial talent would not have counted for much had it not been for 'monetisation', i.e. the availability of precious metal. Indeed the sources mention transactions involving breath taking sums.[37]

The evidence for the existence of all this cash depends on later authors. There is no doubt that the early caliphs were wealthy men and great property developers. Whether some of the sums amounting to 'millions of dirhams' are both realistic and really refer entirely to coins, as opposed to money of account, must as I have already argued be treated with scepticism.[38] The key point is, however, that if Banaji and others are right then the reforms of ʿAbd al-Malik were of no great economic significance, beyond possibly facilitating a process which was already in full swing.

---

[34] 'The monetary reform of ʿAbd al-Malik, its alleged religious or ideological background notwithstanding, must have been undertaken in response to the expanding market conditions', Ehrenkreutz, 'Pirenne Thesis', p. 103.

[35] Banaji, 'Late antique legacies', p. 168.

[36] Benedikt Koehler goes one stage further and dates the process to Mohammad himself, who in an eye-catching first chapter heading he terms 'the richest man in Arabia'. His account of the coinage reform (chapter 12) is full of errors, for example the statement that the post reform dirham was 'precisely' the same weight as the pre-reform Sasanian drachm, and quoting Stefan Heidemann, 'Merger', p 100, as a reference! *Early Islam and the Birth of Capitalism*, p. 103 and fn 18.

[37] Banaji, 'Late antique legacies', pp. 168–71. Banaji does admit that this caused tensions in the ruling elite between the businessmen and the 'theocratic group' of the Quraysh.

[38] The figures are always rounded down to the nearest thousand or million as appropriate. It is always worth bearing in mind the legendary gold nugget of the king of Ghana, first apparently mentioned by the eleventh century author al-Bakri. The twelfth century geographer Muhammad al-Idrisi said it weighed thirty pounds and the king used it to tether his horse. By the time of ibn Khaldun, who reported its sale by a spendthrift prince, it was said to weigh a ton, Bovill, *Golden Trade*, p. 81.

In his careful sifting of the literary evidence James Howard-Johnston highlights a contemporary source which he considers to be basically reliable. There is an account, by George the Monk (fl. 680–700), of the gradual increase in Arab exactions on the wealth of Christian churches in Egypt.[39] This states that Arab demands did not become pressing until the start of the second *fitna* and then only amounted to 10,000 dinars (i.e. solidi). At this stage ʿAbd al-Malik was seriously in need of money to fight the war, though Howard-Johnston thinks that this also marked the first stirrings of a programme of forced conversion. Real pressure only began towards the end of the *fitna* in 691. Ten years later a new governor began what Howard-Johnston calls 'a level [of extraction] close to outright persecution' which in practice meant, among other things, forcing monks to pay the poll tax. Under successive governors the exactions grew steadily worse. This was not just a question of greed but a gradual increase in intolerance on the part of the Arab conquerors. Be that as it may, if George's account is reliable then the stocks of hoarded gold in Christian churches in Egypt did not become significant as source of supply until shortly before the reforms of ʿAbd al-Malik.

I would argue that the numismatic evidence, which I have already referred to, has a decisive role to play here. If gold, whether coined or not, was being systematically extracted from Byzantine churches in Egypt and Syria then it should be reflected in the finds today. The coin hoards should have a 'tail', that is a percentage of older coins going back, in theory, to the time of Constantine. Seventh century gold coins found in Syria (and the hoards are comparatively plentiful) concealed after the Persian invasion essentially start with Focas.[40]

Normally Byzantine coinage was systematically recalled and reminted, but for most of the seventh century Syria and Egypt were out of Byzantine control. Gold coins stayed there and either continued to circulate or be hoarded or melted down. But in the latter case they were not recoined by the Arabs who issued very little gold. The same would apply to uncoined gold. It needed to be turned into coin to fit Banaji's ideas of 'monetisation'. In short, until the reforms of ʿAbd al-Malik the Arabs in Syria were dependent on Constantinople for their gold coins. Broadly speaking Lombard's view was correct.

Copper

The total neglect of the copper coinage by all the authors mentioned so far reflects the sources: it is just not discussed.[41] Copper coins do of course predominate in excavations and there has been some discussion by archaeologists on what the finds tells us about economic activity and the nature of the Arab conquest.[42] In the West pure copper coins, as opposed to debased billon, all but disappeared for nearly a millennium after the sixth century except in areas under Byzantine control. In the East copper coins continued to be used but by the eighth century Muslim jurists were arguing that they were not 'money' in the true sense of the word. This coincided with the time that the first surviving historical annals were being compiled and their authors simply reflected current views.[43] This view of copper coins may have developed somewhat earlier and there are a couple of *hadith* traditions which associate copper with idolatry which may have discouraged early Muslims from working with it.[44]

[39] Howard-Johnston, *Witnesses to a World Crisis*, pp. 309–11. George's account is contained in the *History of the Patriarchs of Alexandria* compiled in the eleventh century.

[40] Material usefully collected in Bijovsky, 'Byzantine solidi from Bet She'an', esp. pp. 180–3 and figure 11. Subsequently published hoards do not alter the picture. By contrast early Umayyad gold hoards do not contain Byzantine gold, indicating that the latter were collected and reminted with remarkable speed and efficiency.

[41] The thirteenth century writer known as bar Hebraeus is an exception, but he was writing in a different tradition.

[42] Phillips, 'Coinage in Syria', *forthcoming.*

[43] Phillips, 'Coinage in Syria'; Ilisch, 'ʿAbd al-Malik's monetary reform in copper', p. 143.

[44] I am indebted to Sdin Vadukut for this suggestion and for information about the hadiths.

Copper coin, however, had been an integral part of the Roman/Byzantine system ever since the reforms of Diocletian. Copper coins were worth hoarding so must have had a value beyond that of small change limited in time and place. According to Hendy's viewpoint their primary function was not simply to provide a small change for everyday transactions but to extract gold from circulation. Thus soldiers and other state functionaries received their wages in high value coins which, for the most part, had to be exchanged, at official rates, so they could spend it. The state, therefore, soon received the precious metal back. Changes to military payments can be associated with fluctuations in the output of copper coins. If a tax payer owed the fisc two thirds of a solidus or above he had to pay an additional solidus and receive his change in copper. This system is only recorded the eleventh century but, Hendy argues, probably existed earlier.[45]

Unfortunately we know nothing from written sources about the role of copper coinage in the Sasanian empire. It was struck at official royal mints and, in the later centuries at least, followed the typology of the silver coins. Recorded hoards, on the other hand, are exceptional. The biggest, 1842 coins, contained a high proportion of imitations.[46] A parcel of 20 copper coins of Hormizd IV (579–90) in the Tehran Museum is almost certainly a hoard or part of one.[47] Since about 2018 relatively large numbers of copper and lead coins of Yazdgard I (399–420), Vahran V (420–38) and Yazdgard II (438–57) have appeared on the market, presumably coming from one of more hoards. Coins that were hitherto ignored may be appearing thanks to demand and it is possible that Sasanian copper was issued in larger quantities than previously thought. The fact remains, though, that it is not nearly as abundant as Roman or Byzantine copper.

These points are discussed in detail by Lutz Ilisch in his article on the role of copper in ʿAbd al-Malik's reform. ʿAbd al-Malik's original intention was indeed to create a copper coinage that would, in theory, circulate from the Egypt to Iran. It had the simplest of designs: the two most important parts of the *shahada.* Style and fabric varied and there was a system of privy marking which still needs to be studied.[48] The whole system was abandoned even in Syria, ʿAbd al-Malik's base, within about five to six years and there is some doubt as to whether it was ever established in the East. Ilisch does not really explain why ʿAbd al-Malik adopted such a drastic programme of centralisation and, perhaps more important, why he abandoned it. Certainly it proved extremely difficult to operate and Ilisch wonders if the expected benefits had simply not materialised, without defining what these benefits might have been. He makes a number of suggestions, one of which hints that it may have been connected with tax, but the total lack of evidence makes it impossible to say more.[49]

Figure 2. Umayyad fals no mint, no date. 2.51 g.
Album Auction 15 (18 January 2013) lot 167.

[45] Hendy, *Studies*, pp. 286–8; 'East and West', pp. 654–6.
[46] Schindel, 'Hoard of late Sasanian copper coins'.
[47] Curtis *et al*, *Sylloge of Sasanian Coins*, nos 1457–1476.
[48] The illustrated coin has a single pellet in the obverse legend. Some coins with more elaborate marks are illustrated on the Zeno web site. https://www.zeno.ru/showgallery.php?cat=5260&page=1
[49] Ilisch, 'ʿAbd al-Malik's monetary reform in copper', p. 142, 'Another alternative might be that the unity of copper coinage, even if found to be useful, was traded away to the governors by the central government in exchange for another tax or for anything more desirable.' Ilisch give examples from later periods of how such a tax operated.

The same article also makes some important points about the reform of the silver coinage and the degree of centralisation. Whereas all the coin evidence indicates that the gold was comprehensively called in and reminted, the position with the silver is less clear. Huge quantities must have been restruck, particularly after the establishment of the mint of Wāsiṭ in 84H, but Sasanian type drachms survive in hoards until the early third century of the hegira. So there was no systematic replacement of the old types by the new one. Ilisch also shows that the coin evidence suggests that ʿAbd al-Malik's original intention was to centralise the minting of silver as well as gold in Damascus since the first silver coins attributable to Damascus do not give a mint. (Fig. 3) This was thwarted in the East by al-Hajjāj's refusal to close active local silver mints. Indeed, it was Damascus that adopted a type initially coined at a few mints in the East rather than the other way round. One factor may have been the relative lack of control that ʿAbd al-Malik was able to exercise in Iran compared to Syria. It was, of course, also al-Hajjāj who took the important decision to allow, or perhaps confirm the legality of, merchants to have their own silver coined at the mints.[50]

Figure 3. Dirham of AH 79 with no mint name. 2.69 g.
Morton & Eden, Auction 99 (2 May 2019) lot 9.

I would suggest that the relative quantity of the respective coinages was also a problem. To judge by the thoroughness with which it was recoined, the quantity of coined gold in circulation must have been manageable. Copper coins in the form of official Byzantine issues and various categories of imitations were present in large numbers and a confusing variety. A wholesale replacement with a single, standard type was obviously desirable and the evidence of overstriking and finds suggests it was, initially, carried out fairly thoroughly.

Acceptable and unacceptable designs.

The design on the reform coins marked a revolutionary break with the Graeco-Roman tradition, being purely epigraphic and anonymous. This followed a very brief period of experimentation. I have left this aspect of the reform until now because it has already been analysed in depth by others. Three of the most important and recent of these, although there is naturally a good deal of overlap, focus of different aspects of the subject. Luke Treadwell has discussed the iconography of the coins of this 'experimental' phase, while Stefan Heidemann concentrates more on the inscriptions: the so called 'war of words'. Michael Humphreys on the 'war of images' deals more with the struggle with Byzantium.[51] This tendency for specialists to concentrate on their respective fields obscures the fact that ʿAbd al-Malik was having to contend with two (or three) sets of opponents simultaneously.

---

[50] In Kennedy's new translation p. 455 'al-Hajjāj gave permission to the merchants and others to have silver struck for them', *History of the Arab Invasions*, p. 455. For the significance of this decision see Phillips, 'Coinage', p. 55. It is not clear what significance to attach to the specific reference to silver but not gold. It could be a reflection of the unimportance of gold in the East but there may have been other reasons.

[51] Treadwell, 'Abd al-Malik's coinage reforms'; Heidemann, 'Evolving representation; 'Humphreys, 'War of images revisited'.

There is a consensus that the decision to abandon any form of images had little to do with objections to representational art as such. Humphreys and Treadwell come close to agreeing that the real difficulty was the Arabs' failure to develop their own iconography. Treadwell emphasises the problems of finding images that made sense to both Iranians and Greeks:

> The problems did not lie in an uneven contest between the elaborate and refined visual repertoire of Byzantium versus the underdeveloped and untested Umayyad visual tradition. Instead it was the insurmountable challenge of creating a new numismatic iconography out of both Sasanian and Byzantine Late Antique traditions which brought the precious metal figural coinage of the transitional period to a close.[52]

Humphreys is quite enthusiastic about the standing caliph coinage but does not discuss the Sasanian style drachm which Treadwell dismisses as 'awkward':

> Nonetheless, it (i.e. Standing Caliph) was a type that was still bound into the world of images inhabited by the Roman empire and Christianity for centuries… In essence, ʿAbd al-Malik was playing a game whose rules were written by someone else.[53]

This essentially coincides with Treadwell's view that the epigraphic coinage was making a virtue out of necessity. This does not explain why ʿAbd al-Malik chose this moment to make his drastic changes in coin design, why he chose to create an anonymous coinage and why he chose the legends he did. Heidemann has an explanation which derives from his insistence that the *fitna* did not end with the defeat of the Zubayrids in 692 but with defeat and death of the Azraqite leader Qatarī ibn al-Fuja'a in 78 or 79/698/9, who, it has to be said, had no inhibitions about striking Sasanian style coins.

The ideological challenges presented by ʿAbd al-Malik's opponents in the *fitna* were in two different categories. The Zubayrid slogans which they placed on their coins could simply be adopted, but those of the Kharajites ('Judgement is God's alone') were another matter:

> For the first time in 66/685–6, Zubayrid governors, as a manifestation of the new Islamic imperial self-consciousness, put on coins the invocation of the messengership of Muhammad, and then – presumably in 70/689–90 – extended it by the profession of the unity of God.
> The Khārijite leaders, too, placed distinctive religious slogans on their coins challenging the claim of the Umayyads to rule, with the expression that there is only guidance by God. The Khārijite beliefs, though, were not at all a common denominator among all Muslims …
> The reform attempts of ʿAbd al-Malik and al-Ḥajjāj b. Yūsuf can be seen as a reply to these challenges, in an attempt to integrate the Zubayrid movement and to face the ideological Khārijite menace …[54]
>
> …On the silver coins, the ruler's side bears the word of God, a variation of the complete *Sūrat al-Ikhlāṣ*, surrounded by the *risāla*, a variation of Qurʾan 9:33, both

[52] Treadwell, 'Abd al-Malik's coinage reforms', p. 379.
[53] Humphreys, 'War of images', p. 243.
[54] Heidemann, 'Evolving representation, p. 188.

representing the sovereignty of God and constituting almost a concession to Khārijite thinking.[55]

The same would surely apply to the decision to issue a purely anonymous coin which, as Brown pointed out, was struck in the name of God.[56] Considering ʿAbd al-Malik had described himself, on his coins, but nowhere else, as 'God's Caliph' (Deputy) this was a considerable volte face.

The problem of the three standing figures

A slightly shortened version of the first sentence of the *Sūrat al-Ikhlāṣ* had already appeared on a coin of Ṭabariya which is usually regarded as a centre of Jewish culture.[57] (Fig. 4) As far as we can tell it would have been contemporary with the Standing Caliph coinage. When this legend was adopted on Islamic coins its explicit denial of the divinity of Christ could be taken as a sign of the influence of Jewish converts.[58]

Figure 4a. Ṭabariya (?) bronze coin with الله احد - الصمد - لم يلد *allāh aḥad al-amad lam yalid 'God is one. The eternal. He did not beget'. Cf. Qurān, sura 112. 3.41 g. Album auction 10 (22 April 2011) lot 145.*

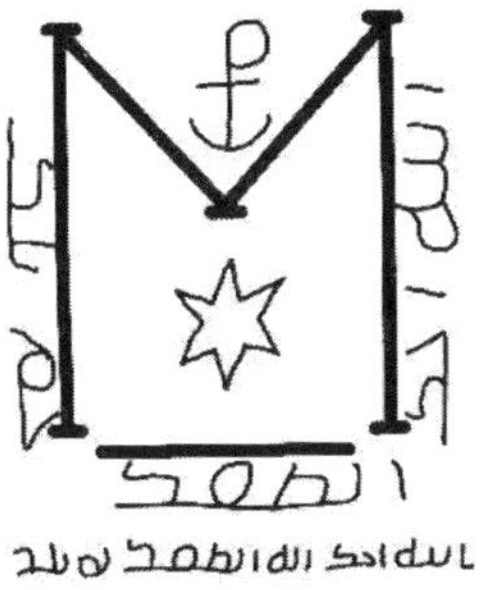

Figure 4b. The complete legend.

Unfortunately for this idea, the obverse type depicts three figures which could have been taken as a reference to the Trinity. The image of three standing figures, copied from a solidus of Heraclius, was also the obverse type chosen for ʿAbd al-Malik's first experiment with an Islamic gold coin, the so-called *shahada* solidus. David Woods has recently argued that this was a deliberate attempt to provoke Justinian II when it was used to pay the tribute to Byzantium in 691.[59]

---

[55] Heidemann, 'Evolving representation, p. 186.

[56] The term *bismillah* (in the name of God) was of long standing use on coins and, as Heidemann points out, not specifically Islamic.

[57] Phillips, 'Islamic legends on pre reform coins of Tabariya'. I know of no example with a complete reverse legend so have reproduced a composite drawing, fig. 4b.

[58] Grierson thought this might be behind Muslim hostility to images, 'Monetary reforms of Abd al-Malik', p. 244, n. 1, but this aspect of Islamic iconoclasm has not been taken up. It is not suggested that the mysterious Sumair al-Yahudi played any role in the choice of designs of the coins.

[59] Woods, 'ʿAbd al-Malik and the *shahāda* solidus'.

In other words, images are very easy to mis-interpret and mis-understand. When Constantine IV (668–85) removed his two brothers from the gold coinage in 681:

> a certain Leo, a valiant and distinguished man, said: 'It is not right to reject now men who have ruled alongside the king. Even our gold currency has three busts portrayed on it. I will not give my support nor will I consent.' The king ordered that his tongue be severed and as he went off followed by the people, he said shouting: 'A trinity rules in heaven and a trinity rules on earth'.

On the other hand, according to the Coptic bishop, John of Nikiu (fl. 660–90), the three figure solidus was unpopular in some quarters:

> And some said the death of Heraclius is due to his stamping the gold coinage with the figures of the three emperors that is his own and his two sons on the right hand and on the left and so no room was found for inscribing the name of the Roman emperor and after the death of Heraclius they obliterated these three figures.[60]

I would suggest that the reason ʿAbd al-Malik chose to copy the type was precisely because it had no inscription on the obverse. He could hardly inscribe the name of the Byzantine emperor and hesitated at that stage to put his own name on the coin. Furthermore the depiction of the figures of Constantine IV and his brothers was hardly suggestive of the Trinity since the two brothers are clearly depicted as small and therefore less important than Constantine. Be that as it may, the story does illustrate how easy it was for images to be misunderstood and how fanatical people could be about them. The advantage of the legends on the reform coins was that they were as unambiguous as it was possible to be. On a more practical level a simple epigraphic design was quicker to engrave than an image and this made it easier to cut more dies and produce more coins.

The result was a de-politicised coinage that avoided not just images that could be misinterpreted but propaganda of all sorts. Michael Bates addresses this in his usual trenchant style:

> There is no indication in any of the many medieval Arabic and Persian political histories and texts on statecraft and administration that Muslim rulers thought of using coins to address a mass audience to win popular loyalty or to communicate to their subjects.[61]

One could argue that 'communicating with his subjects' was exactly what ʿAbd al-Malik was trying to do, but having communicated as emphatically as he could he allowed the message to stand.[62] The ʿAbbāsids, of course, removed the *Sūrat al-Ikhlāṣ* in favour of the simple 'Muhammad is the prophet of God' to stress their kinship with the Prophet. If so, this was a political statement. Recently Lutz Ilisch has argued, in an unpublished paper, that the coins with the legend *ma'din amīr al-mu'minīn* which has been taken to refer to a mine providing gold for caliphal dinars really refers to the mint al-Madīna. This relates to attempts by both ʿAbd al-Malik's successor al-Walīd I (86–96/705–15) and Hishām (724–43/105–25) to gather support and recognition in the holy cities, especially Medina. (Fig. 5) Since the epithet also appears on copper coins it can hardly be considered as propaganda aimed entirely at the elite.[63] Nonetheless, this seems to have been an isolated example as far as Umayyad post reform coinage was concerned.

---

[60] Phillips, 'Coinage and the early Arab state', p. 58.

[61] Bates, 'Who was named on ʿAbbasid coins?', p. 89.

[62] ʿAbd al-Malik's systematic exploitation of Quranic legends is of course most evident on the Dome of the Rock. This is examined in more detail Hillenbrand, 'For God, empire and mammon', pp. 24–6.

[63] Ilisch, 'Mine, residence, or home – the meaning of '*ma'din amīr al-mu'minīn*' on Umayyad coins'.

Figure 5. Al-Walīd (86–96 H) dinar of 92 H with Ma'din amīr al-mu'minīn, 4.25 g. Morton & Eden, Auction 82 (20 October 2016) lot 17.

Conclusion

In this brief survey I have tried to give some idea of the role that coin evidence can play in current debates on some fundamental historical questions. This has necessarily involved some drastic summarising of the issues involved and the views expressed by various scholars. If have misrepresented anyone I can only apologise.

My personal view of ʿAbd al-Malik is that he was a practical politician, not an ideologue, who excelled at assimilating other peoples' ideas. The idea of an entirely centralised minting operation akin to that of the Persian and Roman empires probably never entered his mind. A unified coinage in three metals with a simplified and clarified 'message' was a practical solution to the problems he was trying to overcome. The coin evidence at least suggests that he did not possess the administrative resources to entirely carry it through, but he achieved his basic purpose: a plentiful and independent coinage that, in conjunction with his other measures, cemented the prosperity and stability of the newly unified Arab state.

I have tried to show that in some instances it is possible for numismatic evidence to resolve questions that the written sources do not. As the debates move on, can it be of further assistance? This is partly a matter of the recording of hoards and single finds and here the situation does not look too promising at least in Syria and Iran, but it would help if historians could take more care in their use of the numismatic evidence particularly as it develops.

WORKS CITED

J. Banaji, 'Late antique legacies and Muslim economic expansion', in J. Haldon (ed.), ***Money, Power and Politics***, pp. 165–80. Republished in J. Banaji, ***Exploring the Economy of Late Antiquity***, no. 9.

J. Banaji, ***Exploring the Economy of Late Antiquity: Selected Essays*** (Cambridge, 2016).

M. Bates, 'Who was named on ʿAbbasid coins?', in M. Faghfoury (ed.), ***Iranian Numismatic Studies. A Volume in Honor of Stephen Album*** (Lancaster PA, 2017), pp. 89–99.

G. Bijovsky, 'A hoard of Byzantine solidi from Bet She'an in the Umayyad period', ***Revue Numismatique*** 158 (2002), pp. 161–227.

M. Bloch, 'Le problème de l'or au Moyen Age', ***Annales d'histoire économique et sociale*** 5 (1933), pp. 1–34.

C.E. Bosworth (trans), ***The History of al-Ṭabarī***, vol. V ***The Sāsānids, the Byzantines, the Lakmids and Yemen*** (Albany NY, 1999).

E.W. Bovill, ***The Golden Trade of the Moors*** (London, 1968).

F. Braudel, J. Le Goff, 'Maurice Lombard', ***Annales. Economies, Sociétés, Civilisations*** 21, 3, (1966), pp. 713–16.

P. Brown, ***The World of Late Antiquity*** (London, 1971).

V. Curtis *et al.*, ***Sasanian Coins. A Sylloge of the Sasanian Coins in the National Museum of Iran (Muzeh Melli Iran), Tehran, I*** (Ardahsir I – Hormizd IV) RNS SP no. 47. (London, 2010).

F.M. Donner, ***The Early Islamic Conquests*** (Princeton, 1981).

A.S. Ehrenkreutz, 'Another Orientalist's remarks concerning the Pirenne thesis' ***Journal of Economic and Social History of the Orient*** 15 (1972), pp. 94–101. Reprinted in J. Bacharach (ed.), ***Monetary Change and economic history in the medieval Muslim world*** (Aldershot, 1992), no. III.

A.S. Ehrenkreutz, 'Money', ***Handbuch der Orientalistik*** *Erste Abteilung, Sechster Band, Sechster Abschnitt, part 1* (Leiden, 1977), pp. 54–97. Reprinted in J. Bacharach (ed.), ***Monetary Change and Economic History in the Medieval Muslim World*** (Aldershot, 1992), no. II.

A.S. Ehrenkreutz, 'The silent force behind the rise of medieval Islamic civilization', in C.E. Bosworth *et al.*, (eds), ***The Islamic World from Classical to Modern Times : Essays in Honor of Bernard Lewis*** (Princeton, NJ, 1989).

T. Goodwin, ***The Standing Caliph Coinage*** (London, 2018).

P. Grierson, 'The monetary reforms of abd al-Malik. Their metrological basis and their financial repercussions', ***Journal of Economic and Social History of the Orient*** 3 (1960), pp. 241–64. Reprinted in P. Grierson, ***Dark Ages Numismatics*** (Aldershot, 1979), no. XV.

J. Haldon (ed.), ***Money, Power and Politics in Early Islamic Syria. A Review of Current Debates*** (Farnham, 2010).

S. Heidemann, 'The merger of two currency zones in early Islam. The Byzantine and Sasanian impact on the circulation in former Byzantine Syria and northern Mesopotamia', ***Iran*** 36 (1998), pp. 95-112.

S. Heidemann, 'The evolving representation of the early Islamic empire and its religion on coin imagery', in A. Neuwirth *et al.* (eds), ***The Qur'ān in context: Historical and Literary Investigations into the Qur'ānic Milieu*** (Leiden, 2010), pp. 149–95.

M. Hendy, ***Studies in the Byzantine Monetary Economy c.300–1450*** (Cambridge, 1985).

M. Hendy, 'From public to private: the western barbarian coin images as a mirror of the disintegration of late Roman state structure', ***Viator*** 19 (1988), pp. 29–78. Reprinted in Hendy, ***Economy, Fiscal Administration and coinage of Byzantium***, no. VII.

M. Hendy, ***The Economy, Fiscal Adminstration and Coinage of Byzantium***. Variorum Reprints: Collected Studies Series 305 (Northampton, 1989).

M. Hendy, 'East and West. Divergent models of coinage and its use', ***Il secolo di ferro: mito e realtà del secolo X.*** Settimane di Studi del Centro Italiano di Studi sull' Alto Medioevo 38, (Spoleto, 1991), pp. 637–75.

M. Humphreys, 'The 'war of images' revisited. Justinian II's coinage reform and the caliphate', ***The Numismatic Chronicle*** 173 (2013), pp. 279–44.

L. Ilisch, 'Abd al-Malik's monetary reform in copper and the failure of centralization', in J. Haldon (ed.), ***Money, Power and Politics***, pp. 125–46.

L. Ilisch, 'Mine, residence, or home – the meaning of '*ma'din amīr al-mu'minīn*' on Umayyad coins', paper read to the International Numismatic Congress, Warsaw, September 2022.

R. Hillenbrand, 'For God, empire and mammon. Some art-historical aspects of the reformed dīnārs of 'Abd al-Malik', M. Müller-Wiener, C. Kothe, K.-H. Golzio and J. Gierlich (eds), ***Al-Andalus und Europa. Zwischen Orient und Okzident*** (Petersberg, Hesse, 2004), pp. 20–38.

J. Howard-Johnston, ***Witnesses to a World Crisis. Historians and Histories of the Middle East in the Seventh Century*** (Oxford, 2010).

A.H.M. Jones, 'Numismatics and History', in R.A. Carson and C.H.V. Sutherland (eds), ***Essays in Roman Coinage Presented to Harold Mattingly*** (Oxford, 1956), pp. 15–33.

G.H.A. Juynboll (trans.), ***The History of al-Ṭabarī,*** vol. XIII ***The Conquest of Iraq, Southwestern Persia and Egypt*** (Albany NY, 1989).

H. Kennedy, ***The Armies of the Caliphs: Military and Society in the Early Islamic State*** (London, 2001).

H. Kennedy, 'The Middle East in Islamic late antiquity', in A. Monson and W. Scheidel, ***Fiscal Regimes and the Political Economy of Premodern States*** (Cambridge, 2015), pp. 390–403.

H. Kennedy (trans.), ***History of the Arab Invasions: the Conquest of the Lands. A New Translation of al-Balādhurī's Futūḥ al-Buldān*** (London, 2022).

B. Koehler, ***Early Islam and the Birth of Capitalism*** (Lanham MA and Plymouth, England, 2014).

M. Lombard, 'Les bases monétaires d'une suprématie economique: l'or musulmam du viie au xiie siècle', ***Annales: Economies, Sociétés, Civilisations*** 2 (1947), pp. 143–60.

M.G. Morony, ***Iraq after the Muslim Conquest*** (Princeton NJ, 1984).

A. Oddy, I. Schulze and W. Schulze (eds), ***Coinage and History in the Seventh Century Near East,*** *Proceedings of the 14th Seventh Century Round Table held at The Hive, Worcester, on the 28th and 29th September 2013* (London, 2013).

M. Phillips, 'Islamic legends on pre reform coins of Tabariya', ***Actas del XIII Congreso Internacional de Numismatica*** (Madrid, 2005), pp. 1631–7.

M. Phillips, 'Coinage and the early Arab state', in A. Oddy, *et al.*, ***Coinage and History***, pp. 53–71.

M. Phillips, 'Coinage in Syria before and after the Arab conquest. The results and significance of new research', in F. Montinaro and M. Akpinar (eds), ***Rethinking Conquest***, *forthcoming*.

N. Schindel, 'A hoard of late Sasanian copper coins from the Eretz Israel Museum', ***Sylloge Nummorum Sasanidarum Israel*** (Vienna, 2009), pp. 32–43 and pp. 116–153.

T. Sizgorich, ***Violence and Belief in Late Antiquity*** (Philadelphia, 2009).

A. Smith, ***An Inquiry into the Nature and Causes of the Wealth of Nations***, first edition (London, 1776).

L. Treadwell, 'Abd al-Malik's coinage reforms: the role of the Damascus mint', ***Revue Numismatique*** [6] 165 (2009), pp. 357–81.

R. Tye, 'Sumair and the unity and influence of ʿAbd al Malik's weight reforms', https://www.academia.edu/s/e8e3495997. Posted 30 November 2020.

S. Tyler-Smith, ***The Coinage Reforms (600–603) of Khusru II and the Revolt of Vistāhm,*** RNS SP no. 54 (London, 2017).

J. Walker, ***A Catalogue of the Arab-Byzantine and Post-Reform Umaiyad Coins*** (London, 1956).

D. Woods, 'Abd al-Malik and the *shahāda* solidus', ***Israel Numismatic Research*** 17 (2022), pp. 231–40.